Counsel for the United States

*Also by James Eisenstein*

Felony Justice: An Organizational Analysis of
Criminal Courts (*with Herbert Jacob*)

Politics and the Legal Process

# COUNSEL FOR THE UNITED STATES

## U.S. Attorneys in the Political and Legal Systems

*James Eisenstein*

The Johns Hopkins University Press
Baltimore and London

Manufactured in the United States of America

The Johns Hopkins University Press, Baltimore, Maryland 21218
The Johns Hopkins Press Ltd., London

Library of Congress Catalog Number 77-10562
ISBN 0-8018-1988-1

Library of Congress Cataloging in Publication data
will be found on the last printed page of this book.

*In Memory of*
CHARLES EISENSTEIN
*1904–1967*

# CONTENTS

# PREFACE

Americans possess intriguing notions about the relationship between politics and the application of law. The mythology of American government maintains that "law" and "politics" are distinct, that "law" carries within itself self-enforcing commands that guarantee equal justice, neutrality, and aloofness from mundane pressures arising from social and political conflict. Even when the legal system (as embodied in the Supreme Court) rules on questions of undeniable political origin and consequence, it couches its decisions in legal language and usually remains silent on their political implications. In a sense, we adhere to the notion that everyday political controversies can be resolved by applying a body of neutral and somehow "higher" set of principles embodied in "law." And yet, the reality of American politics constantly belies the validity of the myth. One of the central themes of Richard Nixon's 1968 presidential campaign centered on the performance of the federal legal system. His promise to appoint a new attorney general who would lead a vigorous attack on crime, his criticism of the direction recent Supreme Court decisions had taken, and his pledge to "restore the balance" in the Court's make-up illustrated the interrelationship between law and politics. The ensuing controversy over the nominations of Clement Haynsworth and G. Harrold Carswell, following closely the forced resignation of Justice Fortas, were additional examples. Subsequently, revelations about the Nixon administration's use of the Department of Justice for political purposes that emerged as the result of the Watergate scandal exposed the links between the administration of law and politics to the entire country. More recently, the criticisms accompanying Jimmy Carter's selection of Griffin Bell to be his attorney general refocused attention on the policy impact of federal law enforcement decisions.

If recent events have increased awareness of the political dimensions to federal legal activities, they have also underscored our lack of knowledge in this area. For instance, three assistant U.S. attorneys conducted the principal investigation and prosecution in the Watergate scandal prior to the advent of the Ervin committee and the appointment of special prosecutor Archibald Cox. The Republican

U.S. attorney in Baltimore presided over the investigation of Vice-President Spiro Agnew's conduct while he was governor of Maryland, which led to his dramatic resignation and conviction. His counterpart in San Francisco led the prosecution in the highly publicized Patty Hearst trial. Despite this publicity, however, few people in our country know what a U.S. attorney is or what he does. The general public's ignorance of the role U.S. attorneys and their assistants have played and continue to play in the legal and political systems is matched in the academic realm. Despite their unquestionable significance, little has been published about them.[1]

This book seeks to contribute to an expanding movement in the social sciences to explain the operation and impact of major components of the legal process.[2] The information reported comes primarily from nearly two hundred interviews conducted in 1965 and 1970–71 with U.S. attorneys, their assistants, federal district judges, investigative agents, and private attorneys.[3] Its major theme can be stated rather simply: U.S. attorneys and their assistants make political and legal decisions far more important than the absence of published research on them would suggest. As such, we should know what their contributions to policy-making and political outcomes are and what factors shape their behavior.

Because of the unusual position of the office at the intersection of the legal process with the rest of the political system, the study of U.S. attorneys also serves as an especially productive source of observations about the political process generally. U.S. attorneys perform essentially legal duties. They are members of the Department of Justice and subject to its supervisory control. The department relies upon them to implement national legal policy as it is shaped by the political process in Washington, D.C. Yet, unlike most other field personnel implementing centrally determined policies, they belong to and identify with the community in which they serve. Because their appointment depends upon their political standing in the community, U.S. attorneys frequently feel they owe their position to local political personalities and interests. They perform their legal duties in their home territories and plan to remain in the community and pursue a legal or political career there when they leave office. Thus, local claims on their attention, time, and policies come to rival the demands of national policy and headquarters' directives.

This unique combination of attributes makes it possible to examine several questions of general interest to students of politics. What factors affect the balance of local autonomy versus central control in bureaucratic organizations that depend upon field offices to fulfill their mission? What consequences flow from superimposing a field office structure on a federal political system? How does the performance of agencies so organized differ from that of other administrative agencies of the federal government? These broad questions will be examined as the basic structure of this volume—a description of the dynamics and impact of the office of U.S. attorney—unfolds.

After a brief introduction to the basic structure and functioning of the office in Chapter 1, we shall look at the ways in which U.S. attorneys affect political outcomes. Chapter 3 examines the appointment process and the characteristics of the people appointed. The next five chapters analyze the strategic environment of U.S. attorneys by examining their interactions with the other significant participants in the federal legal process they encounter—the Department of Justice, federal judges, private attorneys, and investigative agents. The final chapter summarizes the strategic position of U.S. attorneys, describes in general terms their patterns of interaction with others, assesses their impact on policy, and examines the role pressures from their district play in shaping their behavior. It concludes with a discussion of the strengths and weaknesses of U.S. attorneys' performance and proposals for reform.

I have accumulated many debts in the years I have studied U.S. attorneys. My greatest debt is owed to the scores of individuals who agreed to be interviewed; I assured them I would not identify anyone, so my appreciation must be expressed to them as a group. Herbert Kaufman first suggested the value of studying U.S. attorneys, and he has continued to offer valuable criticisms and suggestions throughout. David Danelski proved to be a wise and helpful dissertation director, leaving me to my devices when he felt I would benefit and offering guidance and encouragement when necessary. His subsequent assistance has been invaluable. A number of colleagues have read portions of the study and offered useful criticisms. I would like to thank John Kingdon for his especially careful reading of an earlier draft. The Ford Foundation provided support for both phases of the field research, first through a Woodrow Wilson Foundation dissertation fellowship awarded in 1965–66 and then a faculty research fellowship awarded in 1970–71. Finally, I want to acknowledge the extraordinary contribution made by my wife. She played a major role in the conduct of the original research (interviewing federal judges and private attorneys) and offered excellent editorial and substantive criticism throughout. She deserves much credit for whatever contributions this study makes, and I will always appreciate her help.

Counsel for the United States

# CHAPTER 1

# Counsel for the United States

The United States Department of Justice provides nearly all of the federal government's legal representation. The department's actions defending the government's position in the Supreme Court and its initiation of major antitrust, civil rights, or other highly publicized lawsuits dominate the public's knowledge concerning its activities. But it must handle almost ninety thousand routine civil and criminal matters filed annually in the ninety-four federal district courts scattered throughout the United States and its territories. Although they generate little publicity, these cases constitute the heart of the department's legal work. They also create a troublesome administrative problem. How can an agency based in Washington, D.C. effectively provide legal representation in ninety-four widely scattered locations?

Federal administrative agencies have adopted a standard solution to such problems—they rely upon a field service. In a classic work on public administration, Leonard D. White described a field service as "a network of local offices serving the whole country, performing a common and often identical function, organized on a common pattern, enforcing the same laws or performing the same service, and responsible to a single headquarters agency in Washington."[1] United States attorneys and their assistants serve as the department's field service. The department relies upon the office located in each of the ninety-four judicial districts to represent the government in that district. United States attorneys also provide the federal government's representation in state courts, and they sometimes argue federal cases appealed from their districts to the United States Courts of Appeals. The status of U.S. attorneys as the department's field representatives profoundly shapes their behavior and the nature of their impact. This chapter begins with a description of the formal relationship of U.S. attorneys' offices to the administrative structure of the department. It next examines briefly the structure and activity of the ninety-four offices. Then, a brief history of U.S. attorneys and their relationship to the Department of Justice will be presented. The legacy of this history continues to shape relations between the department and U.S. attorneys. The chapter next examines how these lingering effects

1

help explain why department–U.S. attorney interactions differ from most headquarters–field relationships. United States attorneys' resources in dealing with others, which help us understand these relationships, are described next. The chapter concludes by sketching the outlines of the struggle between the department and U.S. attorneys for control of the field offices.

## U.S. ATTORNEYS IN THE DEPARTMENT'S STRUCTURE

The United States Department of Justice encompasses a variety of agencies, bureaus, and divisions performing a number of law-related activities. Congress appropriated over two billion dollars for the department in 1976. Eighty-six percent of this sum went to agencies and bureaus that have little direct involvement in litigation.[2] They include the Federal Bureau of Investigation, the Drug Enforcement Administration, the Immigration and Naturalization Service, the Federal Prison System, and the Law Enforcement Assistance Administration.

United States attorneys' offices fall into the remaining fraction of the budget devoted to general administration and legal activities. The attorney general, deputy attorney general, and a handful of other offices provide general administrative direction to the entire department.[3] As most published descriptions emphasize, the department divides its legal activities into major categories and assigns responsibility for each to a separate division. The solicitor general's office represents the federal government in the Supreme Court and determines whether unfavorable lower court decisions will be appealed. The Office of Legal Counsel, headed by an assistant attorney general, drafts the attorney general's formal opinions, provides informal legal advice to the executive branch, and participates in the drafting and review of proposed legislation. Assistant attorneys general head the remaining substantive divisions: the Tax Division, the Criminal Division, the Civil Division, the Land and Natural Resources Division, the Civil Rights Division, and the Antitrust Division.[4]

Existing statutes grant undisputed supervisory power over U.S. attorneys' offices to the attorney general. Section 507 (b) of Title 28 of the U.S. Code gives him the right to direct U.S. attorneys in the discharge of their duties, including the handling of specific cases. However, the attorney general also may assign a specially appointed attorney to conduct any case. This power, explicitly granted by statute, permits him to dispatch a department attorney from Washington, whenever he desires, to supersede a U.S. attorney.[5] Another section of the U.S. Code requires U.S. attorneys to make all records, accounts, and official papers available to the attorney general's designated agents for audit and review. The attorney general, under authority granted in the Judiciary Act of 1789, may require U.S. attorneys to submit reports.[6] The Supreme Court has strongly affirmed his control over U.S. attorneys.[7]

Despite the attorney general's undisputed authority, the position of U.S. attorneys in the department's hierarchy remains ambiguous. No single division or office within the department exercises day-to-day supervision of all the field offices' work. The government's litigation involves a variety of cases, civil and criminal, that fall within the jurisdiction of the department's six divisions. The appropriate divisions supervise a field office's handling of specific cases within their purview. Consequently, the Tax Division, the Civil Division, and the Land and Natural Resources Division may simultaneously oversee the conduct of cases being tried by a U.S. attorney's assistants. Furthermore, department personnel in the divisions in Washington do not enjoy undisputed authority to oversee and direct the work of U.S. attorneys' offices. Such authority belongs only to the attorney general. Few if any U.S. attorneys interviewed in this study believe that they must follow orders issued by career attorneys in Washington. Most refuse to acknowledge a section head's right to issue binding instructions. In fact, some dispute vigorously the power of the assistant attorneys general to control and direct the handling of litigation.

Almost every administrative detail of running U.S. attorneys' offices falls within the jurisdiction of the Executive Office for United States Attorneys. In fact, the department's organization charts place U.S. attorneys under the Executive Office for United States Attorneys, which reports to the deputy attorney general. The Executive Office provides general supervision and executive assistance, updates the *U.S. Attorney's Manual,* issues the *U.S. Attorney's Bulletin* (which reports important cases in state and federal courts handled by U.S. attorneys), processes all official documents relating to the appointment and promotion of office personnel, oversees financial records and transactions (reimbursements, purchases, payment of fees), conducts inspections to review office practices and procedures, disseminates information among the offices, and serves as a liaison between department personnel in Washington and the field. At the end of the Johnson administration, the department decided to establish four regional branches of the Executive Office, and the Nixon administration implemented the plan. A regional branch monitors offices in its territory to insure conformity with department policy, especially with respect to the keeping of financial and administrative records. Despite

its many important administrative activities, however, the Executive
Office for United States Attorneys provides very little significant direction in the creation and implementation of substantive departmental policies arising from litigation. Furthermore, crucial administrative decisions remain in the hands of U.S. attorneys. They exercise the
dominant influence in selecting personnel (including assistant U.S.
attorneys), determine the office's organization, and allocate its manpower.

The anomalous position of U.S. attorneys' offices in the department's structure may account in part for their low visibility. Many
descriptions of the department's organization and functioning largely
ignore them, focusing instead on the activities of the divisions located
in Washington.[8] The department's allocation of its legal manpower
more accurately reflects U.S. attorneys' contributions to federal legal
representation. Nearly one of every two lawyers employed by the
department works in a U.S. attorney's office.[9]

## AN OVERVIEW OF U.S. ATTORNEYS' OFFICES

The U.S. attorneys' offices span the geography of the United States
and its territories. Each judicial district must have a U.S. attorney's
office. The cities in which they are headquartered read like a bus tour
of the United States, including its major urban cities (New York,
Chicago, Detroit, Atlanta, Los Angeles) and many smaller ones as well
(Macon, Omaha, Asheville, Cheyenne). United States attorneys also
serve in the Virgin Islands, Guam, Puerto Rico, and the Canal Zone.

The federal structure of the American political system guarantees
discrepancies in the amount of litigation handled by the various U.S.
attorneys' offices. Each state, regardless of population, is given at least
one judicial district wholly within its boundaries. Alaska, Nevada, and
Vermont therefore constitute separate districts, and each serves fewer
people, generates less federal litigation, and requires fewer judges
and assistant U.S. attorneys than most other districts. Congress has
exacerbated the malapportionment of population served and cases
handled through its decisions to apportion districts within the more
populous states.[10] One district serves all of New Jersey, and Michigan
and Ohio each have but two. The 1970 population of these five districts averaged over 5,250,000. Congress created two districts in West
Virginia and three in Oklahoma. These five districts serve an average
population of only 860,000, less than one-sixth the size of the New
Jersey, Ohio, and Michigan districts.

Differences in the population served by a district translate into substantial variation in the number of assistant U.S. attorneys assigned to the ninety-four offices. The District of Vermont, for instance, had only one assistant U.S. attorney in 1969, while nearly seventy assistants worked in the Southern District of New York. As late as 1968, nearly half of the U.S. attorneys' offices employed four or fewer assistants.[11] However, the largest five offices accounted for 31 percent of all assistants.[12] Although the number of assistants doubled in the decade spanning the mid-1960s, discrepancies in the relative size of U.S. attorneys' offices persist. In 1975 over half of U.S. attorneys still had only between four and ten assistants.[13]

Differences associated with office size complicate the task of analyzing and describing the behavior of U.S. attorneys and their assistants. In the larger offices they perform quite different tasks than their colleagues in the two- and three-man offices. In the latter, U.S. attorneys undertake most tasks that assistants everywhere do, including handling routine litigation. United States attorneys running large offices devote most of their energies to administration. Larger offices exhibit more differentiation in their internal organization. Most have at least several divisions and levels of supervisory personnel. The manpower resources of larger offices provide the U.S. attorney with greater flexibility in managing the work, and permit him to create special task-forces or to assign a skilled assistant to manage a time-consuming and difficult investigation. Assistants in larger offices specialize in handling specific categories of cases; in small offices, they must handle a broad range of cases.

These differences make generalizations about U.S. attorneys or assistants difficult. United States attorneys in small offices experience the same problems dealing with investigative agents and judges that assistants in larger offices encounter. The problems and behavior of assistants who handle only one or two types of litigation differ from those of assistants assigned a variety of cases. The descriptions and analyses in this book focus on both U.S. attorneys and their assistants. Portions of the following chapters clearly differentiate between the two positions, but at times the analysis applies to both. Consistent differences emerge when offices of varying size are compared. Throughout the book, unless noted otherwise, the term "small office" or "small district" refers to one- or two-judge districts with seven assistants or less; "medium offices" contain from eight to fourteen assistants and three, four, or five judges; "large" districts refer to those with more than five judges and fifteen or more assistant U.S. attorneys. As these definitions suggest, a fairly constant ratio between the number of judges and number of assistants in a district exists.[14] Both, after all, ultimately depend on the caseload in the district.

Differences in the composition of the ninety-four districts' population, their geographical location, the nature of their economies, and their political structures also produce diverse characteristics and behavior. Political structures shape recruitment patterns (discussed in chapter 3), but the primary effect of these differences in composition comes in the amount and content of litigation handled. The Department of Justice publishes no figures comparing districts by the type of cases brought, but the interviews suggest that such differences are a matter of common knowledge. United States attorneys in Border and Southern states prosecute most defendants charged with illegally distilling alcohol. Districts located along the Mexican border or in major port cities handle many immigration cases. Major corporate fraud cases arise in the chief financial centers, like the Southern District of New York (Manhattan). Districts containing Indian reservations and military bases prosecute criminal charges (including murder) commonly found in state courts.

The department does publish statistics that illustrate the substantial differences found in the volume of work put out by the various offices. The sheer volume of cases handled, of course, shows the same magnitude of variation as office size. In the year ending June 30, 1975, for instance, the districts of New Hampshire and Maine terminated 120 and 131 cases respectively. That same year, the Central and Southern Districts of California disposed of 3,018 and 3,215 cases respectively.[15]

Somewhat less than half (44 percent) of the districts concluded less than 500 cases, while nearly 30 percent handled 1,000 cases or more.[16] The proportion of criminal cases disposed of in fiscal year 1976 also varied substantially. About 30 percent of the offices found less than half of their cases involved criminal charges, while 20 percent had 70 percent or more of their cases on the criminal docket.[17] The use of trials in criminal cases also varied substantially. Nationwide, 11 percent of criminal cases terminated in fiscal year 1975 went to trial. Yet the Eastern District of Oklahoma and the Eastern and Western Districts of Tennessee had a trial rate over 20 percent, and the Districts of Wyoming and Rhode Island tried only about 3 percent of their criminal cases.[18] Similar differences emerge in the amount of money collected through fines, forfeiture, penalties, foreclosures, and other civil judgments. The Western District of Washington collected over $17,000,000 in fiscal year 1975; the District of Delaware collected but $98,000.[19]

The Department of Justice has established no uniform internal organization for its field offices. The differences in the volume and content of cases handled make standardization impossible. Consequently, U.S. attorneys utilize a variety of organizational forms and practices. Even offices approximately the same size display substantial variety in organization. In small offices, the degree of internal supervision and control over assistants ranges from practically nonexistent to comprehensive. Some U.S. attorneys delegate most decisions to assistants, back them up in disputes with others, and devote most of their time to handling their own cases, but some strive to supervise assistants closely in addition to handling their own cases. They try to read all investigative reports, scan all incoming and outgoing mail, review prosecutive decisions and proposed compromise offers in civil cases, and even inspect the long-distance phone log. United States attorneys' supervisory policies produce differences in the level of office morale and loyalty among assistants, and this in turn shapes the office's dealings with the department and members of the local federal legal community (judges, investigators, private attorneys).

Despite substantial differences in U.S. attorneys' tasks and administrative style, all share common responsibilities and duties. Running the office occupies a substantial proportion of their time and energy. They recommend appointees to vacancies in assistants' and clerical positions. They assign personnel to specific tasks and bear the general responsibility for supervising their work. The department maintains a computerized case control system which requires filling out forms to report on each case's progress. The U.S. attorney must monitor the reports this system produces to insure that cases do not languish. The Speedy Trial Act promises to increase the pressure on U.S. attorneys to insure cases come to trial quickly. Most U.S. attorneys exercise more detailed supervision over major litigation, conferring frequently with the assistant in charge and participating in strategy conferences. Many hold periodic staff meetings with groups of assistants to discuss the progress of pending litigation. The department holds U.S. attorneys responsible for adhering to its policies and procedures outlined in the *U.S. Attorneys Manual*.

United States attorneys also manage their office's "external" affairs. Much of this task involves dealing with the Department of Justice. Personnel matters (appointments, reclassifications, requests for new positions, salary increases), purchases, and other administrative matters require contact with the Executive Office for U.S. Attorneys or one of its regional branches. Department attorneys dispatched from Washington to assume direct responsibility for litigating a case need office space, secretarial support, advice, and legal assistance. Assistant U.S. attorneys engaged in arguments with departmental attorneys

seek their bosses' assistance. United States attorneys also interact with
several other external organizations and individuals. Major problems
arise in handling the civil and criminal litigation of client agencies.
They often conduct the delicate negotiations required to settle disputes between these agencies when their jurisdictions overlap. Dissatisfaction with an assistant's performance prompts client agencies to
seek the U.S. attorney's intervention. Since the success of his office
depends upon the outcome of litigation, a U.S. attorney must devote
substantial attention to dealing with judges. Judges may demand from
them a number of specific actions, including requests affecting the
scheduling of cases, the reassignment of obnoxious assistants to different courtrooms, and even demands that particular investigations
or prosecutions be undertaken. Finally, most U.S. attorneys handle
contacts with the news media. The extensiveness of this chore depends on the nature of pending litigation. When cases of major importance arise, media relations consume a major part of a U.S. attorney's time.[20] The complexity and variety of tasks imposed on U.S.
attorneys make them more administrators than litigators in all but the
smallest offices.[21] Their other duties limit opportunities to try cases,
although some U.S. attorneys in even the largest offices occasionally
manage to try a case.

Assistants devote almost all their energy to handling litigation or
supervising the work of other assistants. This brings them into contact
with a number of other individuals who significantly affect their work,
including the U.S. attorney or another supervisor in the office, a
"counterpart" attorney in the Department of Justice who monitors the
conduct of the case, a representative from the client agency (an investigative agent in a criminal case), judges, and the opposing attorney.
Assistants also sometimes interact with witnesses, probation officers,
judges' clerks and other court personnel, and the news media. Although the combinations of individuals and subject matter assistants
encounter varies widely throughout the nation, all share the common
experience of having to cope with a heavy workload.[22]

The foregoing description depicts U.S. attorneys' offices as fairly
typical field offices serving a Washington-based headquarters. However, they are far from typical in many crucial respects. These distin-
guishing characteristics make the study of U.S. attorneys' offices and
their relations with headquarters and other important individuals and
agencies important and fascinating. To understand the distinctive
features of U.S. attorneys' relations with the Department of Justice, it
is necessary to examine briefly the history of their association with one
another.

## THE HISTORICAL LEGACY

No one has yet written a definitive history of U.S. attorneys, although a number of scholars provide some intriguing glimpses.[23] Congress established the office of U.S. attorney in 1789 when the federal system was inaugurated. Few institutions continue today with as little change. Three basic features of the position established in the Judiciary Act of 1789 survive: U.S. attorneys represent the federal government in federal district courts; the president appoints them with senatorial confirmation, and only he can fire them; each federal district contains a U.S. attorney's office.[24]

United States attorneys' offices have undergone two significant changes since 1789. First, the number and scope of cases handled has increased dramatically. Prior to the Civil War, U.S. attorneys only prosecuted cases mentioned in the Constitution (piracy, counterfeiting, treason, felonies committed on the high seas), cases resulting from interference with federal justice (purjury, bribery), extortion by federal officers, thefts by employees from the United States Bank, and arson on federal vessels.[25] On the civil side, U.S. attorneys played a key role in litigation over claims to vast federal lands based on Spanish and French grants.[26] After the Civil War, federal criminal jurisdiction began to grow substantially. During reconstruction, federal criminal sanctions were applied to protect civil rights; the Post Office Code of 1872 made it a federal offense to use the mails to defraud, promote or run a lottery, or send obscene materials through the mail.[27] The growth of criminal jurisdiction accelerated in the twentieth century. Prohibition, of course, accounted for many prosecutions, but its demise did not halt growth. The attorney general's *Annual Report* for 1975 listed 115 distinct categories of criminal cases, from poultry inspection and treason (one case each) to motor vehicle theft and bank robbery (1,669 and 2,626 cases respectively).[28] Civil litigation has expanded in scope also. Land condemnation proceedings, defense of tort suits against the United States, litigation arising from the granting and performance of government contracts, and civil fraud actions comprise the bulk of civil cases. The combined volume of civil and criminal cases has increased steadily in recent years. In 1963 U.S. attorneys terminated 59,000 cases; in 1975 the number rose to nearly 80,000.[29]

Second, U.S. attorneys gradually lost much of their independence and autonomy to the attorney general and the Department of Justice. The Judiciary Act of 1789 gave the attorney general no authority whatsoever to supervise or direct U.S. attorneys.[30] They represented the federal government as they saw fit, maintained private practices, and received compensation in the form of a percentage of fees and recoveries. Early attorneys general often failed to reside full time in Washington, discharging their official duties by mail.[31] Indeed, Madison's attorney general, William Pinkney, resigned in 1814 when legislation requiring his residence in Washington was introduced.[32] When William Wirt took office in 1817, he found virtually no files or records of his predecessors' work. He also discovered he had no office and no clerical assistance. Until 1850 Congress provided the attorney general only with a single clerk. In fact, until the Civil War, the attorney general's office was basically a one-man operation.[33] Even if the attorney general had the authority to supervise U.S. attorneys and decided to exercise it, he lacked the resources to do so effectively.

United States attorneys occasionally consulted with the attorney general on a voluntary basis in the republic's early years, but the first official grant of supervisory power over their work went to the Treasury Department, not the attorney general.[34] The Civil War brought legislation that gave the attorney general his first measure of authority over U.S. attorneys. When Congress established the Department of Justice in 1870, it also granted the attorney general power to supervise U.S. attorneys.[35] However, effective control did not come for many years.[36]

The Department of Justice's creation began a long struggle for control of the government's legal functions.[37] The Department of Justice sought to monopolize litigation; the other federal departments struggled to maintain control over the conduct of their litigation. Part of this struggle involved disputes over who had the right to direct the work of U.S. attorneys. Until 1933 the solicitor of the treasury retained his formal rights of supervision first established in 1830.[38] Struggles over control of litigation arising from New Deal programs produced an executive order establishing the Department of Justice's authority over all federal litigation and reaffirming the attorney general's control over U.S. attorneys.[39] But the struggle for control continued, and several agencies retained some supervisory powers.[40]

The department emerged victorious from the struggle and faces few challenges from other federal agencies over the control and conduct of government litigation today. But its efforts to control completely its U.S. attorneys have continued. In 1953 the department succeeded in prohibiting U.S. attorneys and assistants from engaging in part-time private practice. It established the Executive Office for U.S. Attorneys and issued a comprehensive set of formal instructions and policies in the *U.S. Attorneys Manual*. A primitive marked sense card case-reporting system, begun in the late 1950s, has evolved in recent years into a computerized, remote terminal "automated litigation case-load and data collection system."

In many respects, of course, U.S. attorneys' offices exhibit the characteristics Leonard White ascribed to field offices under the control of headquarters. For instance, White notes that "In the eye of the law, all authority is vested in headquarters, and in the single person (or commission collectively) at the head of the agency."[41] Furthermore, the department utilizes nearly all of the standard means of headquarters control identified by White: a body of regulations and instructions periodically combined into an operations manual (the *U.S. Attorneys Manual*); centralized expenditure authority; instructions issued on how to handle specific matters; periodic reports required from the field; the reserving of certain decisions for headquarters only; an inspection service (run by the Executive Office); and regular meetings of field directors (the Annual Conferences of U.S. Attorneys).[42]

But U.S. attorneys' offices deviate in a number of significant respects from most field services. Typically, agencies begin with a strong headquarters organization (usually subdivided into bureaus or divisions with functional specialities) and gradually (and often reluctantly) devolve responsibilities to the field.[43] United States attorneys operated independently of any central control for almost a hundred years. The legacy of this early independence still impinges on current practices in several significant ways, and helps produce a degree of autonomy and independence from the department perhaps unmatched by any other field service in the federal government.

Many agencies with field services determine the district lines and headquarters cities of their field offices. James Fesler, a perceptive student of headquarters–field relations, identifies a number of compelling organizational considerations that administrators should use in drawing field service boundaries: the span of control; the natural physical, social, and economic areas; the desirability of equalizing workloads; relations with other governments, agencies, and private groups; administrative convenience; and political factors.[44] Congress mandated a U.S. attorney for each judicial district in the Judiciary Act of 1789, and it has never altered this arrangement. The Department of Justice inherited a set of district boundaries when it came into being in 1870, and it exerted little influence over the changes and additions made since then. Congress determines the number and boundaries of districts. Tradition and statute dictate that no federal judicial district include more than one state, and each state receives at least one district. The division of the United States and its territories into ninety-four districts impedes the department's ability to control the field offices located in them. Most federal agencies have found twenty regional offices work best. The department must supervise more than four times that many. For some purposes, one district could effectively serve the New York metropolitan area. The department cannot even experiment with such an arrangement. If it wants unified action taken in the metropolitan area, it must try to coordinate the work of four offices. Furthermore, the department cannot rely upon standard techniques of supervision, because its field offices differ widely in the size of their staffs, their workloads, and their internal structures. Because all districts fall within a state's boundaries, U.S. senators of the president's party can invoke senatorial courtesy in the appointment of U.S. attorneys in their state.

Original provisions for the appointment and removal of U.S. attorneys also survive. Most agency heads determine who will run their field offices and whether they should be retained, transferred, or removed entirely. The attorney general, however, lacks such power. The president nominates U.S. attorneys and the Senate confirms the nomination. Only the president can fire a U.S. attorney. The ability of the attorney general to hire and fire his field office supervisors rests on his influence with the president and his willingness to exert it for such a purpose. He cannot assign a U.S. attorney to another district. He possesses considerable formal power over the appointment and removal of assistant U.S. attorneys. He both appoints and fires them. In practice, however, U.S. attorneys select their assistants and forward their choices to the attorney general for ratification, and although he can fire an assistant, he cannot transfer one from one district to another.

The topsy-turvy development of the Department of Justice, with its current field staff predating headquarter's existence, eliminated a major advantage most headquarters agencies enjoy when dealing with the field. When a headquarters establishes new field offices, it frequently reassigns its own personnel from Washington to key positions. These people perform tasks that correspond to those they performed in a functional bureau or division in Washington. The loyalties of these transplanted field specialists remain with the "home" headquarters division, and their familiarity with the people there facilitates communication. This arrangement increases the responsiveness of the field to headquarters' directives, presents the generalist running the field office with serious problems in controlling and coordinating the activities of his putative subordinates, and establishes traditions of accepting Washington's directives. United States attorneys encountered no such problems, and the traditions that survived stressed loyalty to the U.S. attorney, not Washington. When U.S. attorneys have a civil and criminal division within their office, the loyalties of the assistants who head them are attached to the U.S. attorney, not the department's Civil or Criminal Divisions.

## THE RESOURCES OF U.S. ATTORNEYS

Other factors contribute to the unusual degree of independence from Washington of the U.S. attorneys' offices. The resources U.S. attorneys possess that assist them in dealing with other participants in the federal legal process are by far the most important.[45] Four resources in particular contribute to their ability to influence others and win a measure of independence: the "attorney's discretion"—the ability of any lawyer charged with handling litigation to affect its outcome; standing in the community; others' dependence on their offices' work; and a substantial amount of information unavailable to others.

### Attorney's Discretion

Because they possess the power to invoke the formal punitive powers of government, public prosecutors as a group wield awesome authority. Subject to the limitations we shall describe in subsequent chapters, U.S. attorneys (or their assistants) make the following types of decisions in most federal criminal cases:

whether grand juries should be called; what they will investigate; what evidence and witnesses are presented to them;

whether the federal investigative agency working on a case will be authorized to make an arrest, investigate further, or drop the matter;

what charges will be lodged against arrested suspects and (frequently) on how many counts;

whether bail will be recommended and at what amount;

whether some charges will be dropped or reduced in exchange for the defendant's plea of guilty;

if a trial is held, the strategy employed (which in turn influences whether a conviction is obtained).

Put another way, more than anyone else they decide whether to prosecute or not, on what charges, and with what effect. United States attorneys profoundly shape the number, type, and effectiveness of federal criminal prosecutions and federal law enforcement generally.

Though the department exerts closer supervision over civil cases handled by U.S. attorneys' offices, those actually handling these cases retain substantial influence on their outcomes. Decisions on whether to accept compromise settlements in suits against the government, for example, may require the approval of a department review attorney. But he will be hard pressed to oppose the recommendation of an assistant U.S. attorney who argues that on the basis of the plaintiff's witnesses (whom he has probably met), the judge's proclivities, and the typical behavior of local juries, his proposed settlement is a good one.

### Community Standing

Few men become U.S. attorney without the support of politically influential individuals in their district. Most achieved a degree of prominence prior to appointment, and their status increases after they obtain a presidential nomination and Senate confirmation. Those with whom he deals—judges, department attorneys, local mayors and prosecutors, private attorneys—know he possesses political skill and support. Furthermore, U.S. attorneys' knowledge of their district, gained through previous political activities and the contacts established with political and governmental officials, frequently prove valuable.

Because both U.S. attorneys and assistants live in the district and plan to remain, they enjoy substantial career flexibility. They plan to leave the position sooner or later and can usually find other attractive local employment without difficulty.

### The Dependence of Others on His Performance

The department could not begin to fulfill its responsibilities without its field service. Successful implementation of its policies in a number of areas depends upon U.S. attorneys' cooperation and effectiveness. Federal judges also find the work of U.S. attorneys important in meeting their own responsibilities. No judge concerned with keeping his docket current (and most judges are quite concerned) can ignore U.S. attorneys. All of their criminal cases and a significant number of their civil cases are handled by the U.S. attorneys' offices.[46] The number of cases U.S. attorneys bring, the number they settle, the way they schedule them, and the skill with which they handle them all have a profound impact on the work of judges.

## Information As a Resource

United States attorneys sit at the center of a communications web with links to a unique combination of points: local political and governmental agencies; local police departments; federal investigative agencies (such as the FBI); federal agencies' administrative programs in the field; U.S. senators; federal judges (themselves often well-connected politically); and the Department of Justice. As students of influence have noted, information is power. The ability of U.S. attorneys to affect decisions of department review attorneys on compromise settlements provides but one example of how information converts into influence.

## Limits on Influence

Several common features of U.S. attorneys' offices limit their influence and their ability to act independently of Washington. Traditionally, U.S. attorneys' offices have been underfinanced and understaffed. Most offices must allocate their available manpower to handle the civil and criminal cases that are routinely referred to them. "Ready-made" cases that require relatively little additional office time to develop receive priority. There simply is not enough manpower to permit an assistant to devote six months to develop a potentially interesting and significant case. Supporting services also suffer from inadequate funding. Many U.S. attorneys I interviewed complained that the quantity and quality of their clerical personnel created administrative problems.

Furthermore, assistants in most offices lack experience, and while they generally are capable and bright, they compare unfavorably in demonstrated ability with the more skilled attorneys in private practice. Salaries remain too low to attract many capable people wishing to make a career in the office, and in most districts custom dictates that assistants all resign when the party in power changes. The handful of career assistants scattered throughout the country are the exception. As the overwhelming proportion of young assistants gain the experience and skill needed to become effective advocates, they leave the office and their relatively modest salary behind for a lucrative position in private practice. Ironically, they soon find themselves demonstrat-

ing their newly acquired legal skills against their inexperienced replacements.


## THE STRUGGLE FOR CONTROL

The most interesting problem created by the existence of a field
service revolves around the question of where effective decision-
making authority should be lodged. James Fesler neatly captures the
essence of the problem. "It seems evident that what we want is a
reasonable balance between centralization and decentralization.
Complete centralization of a function runs up against the obvious fact
of the diversities in American culture and the need for adapting administration to these diversities. Complete decentralization clashes
with the need for consistency in the application of public policies and
for reasonably uniform standards of equity for people wherever they
may live."[47]

Rarely do we find vigorous proponents of greater decentralization
within a federal agency headquartered in Washington. Although an
agency's field staff may favor devolving decision-power to the field, it
rarely possesses the resources to push effectively for such a policy.
Headquarters agencies usually believe that control over decisions
must remain in Washington, and they typically dominate field personnel with overwhelmingly superior resources. The Department of
Justice presents a notable exception to the general pattern, for its field
staff has the resources, political skill, and motivation to resist complete
domination by headquarters. Thus, although the Department of Justice and the attorney general have largely won the battle to concentrate the government's legal representation within the department,
they have not yet succeeded in establishing complete domination and
control over U.S. attorneys' offices. The behavior of U.S. attorneys
and their impact on the political and legal systems cannot be understood without studying the dynamics of this on-going dispute. Three
subsequent chapters (four, five, and six) examine and analyze this
struggle.

# CHAPTER 2

# The Impact of U.S. Attorneys:
# An Overview

How important are U.S. attorneys in affecting who gets what in American society? The question is central to this book. The reason for studying politics is to understand better what happens to people and society as a result of government's action. The justification for studying U.S. attorneys ultimately depends upon the impact they have on people's lives.

The highly publicized cases which U.S. attorneys handle provide a glimpse of their impact. Some involve crimes dramatic and violent enough to appear on television police dramas. For instance, just five days after graduating from college, Duane Earl Pope walked into the Farmers State Bank in Big Springs, Nebraska, and announced a hold-up. Before leaving, he shot and killed three bank officials, whom he had forced to lie face down on the floor, and critically wounded a fourth. The trial of Patricia Hearst contained even more drama and violence. Other cases attract attention because they expose corrupt practices by elected officials. United States attorneys have prosecuted a number of such cases since 1969, including the nolo contendere plea and resignation of Vice-President Spiro Agnew, the trial of Maryland's governor, Marvin Mandel, the perjury conviction of a top aide of speaker of the House of Representatives, John McCormack, and a series of convictions of top New Jersey political figures from both parties. Members of U.S. attorneys' offices also conducted the original trial of the men charged with breaking into the Democratic National Headquarters in the Watergate Hotel and the "Chicago 7" conspiracy trial.

Most important cases tried by U.S. attorneys attract considerably less attention, but their impact often is as great. Every year, the *Annual Report of the Attorney General* describes important cases completed in the previous twelve months. In addition to describing criminal prosecutions for interstate gambling, prostitution, pornography, and theft, counterfeiting, violence and terrorism, narcotics, political corruption, and significant white collar crimes (including the conviction of per-

and the conditions under which they succeed and fail.) "Nothing was being done in labor cases," a former U.S. attorney in a large district observed, "so I asked the FBI to give me a list of ten union pension funds to be investigated. I couldn't get anything from them, so I got up a list and asked them to investigate. They said they wanted more specific allegations, so I said if I get the grand jury to subpoena the records, will you look at them? They said yes." Some U.S. attorneys attempt to affect the allocation of investigative personnel directly by reviewing agencies' activities with the agency head. One U.S. attorney reported he summoned agency heads for periodic sessions, during which he reviewed the agency's current investigations and suggested what areas should be emphasized. United States attorneys can further affect investigative aspects of federal law enforcement by coordinating the efforts of the various agencies and encouraging the sharing of information. Important cases often develop as a result. A U.S. attorney in a large district put it this way: "If the FBI arrests a known hoodlum, they don't inquire if he has a gun. They don't inform Alcohol and Tobacco Tax. 'Its not our business.' We can ask the agent, 'Did you determine if he carries a gun?' If they won't tell the other agency, they can tell us and we'll tell them." The rivalry and jealousy between agencies implied in his statement is so strong and pervasive that vigorous efforts are needed if they are to be overcome. Significantly, one of the most innovative and effective U.S. attorneys acknowledged with some unhappiness that a major portion of his time was spent dealing with problems created by attempts to achieve essential cooperation between agencies on major cases he was developing.[7]

United States attorneys can avoid relying upon investigative agencies by skillful use of investigating grand juries. The U.S. attorney's office in Baltimore built its case against Spiro Agnew through a combination of testimony obtained by granting "use immunity" before an investigating grand jury, plea bargaining with lesser participants in the kickback scheme, and analysis of subpoened records by assistant U.S. attorneys.[8] These techniques were initially developed and perfected by the U.S. attorney's office in New Jersey during its investigations of official corruption. U.S. attorneys also utilize grand juries to embarrass and entice investigative agencies into continuing investigations begun by the grand jury. The testimony produced also helps agents anxious to work on a new case justify their participation to reluctant superiors.

While the ability of U.S. attorneys to affect the direction and content of the work of grand juries and federal investigative agencies contributes to their impact, their power to control the organization of their office, the allocation of its manpower, and the type of cases brought is even more significant to federal law enforcement. One assistant attorney general in charge of the Criminal Division remarked on the inevitability of choices regarding cases: "I've found prosecutors are a day late and a dollar short. There is always more than you can do. You have to be selective. You make all kinds of policy decisions. . . . The U.S. attorney sets the priority of the docket." U.S. attorneys vary in the degree to which they recognize their role in setting the priority of the docket. However, even those who do not consciously try to influence what cases their offices bring make significant decisions by default. In essence, they leave decisions on the direction of federal law enforcement in their districts to the ad hoc and uncoordinated activities of the various investigative agencies.

Even the most passive U.S. attorney affects the impact of his office through routine prosecutorial decisions and policies. The criteria used in deciding whether to prosecute marginal cases determine who receives what from federal law enforcement. A U.S. attorney in the Middle West gave a typical example of this sort of decision. He started a new policy of filing on every bank embezzlement case, whether the amount was $500 or $500,000. His predecessor had prosecuted only about 50 percent of these cases, due to the preference of the banking institutions to avoid bad publicity. In another district, frauds on Federal Housing Authority home improvement loans were being prosecuted despite the FHA's lack of enthusiasm. "They may not want prosecution," observed the U.S. attorney, "but I don't want somebody going around my district doing this."

As this latter statement indicates, personal values and judgments about right and wrong inevitably affect who is prosecuted. After saying he did not prosecute single instances of interstate car theft, a U.S. attorney added: "Now don't misunderstand me. Even in a single act Dyer case if you've got a bad criminal you prosecute. You do exactly the same thing in an embezzlement case. If it's a small embezzlement but it involves a guy who should be prosecuted simply because he's already abused society's rules all the hell* out of shape, then you proceed to prosecute him." The handling of Dyer Act violations provide the best example of policy-making through routine decisions.[9] In some districts, all Dyer Act violations were prosecuted vigorously as a matter of principle. One southern U.S. attorney allowed how car thieves were "some of the worst criminals." In another district, the U.S. attorney brought Dyer Act cases only to satisfy the FBI's desire to build statistics as part of an unspoken agreement that they would

*Interviewees occasionally used words some people may find offensive. I have preserved their language to convey how these men think, how they interact with others, and how they sometimes reflect local and regional cultural patterns.

cooperate in turn with him on cases he deemed important. His predecessor took a more flexible position and would merely lecture to
youngsters whom he felt "needed a break." In a number of districts,
the U.S. attorney's office prosecuted Dyer Act violations only rarely.
Although some U.S. attorneys made decisions on how to handle such
cases without conscious reference to an overall strategy, others were
more aware of the implications of such choices. "You cannot prosecute every violation of the law that is brought to you," said one such
U.S. attorney. "There were a lot of cheap prosecutions available which
could have just shot your statistics sky high, but would have had no
significant impact on things."

Refusing to prosecute "cheap" cases is not the only way U.S. attorneys consciously shape the emphasis of federal law enforcement in
their districts. By assigning personnel to specific cases or specific
categories of crime, significant prosecutions can result. One U.S. attorney created and publicized a civil rights division within his office. It
was a deliberate attempt to encourage citizens to come to the office
with complaints and information on violations of civil rights legislation. The creation of consumer fraud and organized crime sections in
other districts have had similar effects. Aspects of office organization
far less conspicuous than the creation of special divisions, for example, how decisions to prosecute are made, nevertheless produce important consequences. One small office gave each assistant responsibility for all cases originating in a particular geographical subdivision
of the district. In some districts, investigative agents can bring cases to
anyone in the office who happens to be available. This procedure
permits random factors or decisions made by investigative agents to
determine if borderline cases are prosecuted. Agents can easily arrange to take a borderline case to an assistant who will make the
prosecutive decision he favors. In many of the districts studied, however, prosecutive decisions are centralized. One or two men either
make them all or carefully review preliminary decisions made by others. This procedure effectively limits agents' ability to shop for a favored assistant.

The department's acknowledgment of the role U.S. attorneys play
as executors of its policies does not adequately convey the full importance of such activities. The department can only issue guidelines to
U.S. attorneys in areas in which it seeks to establish policies. These
guidelines do not become enforced policy unless U.S. attorneys implement them. Despite a department policy to the contrary, consenting adults who engage in private correspondence of an obscene nature may find themselves prosecuted in some districts. And while it is
department policy to release defendants on their own recognizance

before trial, the percentage so released varies from district to district. As noted, the Nixon administration downgraded the priority of routine Dyer Act prosecutions. One U.S. attorney admitted that were it not for the department's guidelines, he would prosecute far more of them. Nevertheless, department officials admitted that they failed to win full compliance with the guidelines in some districts. United States attorneys also assist the department by mediating disputes between department attorneys dispatched to the field and local law enforcement officials. One U.S. attorney in a large district revealed the importance of his intercession on behalf of department attorneys dispatched to his district:

For instance, the [local] police ... wouldn't talk to the Department of Justice ... I don't know how many times I've got calls from the Superintendent of Police here. "Do you have a guy works for you by the name of so and so?" And I'd say "Ah, he's down from Washington." "Do you mind if I tell him to go piss up a rope?" "Nah, don't do that." "Look, tell that son-of-a-bitch if he wants to know anything, to ask you to ask us. I'll tell you anything. I won't tell him shit." That's the way it worked.

An official in the Tax Division during the Johnson administration assessed the limited impact U.S. attorneys had in shaping tax policy. "If we are trying to bear a course of 180 degrees," he likened, "a U.S. attorney in a medium-sized district who either doesn't understand or doesn't have any interest in tax cases will move you maybe 10 or 15 degrees off your course." But in some policy areas, high officials in the department claimed U.S. attorneys played a leading role. One such person in the Nixon administration professed shock at the previous administration's policy of permitting southern U.S. attorneys to excuse themselves from participating in civil rights cases. "That was a big mistake.... Before we would take a southern U.S. attorney, we would ask if he was willing to take part in civil rights enforcement. They have done it. They are committed to do it. This has helped in the real desegregation miracle in the South in the past year [1970]."[10]

Undoubtedly, prosecutions of many crimes deter others from committing similar crimes, although the magnitude of such deterrence effects cannot be easily measured. A U.S. attorney's decisions on what type of cases to undertake consequently affect patterns of crime in his district. The deterrent effect of prosecutions depends in part on the publicity that accompanies them. United States attorneys skilled in public relations contribute to deterrence by securing extensive publicity for their prosecutions. Those lacking such skills or the motivation to employ them exert less influence on criminal behavior through deterrence.

*Effect on the Direction and Impact of the Federal Civil Process*

Certainly criminal prosecution provides most of the glamor, publicity, and valuable courtroom experience in U.S. attorneys' offices—a fact those specializing in civil work somewhat wistfully acknowledge. However, in sheer volume and effort expended, civil matters account for about 40 percent of the work of these offices.

By and large, U.S. attorneys act as counsel for the defendant in civil actions. Tort suits against the government arise from a variety of sources, including auto accidents involving government vehicles (particularly postal service trucks), alleged medical malpractice in government hospitals, and aviation accidents. Contractors sue the government over disputes stemming from work performed for a variety of agencies. In addition, there are a number of suits against federal agencies alleging improper enforcement of federal legislation (for example, improper administration of the food stamp program by the Department of Agriculture; illegal ocean dumping of nerve gas by the Department of Defense; discriminatory administration of funds by the Department of Housing and Urban Development). The department dispatches attorneys from Washington to handle some of these cases, but limited manpower forces it to delegate many to the field.[11]

Because much of their civil work is defensive in character, U.S. attorneys are unable to shape the direction and emphasis of civil litigation in their districts as they do in the criminal area. This does not mean, however, that defending civil actions affords no opportunities to affect outcomes significantly. The department seeks to direct the efforts of assistants in these cases, but the actual handling of a case depends upon the ability of these assistants. A politically appointed administrator in the Civil Division acknowledged that how assistants handled a case under supervision from Washington made a "night and day" difference in the outcome. The trial attorney marshals the facts, conducts discovery, and pulls the case together. Failure to conduct adequate pretrial discovery and to obtain depositions can tie the hands of the department official who must authorize settlements in important cases. More than anyone, the assistant in the field determines whether a compromise settlement or trial verdict results and what the size of the award will be.

In isolated but strategically significant instances, U.S. attorneys' offices' participation in civil litigation goes beyond shaping the outcome of a particular case. They can affect both department policy and the content of precedent-setting decisions. The Southern District of New York handles tax matters that the department's Tax Division handles everywhere else in the country, including cases in so-called "prime areas" which involve crucial questions in unsettled and developing areas of tax law. The head of the tax division in this district described why their participation allowed them to shape federal tax policy. "We know what arguments and strategies will win the case," he said. "We are most familiar with the case. Our policy will carry some weight."

United States attorneys sometimes represent the government as plaintiff. The U.S. attorney in the Southern District of New York led the government's efforts in June 1971, to bar the *New York Times* from publishing further installments of its series on the "Pentagon Papers."[12] United States attorneys have represented the Environmental Protection Agency in several significant actions to halt industrial pollution by major corporations.[13] But normally the civil cases the federal government initiates are less exciting and extraordinary. The Army Corps of Engineers or another agency often must go to court to acquire land for a federal project. As trial counsel in land condemnation cases, U.S. attorneys help determine the size of payments of confiscated land. Their efforts to impose civil penalties and fines, effect forfeitures, and collect debts owed the government constitute an even more mundane and low visibility activity. In fact, assistants dislike routine civil work, like collections, so much that the department must constantly prod them to devote time and resources to it. As an assistant in charge of a civil division in a large district observed, "Who wants to become an assistant U.S. attorney and spend all his time trying to collect bad debts?" Astonishing deficiencies in such efforts become established policy in some districts. A newly appointed U.S. attorney in a small district learned that for at least fifteen years, the office made no efforts whatsoever to collect fines imposed by the district court. Despite U.S. attorneys' lack of enthusiasm for such activities, their offices collect substantial sums. In fiscal year 1975, for example, the total amount collected in fines, forfeitures, penalties, foreclosures, bond forfeitures, and other civil judgments surpassed $152 million.[14]

The greater appeal of criminal cases, the active participation of department lawyers in many civil cases, and the essentially defensive character of most of these cases provide few opportunities for U.S. attorneys to develop significant cases in the civil area. In one area with tremendous potential, civil fraud, the department requires the approval of the civil fraud section's chief or the assistant attorney general before allowing the initiation of suit. The politically sensitive nature of such prosecutions results in fewer prosecutions, depriving U.S. attorneys of opportunities to participate in explosive and important cases. Nevertheless, they encounter some opportunities to affect the impact of civil litigation. Some U.S. attorneys seek to forestall attempts to bog down tax investigations by vigorously pursuing tax-payers who fail to comply with subpoenas to appear before IRS agents. The ex-chief of a large office's civil division described to me how he encouraged his men to tackle major projects: "I always try to make mountains out of molehills. It is surprising to see the number of times that agencies would come in with what looked like a small prob-lem but by the time it really was developed, the problems were of greater magnitude."

## The Quality and Public Image of Federal Justice

Framed and hanging on the wall of most U.S. attorneys' offices is a quotation from a Supreme Court opinion of the 1930s commenting on their duties: "The United States Attorney is the representative not of an ordinary party to a controversy, but of a sovereignty whose obligation to govern impartially is as compelling as its obligation to govern at all; and whose interest, therefore, in criminal prosecution is not that it shall win a case, but that justice shall be done."[15] Whether they adhere to these principles or not, U.S. attorneys significantly influence the quality of federal justice in both the civil and criminal areas. The term "quality," particularly when applied to an ambiguous concept like "justice," defies precise definition. Here it is used to designate in a general way the extent to which commonly accepted standards of due process, fairness, and equal treatment are met.

In the criminal area, the quality of federal justice depends in part on the treatment criminal defendants receive. Are investigative agents harsh, impolite, and vindictive in dealing with them or considerate and dispassionate? Do they make a sincere effort to inform them of their pretrial legal rights or merely go through the gestures required to prevent dismissal of the case? Are technical violations of statutes prosecuted rigidly or is flexibility displayed? Are subtle pressures exerted to discourage jury trials? To what extent are the bargains struck during the negotiations for guilty pleas shaped by the social standing of the defendant or the reputation and skill of his attorney? When trials are conducted, how balanced and dispassionate is the prosecutor's presentation? Does he supply information to the defense that bolsters its case if he has it or does he sit on it? If an inexperi-enced court-appointed attorney represents the defendant, does the office cooperate in the preparation of his defense or let him struggle along on his own? Is evidence of questionable admissibility presented in the hopes of slipping it past, or is its possible inadmissibility called to the attention of the court? The answers to such questions shape the quality of federal justice. U.S. attorneys' offices help determine how they are answered.[16]

United States attorneys' experience and expertise make them a useful source to consult when formulating the rules of criminal procedure used throughout the federal court system. A former assistant attorney general in charge of the Criminal Division reported that when he served on the Supreme Court's committee to revise the rules, in the late 1960s, he relied upon the advice of several U.S. attorneys extensively. In one instance, their criticisms of a proposed change altered his position and ultimately affected the final outcome. In 1973, the department established a committee composed of fifteen U.S. attorneys to advise the attorney general. According to the *Annual Report of the Attorney General,* the committee has had a significant impact on the development of the Federal Rules of Civil Procedure.[17]

Civil cases also provide U.S. attorneys with opportunities to affect the nature of federal justice. Are reasonable compromises offered and accepted or do citizens have to endure the trouble, expense, and delay entailed by a trial? Are collection cases handled compassionately and flexibly or is payment demanded and enforced regardless of the consequences to the debtor? Are the superior investigative and financial resources of the government used to "just grind over an individual by dragging out the case for five years and wipe [the defendant] into submission" as one respondent observed was in his power? And how are the difficult moral dilemmas, like the one reflected in the following comments of a former head of a large district's civil division, resolved? "Looking back, when I worked there I thought everything I did was right. You know, 'I represent the United States of America.' But I'm not satisfied now that every single move that we made was the right thing. We got a couple of cases where the plaintiff's counsel—one of them was a tax case and the other a tort claims case—had been incredibly negligent and we managed to get the case dismissed." As in the criminal area, the choices and actions of U.S. attorneys and assistants in such situations inevitably affect the quality of justice.

Finally, U.S. attorneys can improve the quality of federal legal proceedings by helping to train local attorneys. As one judge interviewed put it, "If you have a real good lawyer, the younger ones will learn from him. Other lawyers pick up his techniques. This is especially true of the U.S. attorney." Some U.S. attorneys recognize clearly their potential impact in this respect: "The U.S. attorney has a missionary job to encourage the effective use of the federal machinery. If the

U.S. attorney doesn't do it, the county prosecutor from Groddle Switch isn't going to do it. I would suggest that they serve interrogatories on *me* sometimes."

United States attorneys' activities shape the image of federal justice in general and the image of their office in particular. The manner in which they conduct themselves inevitably influences the attitudes of those in daily contact with them (private attorneys, judges, jurors, the press, defendants). These people form opinions about the vigor, competence, and fairness of the office. An office that is involved in a number of important cases will begin to rise above its typical obscurity to become visible to the general public. Even when it does not, special segments of the public (the legal profession, newspaper reporters, business and labor leaders, and politicians) will form opinions about the office. Thus, an office's image is shaped by what it does and how it does it, regardless of whether or not the U.S. attorney consciously seeks to mold it. Many U.S. attorneys make no conscious efforts to mold their offices' image. Some, however, actively seek to create a specific image. One such man believed his most important decision was to change the image of the office from what it had been. In addition to renovating the office and reorganizing its internal structure, he set about injecting himself into the local community as U.S. attorney. He met with the local city counsel on narcotics problems and devoted considerable attention to his relations with the press, sometimes spending three or four days dealing with the press on big cases. Some U.S. attorneys also accept speaking invitations to try to shape attitudes toward the U.S. attorney's office and federal law enforcement. Thus, a U.S. attorney may appear on a television panel or before a civic organization to explain the structure and functioning of federal law enforcement, to speak more generally on "respect for law," or to affect attitudes toward a specific aspect of law enforcement. Several U.S. attorneys used speaking engagements to encourage compliance with the 1964 Civil Rights Act. One southern respondent reported making over a dozen speeches to manufacturers' associations, the Rotary, and similar organizations on the content and import of the bill. Several U.S. attorneys met with groups of hometown lawyers in communities throughout their districts to explain the legislation.

### Impact on the Legal Process at the Local Level

United States attorneys possess excellent information about the performance of local law enforcement agencies. The FBI and other federal investigative agencies provide information about local criminal activity. They sometimes conduct investigations of local agencies for violations of civil rights or official corruption. They also deal directly with local prosecutors and police on cases with concurrent federal jurisdiction. Since most U.S. attorneys possess considerable political and legal experience in the community, they often have personal knowledge of the local criminal justice system's performance. Some U.S. attorneys I interviewed considered themselves the chief law enforcement officer in their district and willingly utilized the information they possessed to try to improve local law enforcement.

United States attorneys' interest in local law enforcement manifests itself in a number of ways. One U.S. attorney, concerned with local resentment against Supreme Court decisions on the right to counsel before trial, reported visiting a number of state judges to explain the decisions. He arranged with the local chief of police to give a two-hour lecture to the entire police department on the *Escobedo* and *Gideon* cases to try to stop abuses of defendants' pretrial right to counsel. He also helped organize a fraternal organization of local, state, and federal law enforcement officers to build friendships and improve cooperation and the exchange of information and ideas among them.

Investigations and prosecutions of local police officers influence directly the diligence, procedures, and structure of local police organizations. One man deeply concerned about long-standing graft and corruption in the local police department managed to initiate an investigation. The result was prosecution of several officers for evasion of income tax due on graft income. Although only a few convictions were obtained, he felt the system of graft was badly shaken and the overall quality of police administration improved.[18] Another U.S. attorney learned from a federal undercover agent that bets had been placed in front of a policeman. The U.S. attorney quietly contacted the local chief of police and informed him of the situation. The extremely close ties to the local police of some U.S. attorneys facilitate such informal representations, especially when local police violate civil rights laws.[19] But U.S. attorneys without such ties can also influence the local police department's behavior. "If you pick up gamblers," explained one U.S. attorney, "and the local police have been doing nothing, it puts them on the spot."[20]

Finally, U.S. attorneys sometimes shape the behavior of local prosecutors. One U.S. attorney said he had daily conversations with several local prosecutors. A colleague in a neighboring state reported that state prosecutors and judges called him up for advice, especially if they had a problem in a case involving a federal law or a Supreme

Court decision. By serving as a "resource man," this U.S. attorney could influence the interpretation and use of federal decisions at the local level.

Fewer opportunities to affect the civil side of the local legal process exist. But one district brought several important cases that had a direct bearing on the integrity and fairness of civil proceedings in the local courts. The most important one involved the practice of "sewer service," where process servers falsely claimed to have served summonses. Because the unsummoned failed to appear in court, default judgments were entered against them. In addition to prosecuting crooked process servers, a civil injunction was obtained against a jewelry store which made it a practice of routinely resorting to "sewer service" when suing its customers for uncollected accounts. These actions attracted considerable local publicity and set off a chain of further developments. The city council gave itself jurisdiction over the process serving "industry," a new state law was passed giving the attorney general jurisdiction in the area, and local prosecutors were embarrassed into beginning other cases involving "sewer service."

### Impact beyond the Legal Process

Because U.S. attorneys must enforce the civil or criminal sanctions that accompany many federal programs, their position provides an excellent vantage point to observe the quality of administration and the impact of these programs. For example, U.S. attorneys take to court borrowers who default on Federal Housing Authority- or Veterans Administration-backed mortgages. Lax procedures and improper administration of such programs often become evident to the individual handling the case. In one district, the U.S. attorney's office indicted two home siding contractors for preparing a loan application for substantially more than the cost of the work. The surplus, minus a kickback to the contractors, was to go to the homeowner to pay other debts. The U.S. attorney's office discovered that the savings and loan association which granted the federally guaranteed loan did not investigate the loan application, the credit rating of the borrower, or the contractors. The U.S. attorney wrote to the Federal Home Loan Bank Board, setting forth the facts of the bank's laxness, observing that such practices seemed to be widespread, and requesting notification of any action taken to require banks to exercise more prudence.

United States attorneys in several districts complained about the Small Business Administration's "deplorable" procedures for checking the loan security borrowers offered. One informed the new administrator in the region that "they could better protect their own legal rights by filing their liens on time and filing them properly." He indicated that some procedural changes resulted from his efforts. In instances like these, U.S. attorneys can provide other decision-makers with important information that otherwise would go unreported.[21]

In their capacity as legal counsel, U.S. attorneys sometimes inject themselves into the policy-making process of client agencies to shape the decisions rendered. In preparing to condemn land for a federal dam, a U.S. attorney discovered that the agency sought more land than was necessary, and succeeded in having the parcel's size reduced. Another U.S. attorney prevailed upon the Small Business Administration to delay foreclosing on a loan to an insolvent furniture factory. Because he felt his district needed the jobs the factory provided, he spent considerable time and effort in informal attempts to salvage the furniture company or induce another enterprise to take over the premises. Whenever federal agencies deal directly with citizens about matters that lead to litigation (such as the amount to offer in compromise), U.S. attorneys' potential to affect these decisions may come into play.

Some U.S. attorneys engage in public debate on matters of public policy. The U.S. attorney in San Francisco, for example, was quoted in a *New York Times* article as describing the sentences and fines imposed on sit-in participants as "outrageous."[22] Statements U.S. attorneys make in their capacities as private citizens sometimes receive publicity because they hold public office. One who attended the General Assembly of the Presbyterian Church as a delegate, for instance, received mention in another *New York Times* article for his stand in favor of permitting Martin Luther King to address the gathering.[23]

The Hatch Act prohibits U.S. attorneys from engaging in traditional partisan political activities, such as making campaign speeches, holding party office, or acting as a party spokesman. Nevertheless, their activities frequently directly affect partisan politics and the struggle for power. Participation in politically sensitive cases that affect the fortunes of a local party, faction, or prominent politician provide the most dramatic examples. Between 1969 and 1973, the U.S. attorney's office in New Jersey prosecuted and convicted the mayor of Newark and a number of other city officials, obtained a plea of guilty from the Democratic "Boss" of Hudson County, convicted the mayor and other officials of Jersey City, and indicted the former Republican state chairman.[24] The U.S. attorney's office in Baltimore prosecuted the Baltimore County executive and the governor. The Southern District of New York undertook prosecution of former Attorney General John Mitchell and Nixon Campaign Treasurer Maurice Stans. United States attorneys told me about a number of less well-publicized prosecutions with political ramifications—a Republican prosecuted members of the state Democratic administration for misuse of federal highway funds; another Republican participated in an election fraud case against state Democratic officials; a Democrat prosecuted an alleged organized crime boss with ties to the state Republican party; a Democrat won the enduring hostility of a powerful local Democratic organization by prosecuting an embarrassingly high appointive member of the police department. By far the most important "political" case initiated by a U.S. attorney's office in recent times occurred in Baltimore. Evidently, the investigation of possible corruption in Maryland state politics began during the Johnson administration under the Democratic U.S. attorney.[25] It continued under his Republican replacement, George Beall. The investigation grew until it included the vice-president as a principal potential defendant. It was only after the case had progressed that the department, as is typical in "hot" cases, was brought into the picture. There is probably no better example of how an independent U.S. attorney, acting largely on his own, can initiate an investigation that has the most profound impact on the political process.

United States attorneys do not treat such cases as routine matters, of course. No one enters lightly into prosecuting political figures in either party. This does not mean that such cases result in prosecutions or declinations where they normally would not. But the decision on how to proceed is arrived at more cautiously and with more consultation than decisions on routine cases.[26] It is only natural to prosecute cases embarrassing to the other party with a little more vigor and a little more attention to careful preparation.[27] Furthermore, when juicy cases against members of the party that has just recaptured the presidency are in progress, incumbent U.S. attorneys often try to stay in office until they have completed these prosecutions.

The department's practice of playing an active role in politically sensitive cases reduces the likelihood that purely partisan calculations will lead to prosecution of a weak case. Of course, this restraint depends upon the department's ability to resist partisan temptation. Regardless of whether the U.S. attorney or the department makes the final decision to go ahead on a sensitive case, and irrespective of its merits, the individual who brings such a case can expect to become embroiled in controversy. It is exceedingly difficult to dispel effectively charges that partisan political considerations really inspired such prosecutions. A candidate for the gubernatorial nomination in Minnesota in 1966 indicted by the U.S. attorney for fraud illustrated what may happen. He issued a statement during his campaign claiming that he was indicted purely for political reasons, and that the charge was brought "for the sole purpose of advancing the candidacy of the U.S. attorney for U.S. district judge."[28]

Other activities of U.S. attorneys impinge upon partisan politics. Most U.S. attorneys engaged in partisan politics before their appointments, and it is not surprising that many continue to exert influence in party politics. "You are still permitted to contribute to the party while you're in," observed a former U.S. attorney who went on to become a national committeeman, "and you can't be expected to end the friendships that you have with people that you've made over the years. And you can't be expected to give up talking about, or giving observations on an avocation of yours that you've always been interested in."[29] Another politically oriented U.S. attorney illustrated how enmeshed in the local political scene some incumbents are: "You get calls from various people in politics. 'I heard by the grapevine that so and so is going to file for mayor. You got any information that you can help me out?' And you would have information possibly.... It happened with great frequency. Any time that a man in politics was in the building, he would usually drop in and say hello. He might sit down and shoot the breeze for fifteen or twenty minutes and just exchange viewpoints." The appointment of assistant U.S. attorneys also requires U.S. attorneys' involvement in local politics in some districts, especially when strong local and state political organizations of the incumbent's party exist. In these districts, appointments necessitate a complex process of negotiation, bargaining, and clearance of appointees with party leaders.

United States attorneys also provide information to political leaders and friends about conditions in their districts. One respondent claimed that some U.S. attorneys supply their senators with a steady stream of information about such developments. In his book *Crime in America,* former Attorney General Ramsey Clark strongly implies that U.S. attorneys provide U.S. senators with political intelligence.[30] Although I obtained no direct confirmation of this, it is reasonable to suppose that it occurs. A U.S. attorney did confirm that politicians other than senators rely upon them for information. "Robert Kennedy ... used the U.S. attorneys as a sort of political catch-all," he explained. "He wanted to know what was going on in a particular area ... so he'd call up the U.S. attorney and the U.S. attorney would say, 'Well, call up so-and-so, he would know.'" He reported that Kennedy once called him and asked for an assessment of the changes in attitude toward a Catholic president that had occurred in the state.[31]

At times, department officials have gone beyond seeking information to request U.S. attorneys to support publicly the administration's policies and programs. In his book about his experiences as U.S.

attorney in Manhattan during the Nixon administration, Whitney North Seymour reprints a teletype message sent to U.S. attorneys' offices by the department's director of public information in April 1973. It reported the substance of Attorney General Kleindienst's remarks at the Western regional meeting of U.S. attorneys on the "exhaustive" nature of the FBI's Watergate investigation and added some supplementary statistics on the work done by the FBI. The message concluded, "I hope this information will be of use to you in any public comments and speeches you may be called on to make."[32] Seymour reports that Kleindienst told the Annual Conference of U.S. attorneys in June 1971, that it was "of the utmost importance to keep this administration in power and you men must do everything you can to insure that result."[33] Kleindienst repeatedly told U.S. attorneys in the following months to stress the law-and-order record of the administration and avoid actions that would lose votes.[34]

# CHAPTER 3

# Appointment and Prior Careers

Title 28, Section 501 of the United States Code gives the president the power to appoint U.S. attorneys, but it also requires Senate confirmation of his nominees.[1] Only the president can remove an incumbent U.S. attorney.[2] Recommendations of nominees for vacancies come formally from the attorney general to the president, but in practice the deputy attorney general's office assumes the major responsibility for all but the most important and controversial appointments.[3]

Several considerations sharply limit the field of prospective candidates. Appointees must reside in the district to which they are appointed and must be attorneys. In the overwhelming proportion of appointments, the department only considers lawyers belonging to the president's political party. Finally, appointees must be selected with an eye to the reaction of the Senate. The custom of "senatorial courtesy" has transformed the procedural requirement of Senate confirmation into a potent resource for senators of the president's party from the state where a vacancy occurs.[4] Such senators can utilize this resource to exert significant influence on the final appointment if they so desire. In fact, some students of senatorial courtesy believe that senators actually control the nomination of federal officers such as U.S. attorneys.[5] Others contend that the president usually can freely nominate whomever he wants and obtain approval.[6] My research suggests that neither view accurately depicts U.S. attorneys' appointment process.[7] Senators frequently influence appointments, but the deputy attorney general's office overall exerts more influence than any other participant.

## THE STRATEGIC ENVIRONMENT OF U.S. ATTORNEYS' APPOINTMENTS

The field research uncovered four crucial elements in U.S. attorneys' appointments that interact to produce a varied and complex recruitment process. They are the identity of the senators, the point in the presidential electoral cycle when the appointment is made, the nature of the district, and special circumstances that occasionally arise.[8]

## Who Are the Senators?

Only senators from the president's party ordinarily invoke senatorial courtesy successfully. Senators from the "out" party consequently do not usually participate in the selection of nominees to federal posts in their state.[9] Usually, however, a new administration finds at least one senator from its president's party who can invoke courtesy. Eighty-three percent of the Kennedy administration's appointments in 1961 involved at least one Democratic senator, and the figure for the Carter administration in 1977 rose to 86 percent. Despite the weaker position of the Republicans in the Senate, both the Eisenhower and Nixon administrations found over half of their U.S. attorneys came from states with at least one Republican senator.[10]

When both senators belong to the president's party,[11] they may find a common candidate or decide who will take major responsibility for an appointment. If several districts serve their state, the two senators sometimes divide responsibility geographically. In one two-district state, each senator controlled the appointment to one district. The senators from a three-district state each assumed responsibility for the appointment in their home area and consulted on the third. Sometimes, one senator (most likely the senior senator) may possess enough influence to handle all appointments himself. Occasionally, a powerful state political leader can force both senators to accede to his choice. These arrangements seek to avoid conflict and deadlock between senators, but they sometimes fail. One respondent indicated that after making a number of recommendations which failed to win both senators' approval, he reluctantly agreed to take the post himself as a compromise candidate.

A senator's bargaining strength vis-à-vis the administration depends partially on his ability to affect the fate of legislation in the Senate. The department pays particular attention to the recommendations of the chairman and other influential members of the Judiciary Committee. In addition, the respect and esteem a senator commands in the Senate determines the probability of his successfully invoking courtesy. The Senate occasionally refuses to honor the objection of a senator held in low esteem by his colleagues.[12]

## The Appointment's Timing

The strategic environment surrounding appointments changes depending on when in the presidential electoral cycle a vacancy occurs.

When a new administration takes office, incumbent U.S. attorneys normally submit their resignation regardless of when their appointment expires. The president must nominate some ninety U.S. attorneys in the space of a few months. Patronage commitments and political obligations incurred in the nomination and election drives of the new president are numerous and often compelling. Respondents described instances in which political allies of the new president received the nomination despite the fact that key members of the department favored another man. Although patronage claims continue to operate later in the life of an administration, they exert more influence immediately following the inauguration. The policy objectives of the new administration also affect early appointments. Several men chosen at the beginning of the Eisenhower era claimed the administration sought to demonstrate that the Republicans could govern efficiently and cleanly, and looked for men it thought could do so. Prospective nominees may accept the post because they wish to participate in implementing administration programs. "I took the job," an early Eisenhower appointee told me, "because I thought I could do it. The GOP was coming in after a twenty year drought. I felt that if I took over for a while, I could make an impact on the public." The Kennedy administration wanted to attack organized crime, and it examined the ability of prospective appointees in crucial districts to act vigorously and competently in this field. One respondent revealed that in his two-minute interview with Attorney General Robert Kennedy, he was asked only if he supported the program of the president and if he had ever represented anyone connected with organized crime. I interviewed several Republican U.S. attorneys who indicated their strong agreement with Richard Nixon's emphasis on strict law enforcement in his 1968 presidential campaign. Undoubtedly, prospective appointees' agreement with the new president's "law and order" stance figured in the appointment, but the new administration sought men whose agreement with the president went beyond issues of law enforcement. In the words of one high official directly involved in appointing U.S. attorneys, they "were looking for... qualified men committed in support of the policy and leadership of President Nixon." He claimed all prospective appointees agreed to resign at the request of the president or the attorney general, and that they were told to insure that people on their staffs were loyal to them and to the administration.

When a man appointed at the outset of a new administration resigns, a different set of factors comes into play. The department finds policy considerations less salient. The tasks of running the department and handling on-going litigation consume much of its attention. Appointments to sporadic vacancies attract less concern for the policy goals that dominate in the first rush of enthusiasm and excitement after the inauguration. Rewarding the president's supporters also becomes less compelling as the administration ages. Finally, a new contingent of very strong candidates—incumbent assistant U.S. attorneys—can demonstrate proven ability and provide continuity. Evidently, the department finds incumbent assistants very attractive. A study of the careers of U.S. attorneys serving between 1961 and 1973 based on published biographical data (described later in this chapter) provides hard evidence of this. Of the 153 men for whom data are available, 36 received an appointment more than eighteen months after a new president won election. Over one-third of them (13 of the 36) had served previously as an assistant U.S. attorney at some point in his career, and most of them (9 of 13) were assistants at the time they became U.S. attorneys. Only about 18 percent of the men appointed during the first months of a newly elected president's term had served as U.S. attorneys.[13]

Appointments made toward the end of an administration's term present special problems, particularly if the president will not be running for reelection or if his reelection is doubtful. A U.S. attorney in office in 1960 described the problem that arose when his term expired shortly before the election. "It would be very difficult to get anyone to take an appointment like that, when they didn't know what the outcome would be with the election coming up in November." He refused reappointment, but agreed to stay until the election. The dislocation in a private practice that accepting the U.S. attorneyship entails strongly discourages prospective appointees in such situations. Consequently, assistant U.S. attorneys become even stronger candidates. They encounter none of the problems associated with breaking off a private practice. Their experience and known performance appeal to politicians anxious to avoid embarrassment that could come about by misconduct or incompetence in the U.S. attorney's office just before election time. Occasionally, however, other factors dispose an administration to recruit an outsider to take a late-term appointment. In one case, an influential congressman persuaded an elderly and rather inactive incumbent to resign and recruited a younger man to improve the image of the office and groom the appointee for a federal judgeship.

### The Nature of the District

In some districts, members of the federal court community (judges, courtroom personnel, members of the bar, certain local politicians, and the press) develop common views of the nature of the U.S. attorney's office. This consensus helps define the desirability of the post to potential candidates. The office's image attracts men who meet expectations to seek or at least accept the post and discourages others. Common conceptions of the office also guide the efforts of lawyers, judges, and politicians (including senators) in recruiting candidates and lobbying on their behalf. Career officials in the department acquire knowledge of this consensus also, and their input into the recruitment process shapes the department's decisions on whom to recommend.[14] Of course, districts differ in the strength and extent of this consensus. In some districts, apparently little agreement exists.

The content of consensus also varies widely. In some districts it stereotypes U.S. attorneys' stature and legal ability, considering men who have served as U.S. attorney to be among the most distinguished and competent members of the bar. In others it regards them as politically ambitious but professionally mediocre. The consensus in some districts accepts U.S. attorneys with only nominal membership and past service in the president's political party provided they display impressive legal talents. In others, the office is regarded as the province of the party in power, and purely "political" qualifications outweigh legal skills. A former U.S. attorney in one such district described the local view of the office as follows: "Generally, it's a political office . . . I was named by Senator 'Jones' and Senator 'Smith.' . . . I'd never been in federal court before in my life." In another district, an aspiring appointee ran for a political office against a strongly entrenched incumbent in the hope that his "sacrifice" would entitle him to the U.S. attorneyship. A few districts exhibit such a strong tradition of nonpartisanship that party affiliation is not important. In 1976 the two U.S. attorneys from Mississippi, the state represented by the chairman of the Senate Judiciary Committee, James Eastland, had served both Republican and Democratic administrations since 1961. The U.S. attorney in Oregon, who also served during the Kennedy–Johnson era, remained in office through the Nixon–Ford years as well.

Expectations about where U.S. attorneys go after resigning also form part of the consensus in some districts. One incumbent U.S. attorney informed me eagerly that in his district the U.S. attorney "is in a good position—he is usually considered, at one time or another—for a federal judgeship." Occasionally, the federal court community regards the U.S. attorneyship as a jumping-off point to high elective office. More often, however, it is seen as a political dead-end but a real boon to the incumbent's subsequent private practice.

Other characteristics of judicial districts affect who fills vacancies.

As indicated, in some districts powerful local political leaders select the nominee. Sometimes, the type of cases commonly arising in the district (for example, organized crime) cause the department to seek candidates with special skills in handling them.

### Special Circumstances Influencing Appointments

Sometimes, unusual circumstances assume overriding importance in an appointment. When the hint of scandal touches a U.S. attorney's office, the department pays special attention to a new appointee's qualities. In one such instance, a U.S. attorney was implicated indirectly in a serious political scandal. Although his involvement was tangential and did not relate to his conduct in the U.S. attorney's office, the department felt embarrassed by his presence and asked him to resign. His successor, an assistant U.S. attorney with modest political credentials in a district where it was normally important to have them, described the special situation leading to his selection: "Other things being equal, they [the administration, senators, and other political leaders] thought it'd be good if someone acquainted with the office would sort of take over and do a good job—to show that the office itself was not corrupt. . . . If all this had happened the year before or the year after, I'd have never become U.S. attorney."

Another unusual configuration occurs when political factions stalemate over who should receive an appointment. Occasionally, no one can successfully survive the appointment process. In one such case, a court-appointed U.S. attorney with absolutely no political support served a long time while the controversy over who should receive the permanent appointment raged. Local political leaders were incensed because they felt they should have had the dominant role in designating the choice. They were able to prevent the administration from submitting the court appointee's name to the Senate, but they were unable to propose an acceptable alternative of their own. The senator involved, in conflict with the local leaders, came to support the court appointee. But he too was unable to secure his permanent appointment. As a result, the court appointee served as acting U.S. attorney until a new administration came to power.

## PARTICIPANTS IN THE APPOINTMENT PROCESS

The strategic environment of an appointment establishes the key variables that shape the outcome. But enumerating the variations in strategic environments tells us little of the dynamics of the process.

For this, we must examine the interactions of the significant actors in the appointment process.

### The Department of Justice

My research on the appointment of U.S. attorneys indicates that the Department of Justice plays a crucial role. The entire appointment process can best be understood by focusing the discussion around the department and its interaction with other actors. We could add to the complexity of the discussion considerably by investigating the internal dynamics of the selection process within the Justice Department. While the deputy attorney general customarily takes responsibility for recommending nominees, he must rely on subordinates to do the preliminary screening. In at least two recent administrations, this task has fallen upon the director of the Executive Office for U.S. Attorneys. Other department officials, including the deputy attorney general himself, have also played active roles. To make the analysis more manageable, the department will be treated as a unitary actor. Actually, however, appointments can and do sometimes create conflict within it.

The department's influence on appointments rests on its ability to determine whose name the president will submit to the Senate for confirmation. Although the Senate may reject the nominee, no one can receive a permanent appointment without the presidential nomination. In addition, the attorney general can appoint an acting U.S. attorney where there is a vacancy, delay submitting a controversial nomination until Congress adjourns, and refuse to submit the name of a permanent appointee when he wants an acting U.S. attorney or a court appointee to continue in office.

Another important source of the department's strength arises from its strong incentive to see acceptable men receive the post. An incompetent or corrupt U.S. attorney creates trouble for the department. Consequently, it expends considerable time and manpower gathering information on prospective appointees and working for the selection of acceptable candidates.

### U.S. Senators

Significant restraints on the department's discretion in selecting nominees arise from the interactions with other important participants in the appointment process, particularly members of the Senate. They provide by far the most important challenge to the department's hegemony, particularly if one or both senators from a state where a vacancy exists belong to the president's party. As indicated, the ability to veto an appointment by invoking senatorial courtesy has led some political scientists to believe that senators exert the predominant influence. This is an overstatement, but courtesy provides enough leverage to offset partially the resources of the department so that a good deal of give-and-take bargaining occurs.

This bargaining takes place before the appointment is submitted to the Senate for confirmation. Both parties anxiously seek to avoid a situation where courtesy is actually invoked. If a senator rises to declare one of his president's appointees "personally obnoxious" to him, it is a costly and embarrassing situation for all concerned. In practice, senators can usually block an appointment more quietly. The Judiciary Committee sends the senator a "blue slip" reading, "I have no objection to ———— as U.S. attorney." It will not act on the appointment until the slip is returned to them.[15] If the senator fails to return it, the Department of Justice finds itself in the position of having a candidate whose appointment languishes in committee throughout the session.[16]

Senators differ markedly in their interest in pushing a particular candidate. Some conform to the pattern described in accounts of senatorial courtesy. They actively recruit men interested in the post and present their names to the department as their choice. "I was a good friend of both my Senators," a Nixon appointee told me. "(The senior senator) first mentioned it to me. I really hadn't seriously considered the appointment until he asked me if I wanted to be U.S. attorney." A man appointed during the Johnson administration had a similar experience. "I got a call from Washington one day and they wanted to know when I was coming in town next . . . [the senator] told me what he had in mind. I said, 'I'm not interested,' and he began to go to work and put pressure on me." Some senators, however, appear genuinely uninterested in pushing a personal choice for U.S. attorney. In one instance, the successful candidate claimed that he did not know the senator prior to his appointment. The first contact came after he solicited support from people he learned the senator respected when the senator called and informed him he would be nominated. Others find it impossible to make the choice themselves because of the political situation in their state. One very influential southern senator found that although he had the ultimate say, he had to ratify a man chosen by a powerful political faction in the state. According to the appointee, several factions had agreed to a patronage split. The U.S. attorneyship went to the eventual appointee's faction, which in turn selected him for the post.[17] Some senators find they must accept the choice of powerful local politicians. In one district, such a figure with close ties to the president also happened to be an indispensable electoral ally of the senator. The local politician, a mayor, really decided who the appointee would be. The senator's support was sought and obtained, but the mayor convinced the administration to choose his man over someone favored by top department officials.

Though locally based factions or individuals may dictate the senator's choice, he can still demand that the department nominate this individual. However, most senators refrain from submitting just one name to the department. An official in the Kennedy and Johnson administrations estimated only 15 to 20 percent of appointments involved this procedure.[18] Instead, most senators submit a list of about five names. Sometimes, the senator designates whom he prefers, but often he states that all are well qualified and indicates no preference. Such neutrality absolves senators under conflicting pressure from friends and supporters from responsibility for the final choice. Some senators fail to designate a choice because they do not care who becomes U.S. attorney. Others, particularly those who practiced in the federal courts, genuinely feel that the attorney general ought to choose the appointee.

Occasionally, a senator designates a nominee unacceptable to the department. When that happens, the department has a problem. If the list contains a better nominee than the man designated by the senator, it must come up with a reason to give the senator for rejecting his choice. Sometimes, the department states its objections bluntly to the senator, but it more often relies on indirect tactics. If the senator's list contains no suitable alternatives or only one name, the department can recruit someone else. By emphasizing the shortcomings of the senator's choice and presenting an alternative, the attorney general can seek to change the senator's mind. Sometimes the department locates someone so good that the senator finds it difficult to oppose him.[19] It also resolves impasses with senators, at least temporarily, by by-passing the Senate. When the previous incumbent has already resigned, the attorney general can call the chief judge, inform him that the department's choice will be nominated, and request the judge to give him a court appointment until the nomination is approved. As one respondent observed, the department largely accomplishes its purpose in such situations. Its man is serving as U.S. attorney. It also puts the individual in a stronger position to gather support for the permanent appointment. However, to work this tactic requires the chief judge's cooperation.[20] Recess appointments provide another device for by-passing senators, and they require no formal approval or action from judges. Several factors limit the usefulness of recess appointments, however. Congress now sits for most of the year, restricting the time when such appointments can be made. Since recess appointments must be submitted to the Senate at its next session, a senator can block confirmation then if he chooses. Court appointees can (and have) served for years while their appointment lingers in the Judiciary Committee, but the department finds it awkward to give a second recess appointment to someone who fails to obtain Senate confirmation. A third means of by-passing a senator can be used when a new administration has just taken office. The department can avoid the necessity of making any appointment by convincing acceptable holdovers from the previous administration to remain.

Although a senator's insistence on his own nominee or disapproval of the department's choice creates serious problems, few senators control appointments absolutely. A senator from the president's party can veto any man proposed by the department, but to control the selection a senator must persuade the administration to nominate his man. Even if he convinces the president to nominate someone opposed by the department, his problems may not be over. Poorly qualified nominees may encounter vigorous opposition in the Senate and fail to win confirmation.[21] If the administration refuses to nominate the senator's choice, he can wage guerrilla warfare against the administration and its programs generally, play "dog in the manger" with regard to the U.S. attorneyship by vetoing all other candidates, or give in. Few senators find dissatisfaction over a single U.S. attorney's appointment justifies prolonged, bitter, and relatively ineffective opposition to the president. Pursuing a "dog-in-the-manger" strategy provides a more attractive option, but it too usually fails ultimately. The department can operate quite well with court appointees, recess appointments, or "acting U.S. attorneys" dispatched from Washington serving in a few districts. Occasionally, the administration determines that wisdom dictates it accept an undesirable appointee. Department officials acknowledged to me that occasionally such capitulation occurs.[22] Fortunately for the department, some senators with enough power to insist on their own nominee pick men acceptable to the department. One Kennedy administration official informed me that "it so happened that Senator Kerr had three fine U.S. attorneys."

Few senators wield as much influence as the late Senator Kerr. For most senators seeking the appointment of someone adamantly opposed by the department, the best choice is to give up and seek a compromise. Similarly, the department finds accommodation and compromise the most effective tactic. Undoubtedly, the department's standards for determining what men are acceptable loosen as the power and influence of the senator increases. Generally, neither senators nor the department can force the other to accept a nominee, and both know it. Each finds it best to avoid disagreements in the first place. When they arise, a compromise solution generally results, in which the eventual appointee is acceptable to both but the first choice of neither.

### Local and State Political Figures

When both senators belong to the other party, the department consults state party leaders and members of the House of Representatives on appointments. Although such individuals may be as important as senators to the president's political coalition, they lack the power to block Senate confirmation of nominees and consequently exert less influence on appointments. In one case, the dean of a congressional delgation tried to insist on a candidate absolutely unacceptable to the department. An official involved in this episode exclaimed, "He was acting like he was a senator!" He was ultimately by-passed, and the department's choice selected. The department sometimes finds itself in the middle of squabbles between competing factions and must engineer a compromise or choose sides when there is no senator to shoulder the task. A Nixon appointee described how his state's Nixon campaign director succeeded in winning department support for him over a candidate favored by both the national committeeman and the state chairman. The available evidence suggests that particularly at the beginning of a new administration, candidates supported by leaders in the campaign effort of the president receive preference. Certainly, such considerations provide decision rules for resolving conflicts like one described in which the governor had not supported the president, but another faction had. Both had candidates for U.S. attorney, and in the words of the department official involved, "There wasn't much question of whom you went to for the appointment."

Of course, local political leaders and congressmen affect appointments even when a senator belongs to the president's party. They may themselves be able to dictate a candidate to the senator or prevent him from vetoing their choice. Local leaders who enjoy no direct access to the administration may utilize the senator's leverage to influence an appointment. Such situations most often arise in states where political factions or urban machines dominate the politics of the presidential party.

### The Federal Court Community

Federal judges possess both formal powers and informal attributes that permit them to affect the appointment process. Judges select "court appointees" to fill temporary vacancies when a U.S. attorney resigns before his successor receives Senate confirmation. When a judge receives a request from the department to appoint its intended nominee, he retains the power to refuse. Sometimes, the department takes no initiative in seeking to get its choice appointed by the court or in designating an "acting" U.S. attorney. When this occurs, judges have an opportunity to affect the final selection through their appointment, and some seize it. If they select a candidate or potential candidate for the permanent appointment, his chances improve considerably with the experience, publicity, and opportunities to build support that accrue to him as the court's appointee.[23] Sometimes, a judge's initiative may spur someone to seek the permanent appointment. A former U.S. attorney described his "flabbergasted" reaction when the chief judge, for whom he had served as a law clerk, called out of the blue to ask if we would serve as the court's nominee. Not wishing to jeopardize his private practice for a short stint as U.S. attorney, he set about determining whether he could secure a permanent appointment.

Two other attributes of judges enhance their effectiveness in affecting appointments. First, the department recognizes very well the importance of U.S. attorneys maintaining good relations with the bench. Consequently, when judges make strong positive or negative recommendations, the department cannot ignore them. Special circumstances sometimes compel a judge to take such an initiative. A respondent in a two-judge district described his judge's efforts on his behalf when he served as an assistant. The U.S. attorney resigned and at about the same time, the chief judge died. The surviving judge went directly to the attorney general and asked that the assistant be appointed. Second, many federal judges wield considerable political influence themselves and have extensive experience in the politics of federal appointments.[24] Of course, judges frequently know their senator extremely well and can effectively communicate their wishes and views directly to him. One U.S. attorney's appointment illustrates a judge's use of several of these resources. The chief judge called this individual and pressured him into taking a court appointment. After a month, he called again, revealed he had talked to the powerful local Democratic mayor and the equally powerful Republican senator and cleared him for the permanent appointment.

A second significant component of local federal court communities, private attorneys, also participate in the selection process. Interestingly, the organized bar as such plays no role in the appointment of U.S. attorneys despite its active participation in the selection of federal judges.[25] However, individual lawyers or informal temporary coalitions of attorneys do seek to influence the appointment of U.S.

attorneys. In a few districts (such as the Southern District of New York) leading members of the bar traditionally seek to affect the process. Occasionally, special circumstances mobilize normally inactive attorneys to enter the process. In one rural district members of the bar who practiced in federal court considered the only man actively seeking the vacancy "totally unacceptable" because he could not be trusted to adhere to verbal agreements. A former U.S. attorney in the district described how he and other attorneys practicing in federal court "got busy and got together. We made our views known to the senator." They succeeded in vetoing the unwanted candidate and then prevailed upon the eventual appointee to take the position as a public service.[26] Finally, private attorneys may make their views known individually to the department or senators through personal contact or letters.

When a U.S. attorney resigns before an administration's term expires, he often seeks to determine who his successor will be. Frequently, an out-going U.S. attorney urges the appointment of an assistant. In one district, the outgoing U.S. attorney engineered a court appointment for an assistant after winning the department over to sponsoring him for the permanent appointment. Local politicians who felt entitled to influence the appointment objected so strongly that they successfully blocked his permanent appointment. The best documented instance in which a U.S. attorney lobbied vigorously and successfully for an assistant's appointment occurred in 1970 in the appointment to the New Jersey office described in the previous chapter.[27] The assistant, Herbert Stern, was a native New Yorker, young, without political contacts in New Jersey, and roundly disliked by a number of important New Jersey politicians of both parties who found themselves the targets of federal criminal investigations initiated by the U.S. attorney's office. The outgoing U.S. attorney, Frederick Lacey, convinced Republican Senator Clifford Case to support Stern's appointment even though Case had never met Stern. The Nixon administration dragged its feet and made no recommendation before Lacey resigned to take a seat on the federal bench. However, the judges gave Stern a court appointment in February 1971, and he served in that capacity until the department finally formally nominated him in September.

*Eventual Appointees*

A mail survey of U.S. attorneys serving between 1961 and 1973 provides some indication of appointee's interests in and efforts to obtain the office.[28] Nearly half (46 percent) reported they were extremely interested in obtaining the appointment. A handful (11 percent), however, said they were not at all or only somewhat interested. A third claim to have made no personal efforts whatsoever to secure the appointment, but nearly a quarter said they made very extensive or fairly extensive efforts on their own behalf. These findings confirm the patterns suggested by the field interviews. A few men professed no interest in the office. Others found they became interested and began active efforts to obtain it only after someone else began to promote them. A few described intensive campaigns begun even before the previous incumbent had resigned.

Several factors shape the efforts appointees make to secure their appointment. Personality plays a crucial role. Aggressive, outgoing men engage in activities that more passive and introverted men find distasteful or even impossible.[29] Career ambitions and the office's reputation in the district interact to shape potential appointees' behavior. In many districts, leading members of the legal profession regard the post as too "political" for someone of their stature to assume. Sometimes, men interested in the appointment believe that they lack the political connections and background required to obtain the appointment. I encountered some evidence that men without good political qualifications overestimate the importance a political background plays. One Eisenhower appointee described himself as a newcomer to the state who knew neither of the Republican senators and who supported Taft rather than Eisenhower at the state convention. He received the appointment nonetheless, despite the fact that the other major contender supported Eisenhower and had served as state chairman of the Young Republicans. But in a few districts, a tradition has developed which encourages outstanding members of the bar to serve as U.S. attorney. Politically active attorneys hesitate to compete for the appointment in these districts.

Finally, the career prospects of incumbents, as evidenced by what has happened to recent incumbents, affect which men desire it.[30] Where it is regarded as a political dead end but useful for improving one's earning power in private practice, the politically ambitious may shun the office. If it is regarded as a steppingstone to a judgeship, a man may be willing to seek the U.S. attorneyship even though he really does not relish the prospect.

## THE PRIOR CAREERS AND PERSONAL CHARACTERISTICS OF APPOINTEES

What kind of people does the appointment process just described select to become U.S. attorneys? To answer this question, I examined the published biographical information available on U.S. attorneys who served between 1961 and 1973.[31] After compiling a roster of 261 names from the *U.S. Government Organizational Manual* and *The Department of Justice Register,* several major biographical sources, including *Who's Who in America* and *Who's Who in Government* were examined. At least some data were located on 163 of these individuals (over 62 percent of the roster). A mailed questionnaire sent to this same group sought to supplement the information available from published biographies.[32]

Middle-aged white males clearly dominate the ranks of recent U.S. attorneys. No woman served between 1961 and 1973. No information on the race of U.S. attorneys exists, but only a handful of blacks (very likely less than five) have ever received an appointment.[33] Men less than thirty-six years of age or more than fifty constitute only 30 percent of the group. They average between forty-two and forty-three years of age, a time in life when they have established themselves politically and professionally, but retain the vigor and desire to advance themselves further.

Data on the birthplace and schooling of these U.S. attorneys confirm their status as established, long-time residents of the area they serve as U.S. attorney. Seventy percent list the state in which they served as their birthplace, 64 percent attended undergraduate school and 59 percent law school there. In fact, almost one-third for whom data exist are both native born and schooled exclusively in the state where they become U.S. attorney. And practically every one (93 percent) indicates he first began the practice of law in that state. U.S. attorneys' reported participation in community affairs also suggests their integration into the life of their communities. Over half list membership in various civic, service, fraternal, relgious, or other organizations; nearly half indicate service on a board or commission (zoning board, school board, library board, and the like). Undoubtedly, these proportions underestimate the actual level of participation in such activities, since many men fail to list such activities when they submit their biographies to *Who's Who in America* and similar publications.

Although most U.S. attorneys engage in the private practice of law prior to appointment, they come to office with a substantial record of prior political activity. A high proportion (30 percent) indicate holding a political party post in their published biography, but the mail questionnaire provides a more accurate measure of just how much political experience U.S. attorneys bring with them to office. Eighty-eight percent of the 144 men responding to the mail questionnaire reveal having engaged in active political campaigning; 60 percent

report holding a political party post; nearly 60 percent have themselves run for elective office. Almost all identify themselves as at least
"average" Republicans or Democrats, and over 60 percent say they
held a "strong" preference for one of the two parties.

Three-quarters of the men for whom biographical data was located
had prior governmental experience. They held an average of more
than two posts each and served at all levels of government, though
more (33 percent) held jobs at the federal level. Most obtained their
position by appointment, but a substantial minority of 22 percent
demonstrated their voter appeal by winning an elective office. Not
surprisingly, a substantial majority (almost 70 percent) of these positions involved the utilization of legal skills in representing a governmental unit or agency, particularly as a prosecutor or assistant
prosecutor. In fact, almost four of every ten prior governmental positions held involved prosecution. Twenty percent of the U.S. attorneys
in the biographical study could point to experience as an assistant U.S.
attorney as a primary qualification for the job.

Analysis of the position held immediately before becoming U.S.
attorney confirms that many primarily pursued a political rather than
legal career. Half held public employment, primarily at the state or
federal level. Although the largest single group served as assistant
U.S. attorneys (22 percent), 15 percent of the public employees served
as district attorneys or state attorneys general, 10 percent held a legislative post, and 10 percent occupied a judicial position. In all, nearly
one-third of these positions were elected rather than appointed.
Nevertheless, the appointment process displays enough variability
and flexibility to recruit a significant number of U.S. attorneys who
come to office with no prior experience in government; one-quarter
list nothing but private practice before becoming U.S. attorney, and
half engaged in private practice at the time of their selection. A handful (13 percent) report never holding a government position or a
political party office, and never ran unsuccessfully for office.

Studies of political decision-makers in the United States consistently
find that they come from the higher strata of society, and U.S. attorneys are no exception. The educational requirements established by
the legal profession guarantee an unusually high level of education.
Nine out of ten indicate some undergraduate training, and three-
fourths list an undergraduate degree; 96 percent received a law degree. They attain considerable status in the legal profession as well.
One-half list membership in the American Bar Association, and one-
quarter served as officers of one or more bar associations. Over one-
quarter mention in their biographies that they attained the status of
partner in a law firm before becoming U.S. attorney, and this figure

undoubtedly underestimates the actual proportion. A disproportionate number (49 percent) of protestant U.S. attorneys belong to the higher status denominations (Presbyterian, Congregationalist, Episcopalian).

However, because political factors shape their recruitment, recent appointees display some characteristics that differentiate them somewhat from other decision-makers. Unlike many decision-makers, the proportion of Roman Catholics (28 percent) and Jews (nearly 11 percent) matches or exceeds respectively their share of the general population. Nor do they go to particularly exclusive educational institutions. Only 15 percent attended law school at Harvard, Yale, Columbia, Michigan, or Chicago; by contrast, nearly one-third of Supreme Court appointees have attended prestige law schools.[34] Nearly one-half went to a state-supported law school. Only 10 percent attended a private, prestigious undergraduate institution.

United States attorneys display a few differences in background characteristics. For the most part, however, the differences found sometimes fail to display a high level of statistical significance, and in almost all instances the relationship is not strong. The modest nature of the findings should be kept in mind. Table 3.1 summarizes the relationship between district size and several background characteristics. United States attorneys from large districts appear to graduate from private undergraduate institutions, including so-called "prestige" schools, slightly more often. This pattern holds for the law school attended as well. Not surprisingly, Roman Catholic and Jewish U.S. attorneys receive appointments somewhat more frequently to large offices which serve major metropolitan areas. Men serving in small offices more often have had prior experience as elected officials. Over one-third of U.S. attorneys in small districts have held elective office, compared to less than one in ten in large offices. Finally, men from large districts are slightly more likely to receive a promotion directly from the ranks of assistant U.S. attorneys in the office.

With only two exceptions, the Kennedy–Johnson administration appointed men with characteristics similar to those the Nixon administration chose. Each, of course, chose men from its own political party. Religion provides the other exception. Although the data must be interpreted cautiously, because only one-half of the biographies indicate a religious preference, the results coincide with established patterns of support for the two parties among religious groups. Roman Catholics and Jews received many more appointments from the Democrats (50 percent of the men appointed) than from the Republicans (20 percent).[35]

Finally, a few small differences emerge among U.S. attorneys'

Table 3.1. Relationship between Size of Office and Selected Characteristics of Appointees

| | Size of office[a] | | | N |
|---|---|---|---|---|
| | Small (N) (%) | Medium (N) (%) | Large (N) (%) | |
| Type of undergraduate school attended | | | | |
| Public | 32 (52.5) | 19 (39.6) | 7 (25.0) | 58 |
| Private, nonprestigious | 24 (39.3) | 23 (47.9) | 16 (57.1) | 63 |
| Private, prestigious[b] | 5 (8.2) | 6 (12.5) | 5 (17.9) | 16 |
| | 61 (100.0) | 48 (100.0) | 28 (100.0) | 137 |
| Chi Square[c] significance level = .16 Cramer's V[c] = .15 | | | | |
| Type of law school attended | | | | |
| State law school | 33 (58.9) | 28 (52.8) | 9 (33.3) | 70 |
| Private law school | 23 (41.1) | 25 (47.2) | 18 (66.7) | 66 |
| | 56 (100.0) | 53 (100.0) | 27 (100.0) | 136 |
| Chi square significance level = .09 Cramer's V = .18 | | | | |
| Religion | | | | |
| Roman Catholic | 8 (26.7) | 7 (24.1) | 5 (41.7) | 20 |
| Jewish | 0 (0.0) | 4 (13.8) | 3 (25.0) | 7 |
| Protestant | 22 (73.3) | 18 (62.1) | 4 (33.3) | 44 |
| | 30 (100.0) | 29 (100.0) | 12 (100.0) | 71 |
| Chi square significance level = .05 Cramer's V = .26 | | | | |
| Any elective post prior to appointment listed? | | | | |
| Yes | 24 (35.3) | 14 (23.7) | 3 (9.7) | 41 |
| No | 44 (64.7) | 45 (76.3) | 28 (90.3) | 117 |
| | 68 (100.0) | 59 (100.0) | 31 (100.0) | 158 |
| Chi square significance level = .02 Cramer's V = .22 | | | | |
| Was assistant U.S. attorney occupation listed immediately prior to becoming U.S. attorney? | | | | |
| Yes | 5 (9.3) | 5 (9.6) | 6 (24.0) | 16 |
| No | 49 (90.7) | 47 (90.4) | 19 (76.0) | 115 |
| | 54 (100.0) | 52 (100.0) | 25 (100.0) | 131 |
| Chi Square significance level = .13 Cramer's V = .18 | | | | |

[a]For this analysis, small offices are defined as containing four or fewer assistants, medium offices between five and eight, and large nine or more. The Executive Office for U.S. Attorneys kindly provided me with information on the number of assistants in each of the offices.

[b]Harvard, Princeton, Yale, Williams, Wesleyan, Columbia, Dartmouth, Cornell, University of Pennsylvania, Brown, Stanford.

[c]For a discussion of chi square significance levels and Cramer's V, a measure of the strength of association, see Herbert M. Blalock, *Social Statistics* (New York: McGraw-Hill, 1960), ch. 15.

Table 3.2. Relationship between State of Birth and Region

| Location of birth in relation to state of service | Served elsewhere | Served in Pacific or Mountain state | |
|---|---|---|---|
| Same state | 96 (76.2) | 15 (48.4) | 111 |
| Out of state | 30 (23.8) | 16 (51.6) | 46 |
| | 126 (100.0) | 31 (100.0) | 157 |

Chi square significance level = .005
Cramer's V = .24

characteristics by region. As Table 3.2 suggests, districts in the Pacific and Mountain states appoint fewer men born in the state they serve as U.S. attorney, reflecting the more recent settlement of the region. The fact that in the West fewer men born out of state came originally from another region supports this hypothesis.[36] Men serving in New England, the Mid-Atlantic states, and Border states attended private, prestigious undergraduate institutions and elite law schools somewhat more frequently than other U.S. attorneys.[37] Roman Catholics and Jews serve in New England and the Mid-Atlantic states, but not in the South or Mountain states. U.S. attorneys in the North Central states won elective office prior to their appointment at a much higher rate than those serving elsewhere (41 percent versus 19 percent respectively). These regional differences generally reflect variation in the social composition and nature of educational institutions, demonstrating again how the appointment process ties U.S. attorneys into the American political and social system.

Appendix B presents an analysis of U.S. attorneys' subsequent careers. Two significant statistics convey the general conclusion of that analysis. First, about one of every eight U.S. attorneys appointed between 1961 and 1973 and no longer in office in 1975 became a federal judge. Second, if we count other important posts held in addition to judgeships, the proportion of "successful alumni" rises to 17 percent. Thus, U.S. attorneys' activities after leaving office offer additional compelling evidence of how closely they are linked to the American political process.

# CHAPTER 4

# Mutual Perceptions of U.S. Attorneys and the Department of Justice

The Department of Justice influences U.S. attorneys' behavior more than any other participant in the federal legal process. This is not surprising, since headquarters agencies typically exert substantial control over personnel stationed in the field. However, U.S. attorneys' offices differ substantially from most other field offices, and these differences are reflected in the fascinating and complex relations between them and the Department of Justice described in this and the following two chapters.

## A VIEW FROM THE FIELD

An outspoken U.S. attorney who headed a large office in the Kennedy–Johnson era offered some unusually useful insights into many of the major features of headquarters–field relations that differentiate the Department of Justice from other agencies with field services. His observations provide a useful informal introduction to the more systematic analysis that follows.

Several comments suggested that the control exercised by the department over him fell short of what most headquarters agencies expect. When I mentioned I was interested in the degree of autonomy U.S. attorneys had, he interjected, "You get as much autonomy as you take." He believed department officials often acted in a high-handed manner and he displayed little deference to them. "If you come from one of those five (big) districts, you don't have to worry about some damn assistant attorney general. If you aren't as strong as he is in your district, then by God you shouldn't be there." He also indicated that he defied the department on occasion. Yet, he clearly did not enjoy complete autonomy and complained that he "chafed" under the department's regulations. He also acknowledged the ultimate authority of the attorney general when he explained why he acquiesced in a decision that he strongly disagreed with. "I felt that in our position I couldn't be a member of the Department of Justice and not follow the order of the attorney general. So I swallowed everything and did what he told me to do." When I asked what would have happened if he had gone ahead and defied the attorney general, he replied, "Nothing." What about being fired, I asked. He replied, "How could the attorney general fire me? I'm a presidential appointee." I suggested the attorney general might convince the president to fire him. "If he could have gotten the President to fire me, that would have been an achievement."

The independence this individual felt due to political support from his district emboldened him in his dealings with department officials. He successfully refused to accept attorneys dispatched from Washington to handle organized crime cases in his district. "I said you're not going to run anything from Washington. I'm the U.S. attorney. It will be run by me or there won't be any here . . . I sent back two or three men to Washington because I wouldn't have them with me." When pressed as to how he succeeded in forcing these attorneys to leave, the U.S. attorney revealed that the chief judge would have refused to accept indictments signed by the department attorneys. "I had tremendous support from a good aggressive judge who . . . knew the system, and who was interested in an effective office. . . . Thank God for him."

## THE CHALLENGE OF STUDYING CENTRALIZATION

These remarks suggest that U.S. attorneys do not behave as typical subordinates who head regional offices in a field service. Crucial differences in the recruitment, resources, political support from the community, and organizational status of U.S. attorneys described in the first chapter translate into substantial autonomy. But the stubborn conceptual and methodological problems in measuring precisely the amount of centralization attained in field organizations prevent any easy identification of the degree of central control achieved by the department. As numerous authorities on public administration have pointed out, administrative organization and the pattern of formal authority tell us little about who actually makes decisions. As one student of decision-making in organizations observed, formal authority (legitimacy, position, and the sanctions inherent in office) competes with functional authority (expertise, experience, and human relations skills).[1] Those with *functional* authority may in fact be the center of effective decision-making in an organization.

It is also impossible to locate effective decision-making by examining where the actual work of an agency is performed. We cannot assume the department controls U.S. attorneys merely because it possesses formal authority over them. By the same token, the fact that U.S. attorneys perform much of the department's work does not necessarily mean the department is decentralized. As James Fesler points out, "The field office may be performing only a routine clerical function wholly devoid of any element of discretion."[2] Nor can we assess the degree of centralization by relying on the perceptions of key participants. The field research revealed that officials at the very highest level of the department learn about a very unrepresentative sample of encounters with U.S. attorneys. Controversies elevated to the level of visibility of the attorney general are normally resolved in accordance with his wishes, leading to an exaggerated sense of control. Thus, one attorney general observed that U.S. attorneys "really don't have much say." But some career attorneys in the Department of Justice reported losing long, heated, and frustrating arguments with U.S. attorneys and conveyed the image of department impotence. United States attorneys themselves define autonomy so differently that their assessments cannot be compared. When asked if he felt the pressure of control from the department, one replied, "No. No. I was stunned by the autonomy I had." Yet he cooperated fully with the same organized crime strike force dispatched from Washington that his predecessor regarded as a major infringement on his autonomy, calmly declaring that, "I was not jealous of my prerogative."

These problems suggest the utility of looking at actual behavior rather than perceptions to determine the balance struck between autonomy and control. Here too, however, serious problems arise. Some U.S. attorneys willingly do what the department requires of them because they happen to agree with the policy. The identity of the effective decision-maker in such situations is indeterminate. Even when he can be identified in a specific instance, the problem of aggregating situations of varying importance remains. One U.S. attorney may defer to the department in nine unimportant matters and prevail in a single important one. Is he more or less autonomous than his colleague who prevails in nine unimportant matters and acquiesces in the tenth (and important) one? Even if these conceptual problems could be overcome, the exploratory nature of the field research does not provide data capable of permitting the identification of the precise degree of control achieved by the department. It does, however, establish a basis for answering two significant questions: (1) What are the principal variables that determine the balance between autonomy and control? (2) What are the major patterns (irrespective of their frequency) found in relations between the department and U.S. attorneys' offices? Both will be examined in Chapter 6.

The analysis in this and the following two chapters focuses primarily on the sources and dynamics of conflict between U.S. attorneys and the department, despite the fact that on balance their interactions exhibit a preponderance of cooperation. Analyzing conflict lays bare the basic dynamics underlying their interaction. Anticipation of the costs and probable outcomes of the conflict that would arise in lieu of cooperation and mutual accommodation shapes much of the cooperation typifying day-to-day interaction. Furthermore, this anticipation depends in large part on recollections of the outcomes of earlier disputes. Thus, cooperation is accompanied and sustained by an underlying tension which itself rests on a conflict orientation. Finally, analyzing conflict, however infrequent, provides insights into the problems of identifying where effective decision-making is lodged in those indeterminate situations where the man in the field chooses to do what headquarters would like him to do.

## THE STRUCTURE OF MUTUAL PERCEPTIONS

In his *Introduction to the Study of Public Administration*, Leonard D. White observed that the physical separation between headquarters and the field services generated a different (and often critical) psychology in their attitudes toward one another: "Two separate bodies of employees consequently emerge, without common experience or a common point of view. There is a field way of life and a headquarters way of life, each different from the other, both essential to the best conduct of the public business and each needing an appreciation of the functions and contributions of the other."[3]

Perhaps the best statement of this divergence from the Department of Justice came from an official with experience in one of the department's divisions who later worked in the Executive Office for U.S. attorneys.

I detected . . . an enormous gulf between the Department and the U.S. attorneys. Part of it was just the inherent difference between the home office and the field office. And part of it, seemed to me, came from a very strong current of resentment (and I think resentment is not too strong a word) on the part of the men in the U.S. attorneys' offices who felt that over the years discrimination had been allowed to creep in between themselves and the attorneys in the Department of Justice. . . . So when the two faced each other, the departmental man and the assistant U.S. attorney, there was, I felt, a deep-seated different viewpoint and a certain amount of hostility.

Although he based his observations on knowledge of relations between the criminal division and the field offices, his views reflect opinions expressed throughout the department's various divisions.

Like all gross generalizations, the one quoted above obscures considerable variation and subtleties. Though on balance resentment and hostility probably dominate basic perceptions, interviews both in the field and in Washington revealed shared perspectives, instances of mutual respect, and geniune friendships that blurred the sharp distinction between headquarters and field. Furthermore, regardless of the extent of mutual resentment and hostility, the overwhelming majority of the interactions between department attorneys and members of U.S. attorneys' offices are conducted in a polite and restrained manner, and accommodation rather than argument and appeals to superiors resolve most differences. Nevertheless, an undercurrent of tension and subdued hostility appears to coexist with and indeed shape most interactions between them. These undercurrents do not determine behavior, but they affect the perceptions and predispositions of both parties and consequently exert a consistent if subtle influence on their dealings with one another.

### Headquarters Perceptions of U.S. Attorneys' Offices

The perceptions of department attorneys toward the role and performance of U.S. attorneys contain five basic elements. The composite picture that results does not depict the "typical" view, since no single individual articulates all five of them. In addition, differences emerge in the perspectives of the various divisions of the department, among individuals at different levels in the hierarchy, and between different national administrations. Finally, the department contains individuals who differ markedly in their whole outlook toward U.S. attorneys. The exceptions and qualifications to the composite view will be discussed after its five components are presented.

Most attorneys in headquarters believe in the value and necessity of uniform national policy in the execution of the department's responsibilities. A political appointee in an administrative capacity in the Civil Division expressed the content of this first element: "If what one is working on has national implications, then I think that it should be followed through Washington. Does the case have precedent value?

Does it involve a large sum of money? What are the ramifications? . . . There is just no doubt about it, the ramifications nationally really require that you've got to have one policy and one policy only. You can't have one U.S. attorney's office taking one tack . . . and another taking another tack."

The second component, directly related to the first, holds that the Department of Justice must formulate policy and control litigation if uniformity is to be achieved. For many, to permit ninety-four U.S. attorneys to set policy and simultaneously achieve a uniform policy is more than just an administrative impossibility, for it would preclude the department from exercising its responsibility to set the tone and direction of the administration's law enforcement policy. Department personnel believe that if uniform policy is to be a reality, central control over litigation cannot be relinquished.

The department understands, however, that some decentralization in the implementation of policy is inevitable. This third tenet recognizes the physical impossibility of handling all litigation from Washington and acknowledges the positive benefits of relying on local U.S. attorneys. The sentiments of Attorney General Jackson, expressed three decades ago, still accurately reflect this view: "It is also clear that with his (the U.S. attorney's) knowledge of local sentiment and opinion, his contact with and intimate knowledge of the views of the court, and his acquaintance with the feelings of the group from which his jurors are drawn, it is an unusual case in which his judgment should be overruled."[4] An ethic of paternalistic solicitude and helpfulness accompanies this attitude. "We're ready and able to render assistance," observed a former department attorney. "We'll go out and try the case for them or review the facts. I felt we should give a lot of weight to the U.S. attorney's opinion."

This viewpoint in no way diminishes the intensity of the belief in the necessity for central control, however. In fact, the fourth tenet of headquarters' ideology is the conviction that the various specialized divisions of the department must retain and utilize if necessary the capability to enforce adherence to its policies. Because the divisions have responsibility for the development and implementation of uniform policy, they have the incentive that individual U.S. attorneys lack. They also possess the information needed to form policy and the special competence required to implement it. In practical terms, this leads to a belief that the assistant attorneys general in charge of the various divisions have a clear duty and right to direct the work of U.S. attorneys. The political official in the civil division quoted earlier (not an assistant attorney general) put it this way: "As far as I'm concerned, an assistant attorney general makes the policy in a civil matter. Those section chiefs in the big (U.S. attorneys') offices of the civil sections, while they have an obligation to the U.S. attorney, they also have an obligation to the assistant attorney general in the Civil Division. And I think unless shown otherwise . . . the policy of the assistant attorney general of the Civil Division should hold."

Despite recognition of the necessity to rely on U.S. attorneys to implement centrally determined policy, department personnel question the willingness of field personnel to do so faithfully. In practical terms, this fifth element in the department's ideology plays a central role in fostering the suspicion that U.S. attorneys cannot match the zeal of the various divisions in adhering to national policy. The department believes that U.S. attorneys lack specific responsibility for formulating national policy and consequently encounter few incentives to follow it. Furthermore, the divisions feel a variety of direct pressures and incentives impinge on U.S. attorneys that positively detract from their ability and willingness to follow national policy faithfully. For instance, headquarters personnel believe the political nature of the selection process, and the participation of senators in particular, results in significant political pressure on U.S. attorneys. A former attorney general expressed concerns widely held in the department in strong terms: "It's intolerable that he [a U.S. attorney] gets his job through political interests. I found frequently Senators were knowledgeable about things they had no business knowing about. . . . The effective power is in the hands of senators or other political forces."[5] He cited an example of a U.S. attorney who behaved "unsatisfactorily" in handling a case against officials of a local union. "These people were his friends. He had seen them face to face for twenty years. Now all of a sudden he couldn't stop recognizing them anymore." He felt that the unhealthy effects such pressures generated sometimes caused U.S. attorneys to prosecute when they should not just to prove they could not be improperly influenced. An assistant attorney general identified another significant source of pressure from U.S. attorneys' districts. "U.S. attorneys really become, in some instances, the hand-maiden of the chief judge in the district for which they serve and are more responsive to his needs and desires than anyone else's." Department officials believe judges tell the U.S. attorney what cases to bring in some districts. "I know of one case," observed an official who dealt with organized crime, "where a U.S. attorney told me, 'I don't think we should bring this case. The judge doesn't like this sort of case.' Well, who gives a good god damn!" Several officials in the Tax Division expressed the view that judicial hostility toward tax refund cases inhibit U.S. attorneys' vigor in handling them. Pressures generated by heavy caseloads and limited staff lead department attorneys to question the ability of U.S. attorneys' offices to devote sufficient effort to specialized litigation. A former department attorney with responsibility for medical malpractice suits reported he got the feeling that U.S. attorneys didn't have time to do the things that needed to be done to prepare such cases. The concern of a Tax Division attorney for this problem suggested some unhappy experiences: "Tax problems are not the most important thing to them. If they have an Indian murder case come up, they'll pull their man off tax and he'll be spending all his time on the reservation. The tax docket goes to hell."

Even when specialists in Washington acknowledge that a U.S. attorney's office does not succumb to such pressures, they still question the ability to implement policy faithfully. Although admitting that a handful of U.S. attorneys are competent or even outstanding, they regard most of them as mediocre or worse.[6] But even competent generalists have difficulty handling what specialists see as the intricate and arcane peculiarities that litigation in their areas of responsibility presents. James Fesler's general comments on this phenomenon describe the situation in the Department of Justice well: "Specialists distrust generalists, particularly those generalists that appear at the bottom rather than at the top of the organization chart and that receive lower pay than the central specialists. Distrusting field generalists' competence to handle specialized problems, the Washington specialists are reluctant to have decision-making authority lodged in the field."[7]

### Why Department Attorneys Resent U.S. Attorneys

A number of specific characteristics of interactions with U.S. attorneys generate the resentment in the department that produces much of the tension and hostility that underlies relationships with U.S. attorneys' offices. The fact that the department cannot control U.S. attorneys' offices as tightly as it would like is itself a major sore point, particularly given the strong desire to exert such control. The inability of the attorney general to fire U.S. attorneys also rankles attorneys in Washington. I asked a veteran career attorney at the end of a protracted interview if he would like to make any general comments. "Yeah," he replied, "I'd like to appoint them. I'd like to subject them to the same standards that I subject the people that I hire." A colleague of his expressed a similar sentiment. "I can be fired by the attorney general, and if they could, the system would work much better." He viewed U.S. attorneys somewhat contemptuously with a tinge of jealousy. "Some are small individuals. They feel that the presidential appointment gives them some magical ability and experience to handle cases on their own. They don't have any competence, really."

Department attorneys resent what they believe to be the parochial and narrow perspective of U.S. attorneys that leads to resistance of department directives. For example, it is desirable to prosecute even when the chances of winning a case are dim if the fact of prosecution will deter others.[8] A sure loser in the district court may help develop favorable precedents or contain facts that will prove valuable in resolving a conflict between circuits at the Supreme Court level. When U.S. attorneys resist filing weak cases that make them look bad in their district, it antagonizes Washington attorneys who are struggling to implement coherent national policy. The department also finds it necessary to centralize prosecutive decisions when a new statute is enacted in order to establish favorable precedents. If U.S. attorneys insist on injecting their own considerations into prosecutive decisions here, it may be difficult to prevent initial adverse rulings. Strategic considerations also cause the department to turn down compromise offers in civil litigation, forcing the U.S. attorney to trial. For example, the department has found that the outcomes of the first few cases in projects requiring the acquisition of large areas of land affect the sizes of later awards. U.S. attorneys' vociferous protests over Washington's refusal to approve compromises in such cases angers department attorneys.

Because department lawyers regard themselves as specialists in their fields, they resent it when U.S. attorneys fail to acknowledge their expertise. "Where can they get better advice?" a career official asked me. "It's not necessary for a U.S. attorney to do a long study and research job. They can rely on us, but—if there is any weakness in the system it is that our resources are not being tapped as often as they could be." Conflicts over who should handle prime cases produce even more resentment. Department lawyers feel affronted when poorly qualified—even clearly incompetent—assistants insist on handling cases themselves. An official in the Lands Division described with grim satisfaction what he felt was the outcome of a U.S. attorney's successful effort to retain control over a series of complicated condemnation cases: "He had a green assistant who thought he knew what he was doing, and he convinced the U.S. attorney to let him handle it. The U.S. attorney told me, 'I can run my own office. I'll do it my own way.' The awards were disastrous!"

Though the dollar loss to the government distresses the department, incompetent handling of a civil case has far more serious repercussions if it results in harmful precedents. This fear prompts the department to supervise seemingly minor preliminary matters in sensitive cases. Specification of the form a pleading should take may seem like petty and unwarranted interference to an assistant; the department regards it as an essential precaution against costly blunders. As a Tax Division attorney put it, "The formulation of issues, selection of evidence, and legal arguments have to be carefully controlled. You don't make all of the arguments in these cases that will help you win." Department attorneys naturally become annoyed when attorneys in the field they regard as incompetent resist supervision. Competent U.S. attorneys who insist on trying cases department personnel want to try upset attorneys in Washington at least as much. Even though his staff attorneys have put in months of work on an investigation, one official said, "The U.S. attorney wants to try it—no matter how little work he has done on it." This causes serious morale problems in the department. As an official in the Civil Division during the Nixon administration put it, "If it is an attractive case, that section chief will want that case for his boys because in order to keep his boys he's got to keep feeding them good cases."[9]

Much of the department's resentment, then, results from its perception of U.S. attorneys as obstructionist, parochial-minded interlopers who fail to appreciate the need for establishing national policies. The results, in the eyes of the department, are that important cases are lost, bad precedents set, morale within the department weakened, and difficulties created with Congress and the public.

As noted earlier, this description of the "department view" is a caricature. Department personnel do not express monolithic views toward U.S. attorneys and assistants. Most department personnel who deal with U.S. attorneys on a regular basis come to differentiate among them according to their cooperativeness, competence, reliability, and personality. Both U.S. attorneys and assistant attorneys general, for instance, described warm friendships that had developed with specific individuals. Suspicion, hostility, jealousy, and fear of incompetence sometimes give way to trust, friendship, and respect, and permit discussion of litigation on a coequal, professional basis. Different levels and divisions within the department also display different attitudes toward the field. Because the nature of the supervision over U.S. attorneys varies,[10] some divergence arises in the content of consensual views that result from interaction with the field and internal communication about it within the division. Many career attorneys in the lower ranks of the divisions develop attitudes toward U.S. attorneys that remain stable when politically appointed supervisory personnel change. Even some career attorneys, however, stray from the norm. A man with many years experience in the department (including some in positions with considerable responsibility) dissented from the widespread belief that U.S. attorneys should be appointed by the attorney general and made more responsive to the department. He approved of the conflict generated by the appointment process and felt greater department control would mean the end of "constructive conflict" and the benefits derived from it. Department colleagues, he believed, sometimes exaggerated the expertise required to handle certain types of cases. And he expressed an unusual degree of sympathy and understanding for the strategic position of a U.S. attorney: "I understand that the U.S. attorney has a district. And once you understand that, then you understand everything else. He is, to that extent, a local person. You have an obligation, back in the Department, to enhance, legitimately enhance his stature in that local area."

### U.S. Attorneys' Perceptions of the Department

United States attorneys acknowledge the necessity for some central direction in federal legal policy. Very few dispute the attorney general's authority and responsibility for providing it. They recognize and accept that they are subordinate to his direction. The position of the most independent U.S. attorney encountered during the field research demonstrates how widespread agreement is on this point. "There is no *question* we are a part of the Department of Justice. We have got to carry out the policies of the Department. We have a right to argue about what the policy should be, but when it is made, we go along."[11] Even on fundamental questions such as this, however, agreement is not complete. With respect to the need for national policy, one assistant asserted that, "In certain areas the department ought to stay out of it. I'm representing a client. I can do as any attorney. If I'm wrong, I'm wrong." A U.S. attorney took the position that he owed his primary responsibility to his oath of office and that he had an obligation to the government as such, but not to the Department of Justice. One assistant even denied that U.S. attorneys are subordinate to the department. "We are *not* a field office. We have independent statutory authority."[12]

The absence of agreement on the department's ultimate responsibility and control indicates the failure of U.S. attorneys as a group to achieve the degree of consensus in their attitudes toward headquarters that members of the department have toward them. This failure is not surprising. The appointment process guarantees that the diversity of local attitudes toward the federal government found throughout the country will be at least partially reflected in the views of the men who become U.S. attorneys and assistants. The rapid turnover of personnel in U.S. attorneys' offices, combined with the physical obstacles to face-to-face communication among U.S. attorneys and assistants, inhibits the development of shared perspectives found among career attorneys in Washington.

As a result, we cannot isolate a single core of beliefs shared by U.S. attorneys and assistants. In fact, at least three distinctive outlooks toward the department exist.[13] The "field officer" view accepts U.S. attorneys as nonautonomous arms of the department, carrying out its directives in the various districts. The opposite position, the "autonomous" view, acknowledges the department's role in setting broad policy, but holds that a U.S. attorney should be free to exercise wide discretion in individual cases. The third or "middle" view falls between the other two.

United States attorneys' statements in response to questions about the proper relationship with the department illustrate these three views. When asked about the duties and obligations of U.S. attorneys, an adherent of the "field officer" view replied: "It's rather obvious. The U.S. attorney is part of the executive branch. . . . Our home office is Washington. I know there are different attitudes in different districts toward Washington. . . . I defer to them when they feel something should be handled by the department. I do everything to accommodate them." A like-minded individual observed: "These things they lay down—they're more than just guidelines. They're directions."[14] Men adhering to the "middle" view accept departmental authority and control, but they impose conditions on their acceptance that attorneys who regard themselves as field officers do not. One southern U.S. attorney acknowledged he was part of the department and that the department's objectives included a mandate in the field of civil rights. But when the department dispatched an attorney from Washington who began to tell him how to try a civil rights case, he reacted strongly. "I called him in here and I told him, 'You do what I tell you. After all, I'm your boss down here. You're like one of my assistants when you're down here.'" Another U.S. attorney in this category indicated he generally accepted department control because of the need for uniform policy, but he did not accept the department's right to dictate decisions in all matters. In fact, after fighting vigorously (and unsuccessfully) for approval of a compromise in a civil suit, he told the department he was going ahead and accepting it regardless of what they said.

Those subscribing to the "autonomous" view do not reject departmental authority, but they consciously restrict the conditions under which they accept it. They dislike having department attorneys come to observe the handling of cases. They object to the taking over of cases even more. Referring to tax cases, one such independent-minded individual acknowledged that he couldn't interpret the internal revenue laws. "We have to follow policy. But the day-to-day handling of cases we want to control. We have what we call the primary trial responsibility." Referring specifically to the department's policy of handling these cases by dispatching an attorney from the Tax Division, he added: "It isn't a question of how to handle the case [i.e., the office follows policy], but *who* is to handle it. If we are not qualified to handle the case, o.k. But if we are qualified, then we should handle it." The occasions when this office did not feel qualified were rare indeed.[15]

Variation in U.S. attorneys' attitudes and behavior along several other dimensions corresponds rather closely to their position on autonomy. One involves beliefs about who speaks for the department in determining what policy is. Less independent-minded U.S. attorneys fail to distinguish between levels within the department. For them, the department appears to be anyone in Washington who issues instructions. "Although I am a presidential appointee, I really think of my boss as the attorney general," one such individual told me. "And inherent in that would be those subordinates who are delegated certain of his responsibilities." Those tending toward the "autonomous" view take a different position: "There is a question of *who* in the department makes policy. If it's the attorney general or an assistant attorney general, o.k. But some guy way down the line? It's important, and we have an obligation to follow policies, but not if they are made by some section chief in the Civil Division. People of this position should not be the ones to make policy." An assistant, describing a dispute he had with the department, expressed the same view in less restrained terms. "If the attorney general orders it, then all right. But I'm not going to do it just because some schmuck in the Tax Division thinks I ought to do it that way."

United States attorneys differ in their willingness to appeal directives and decisions from the department. "Field officers" hesitate to go beyond a section chief and may do nothing more than seek to change a career attorney's mind. At the other extreme, some U.S. attorneys go directly to the attorney general or deputy attorney general whenever a dispute arises with an assistant attorney general.

Several other attitudes provide a good indication of a U.S. attorney's general orientation toward the department. Those inclined to accept the domination of the department follow policies spelled out in the *U.S. Attorneys Manual*. Several referred to it as "the Bible." One observed that he followed the *Manual* "religiously." The independents largely disregard it. "In all my time there," bragged a former U.S. attorney, "I never did read the damn *Manual*." Those in the middle may refer to it as a general guide and source of suggestions, but believe it is open to flexible interpretation. The independents dislike relying on the department for information, research, and advice. "We don't like to talk to them every day in Washington. Otherwise, what the hell are we here for if we can't handle things ourselves." This contrasts sharply with the view of field officers. "As a matter of fact, I welcome the Department's help on many, many things. . . ." The reception given department attorneys sent out to handle cases also reveals attitudes toward Washington. A department lawyer telephoned an independent-minded assistant and asked him to obtain a postponement because he had a conflict in travel plans. The assistant politely refused. After he hung up, he turned to me and grinned. "Screw him! He'll just have to cancel his trip!" This attitude contrasts sharply with that of a more sympathetic U.S. attorney: "I've been in Washington and I know the problems of the federal government. I want to work with them."

The U.S. attorney's attitude toward the department sets the standard for his assistants. In part, this results from a combination of indoctrination and loyalty to the U.S. attorney. Internal office procedures also shape attitudes. A department-oriented U.S. attorney, for instance, read all correspondence between his assistants and the department to insure headquarters' policies were being followed. One official in the Executive Office for U.S. Attorneys, however, suggested the possibility that attitudes of U.S. attorneys toward the department may differ from those of assistants in some respects. "Most of the U.S. attorneys felt a pride in being the president's man, if you will, in the district—and perhaps a better feeling for the Department of Justice . . . really more than the assistant U.S. attorneys. I think there was more feeling on the part of the assistant U.S. attorneys that the Department was unreasonable and imperfect.[16]

### Why U.S. Attorneys Resent the Department

Like their counterparts in the department, U.S. attorneys and assistants express a variety of complaints that contribute to the underlying tension in their dealings with Washington. Once again, it is important to remember that such tension infrequently results in open conflict and hostility. Thus, the following paragraphs catalogue the variety of the sources of resentment, but do not indicate the frequency of their occurrence. Even men in the field who expressed deep resentment and hostility toward members of the department reported having amiable relationships with other individuals and even whole divisions.

Resentment of Washington arises from three sources. First, U.S. attorneys resent attempts to control their behavior. Second, they find the bureaucratic tendencies of the department annoying. Finally, they feel that department actions, over which they have little control, make their task harder by creating difficulties with important individuals and groups in the district.

1) Departmental Control of Behavior.   Departmental supervision and directives create the strongest resentment. Men in the field who feel capable of acting on their own seldom enjoy being told what to do. "It almost seemed," reflected a former U.S. attorney, "in a job of that calibre where you're a presidential appointment with Senate confirmation that you ought to be delegated wider discretion than you were."[17] The professional status of U.S. attorneys and assistants reinforces these feelings. As lawyers, they feel degraded by being told how to handle legal work by other lawyers.

United States attorneys find a number of department actions insulting. The department, not the U.S. attorney, makes prosecutive decisions in some types of cases. Naturally, occasions arise when the department orders prosecution of a case which the U.S. attorney feels is a minor violation or a sure loser.[18] The department's refusal to accept U.S. attorneys' recommendations for compromise settlements in civil cases also creates resentment. In district after district, U.S. attorneys related instances in which they had been forced to trial and ended up with judgments substantially higher than the compromise figures they originally recommended. They resented the actual dollar loss to the government, but the resulting blow to their self-esteem after "losing" these cases obviously hurt more. United States attorneys consider the department's rejection of a recommendation to accept a settlement as an insult to their judgment. "I had settlements that I knew were very good as a lawyer and as someone who knew the case and the factors involved. And it was passed around in the Department of Justice and some guy would say, 'No. You can get more out of it.'" Frequently, a department attorney makes suggestions or issues directives to the assistant handling a case. Assistants often find such suggestions valuable, but many remember instances where they thought the department's suggestions were wrong, stupid, or merely insulting.

A former Justice Department official who dealt extensively with U.S. attorneys found the biggest source of conflict arose when divisions sought to handle a case themselves rather than letting the U.S. attorney handle it. It is not difficult to see why. Most U.S. attorneys feel it is their job to handle cases in court, not the department's. Asked what difficulties he had with the department, a first assistant replied, "It's not a question of difficulties. It's when they usurp our prerogative and take over our cases." Field personnel also suspect the department's motives. A former U.S. attorney felt the Tax Division handled its own cases because they had "built a damn empire." And an assistant in an office located in the Second Circuit believed Tax Division attorneys tried to take over cases because the most important and interesting cases arose there. Important cases represent a scarce resource. They provide opportunities to obtain excellent experience. When a lawyer from the department tries one, it deprives someone in the field. "I'm here to learn all I can," explained an assistant. "The people that they send out are young men also, and I might as well try them. I'd like to try them." The resentment goes beyond remorse at lost opportunities to try interesting cases, however. "We all have our sensitivity out here. We're sensitive to anyone coming out from Washington. It's sort of a reflection on our competence—that we aren't competent to do the job." The belief that the department often takes a cavalier attitude toward people in the field compounds this sensitivity. "They seem to feel that the boys in Washington have some God-given intellect that people out here in Cowship just don't have."[19] Furthermore, department attorneys can become a nuisance. "They didn't know how to litigate a case in this court," lamented an assistant, describing what happened when several department attorneys handled a case. "I was getting two or three calls each day. They were asking me about everything—the size of the paper, forms . . . ." Not only do most U.S. attorneys feel their offices are capable of handling their own cases, they also question the competence of department attorneys. An independent-minded U.S. attorney defended his efforts to maintain autonomy on the grounds that his people could handle cases better than department attorneys.[20] Another felt that the most ambitious, hardest working, and courageous attorneys avoided the career ranks in the department. The noncareer attorneys suffered from inexperience. His summary judgment was harsh. "I have never—and I've had some experience with this—seen a really able trial lawyer in the Department of Justice."

2) The "Bureaucratic" Nature of the Department.   United States attorneys and assistants complained frequently about the "bureaucratic" behavior of the department. The following comment is typical of the attitude of assistants. "If there's anything that strikes me about working for the government, it's the fantastic amount of red tape you've got to cut through. And dealing with people from the Department, this has become terribly apparent . . . I can practically feel it and

touch it." When dealing with the department, U.S. attorneys experience timidity of lower level officials, confused lines of authority, and long delays in transmitting decisions or replies to inquiries. "You waste so much time," observed an assistant sadly. "You wait for an opinion sometimes three or four months. I've quit asking them now." Attempts to get action from the department on requests or suggestions are usually regarded as doomed to failure. "They listen to your problems and are sympathetic," said a U.S. attorney, "but nothing happens." The passage of time and the change to a Republican administration apparently brought few changes. A Nixon appointee complained about the department's internal rules, adding, "I suppose what disturbs all U.S. attorneys is the lack of urgency shown problems sent to Washington."[21]

Many U.S. attorneys consider the routine reports and memos required by the department little more than time-consuming bureaucratic exercises in paper shuffling. They disdainfully describe the department as "statistics happy." Small offices find the time they must spend on reports and memos burdensome. "You can be worn out, writing back and forth to the department on every routine case. You can spend all your time."

United States attorneys also become exasperated with what they feel is inflexibility and rigidity in the department's supervision. Several lamented their lack of discretion in such administrative matters as salaries, travel costs, and miscellaneous expenditures. They consider the amounts provided for these purposes too small: "Men, when they went to Washington—you had to in effect pay half of your own way just to go to a conference. You weren't even compensated so that you could live at the normal level they want you to. That's ridiculous. Ridiculous." Such feelings are exacerbated when U.S. attorneys discover that department attorneys trying a case in their district can, in the words of one indignant assistant: ". . . go to the court reporter and say, 'We want this transcript by next Monday and by the way we are authorized to pay you for expediting . . .' and that gripes my ass . . . because it is an insult to me that they can say we can do what the U.S. attorney can't." United States attorneys also complain of the department's timidity in undertaking investigation or instituting prosecution.

Although they formally constitute part of the government bureaucracy, most U.S. attorneys and assistants rarely think of themselves in these terms. Rather, they regard themselves as lawyers "on the firing line," handling cases for a very big and important client. But they consider their counterparts in the department to be bureaucrats more than attorneys. After describing how he managed to collect most of a debt by not foreclosing a lien, an assistant observed that every so often another lawyer from the department asked him to foreclose. "All they can think of is closing the case. And my time is taken up educating them as to the practical problems of business affairs." An assistant expressed the sentiments of many field personnel when he described department attorneys. "What's annoying is that some of these people, who only have their canned cites and have never tried a case, get the feeling that they're all-knowing. . . . They get very impressed with themselves in the Department of Justice. They have the attitude that out here in * * *, we're fighting cowboys and Indians."

3) Creating Difficulty in the District.   The third major cause of discontent results from the adverse reactions of judges, the local bar, and other salient individuals to the department's actions. "How would it be," a former U.S. attorney asked me, "if someone would drop in on you saying, 'I'm so-and-so from the Antitrust Division. We're getting ready to file antitrust suits against the ten top building contractors in the city.' I resented this, and felt I should be consulted." At least, he added, he could have been prepared for newsmen when they besieged him. The refusal of the department to accept recommended compromises causes difficulties by undermining the U.S. attorney's bargaining reputation. In several districts, private attorneys indicated that it was a waste of time dealing with the local office; they dealt directly with Washington when they wanted to effect a compromise. The failure to appeal lost cases particularly annoys members of U.S. attorneys' offices. The department informed one assistant that it would not appeal a case to the Supreme Court because the Court would probably deny certiorari and it wanted to maintain its high acceptance rate. "I thought that it was really terrible that my case was shot down to help somebody's batting average." When a department attorney performs poorly in the local courtroom, it embarrasses members of the local office. "I feel that I am the government's attorney here," observed a U.S. attorney, "And I hate to see an ass stand in front of the judge and try to conduct the business of the government. It's just that simple." An assistant in charge of the civil division in a large district claimed that such performances damaged the office's local stature. " 'Say, where did you find this fellow?' They'll say, 'Where did you find him?' even though we had nothing to do with it. This is a source of embarrassment to us."

Local offices become particularly concerned when they feel that actions taken on behalf of the department are eroding relations with the judges. In one district, the department directed the handling of pretrial matters in organized crime cases from Washington and dispatched its own men to try them. The arrangement created numerous difficulties for the U.S. attorney's office. In one instance, the department ordered a case brought which neither the local office nor the judges felt worthy of prosecution. When the department ultimately decided to drop it, the local office had to take responsibility for the dismissal. Over time, relations with the judges deteriorated, affecting all of the office's work. Asked if the judges didn't understand that the local office was not responsible for these actions, an assistant there replied: "They kind of understood, but they lumped us together. We are the Department of Justice, and we have to stand up for them . . . normally, we have to defend the DJ. Anything done is a reflection on our office." Other actions ordered from Washington create problems with the judges. "For example, they write and ask you to request for extensions of time. They don't understand that's a swear word in this district. It's not all that easy. . . . We're on the firing line, and because of that, we catch all of the static." And an assistant explained why his office strenuously objected to a department suggestion that they state as appellees that the arguments in the district court were wrong. "[We] were supposed to undercut the trial judge. If we did that, the judge would get the impression he was led down the primrose path. . . . We have a reputation to maintain."

In more extreme instances, carrying our department instructions can do more than injure one's reputation with a judge. A number of years ago, the department ordered a U.S. attorney to disobey a court order to sign grand jury indictments of civil rights workers in Mississippi. The U.S. attorney soon found himself standing before the judge being sentenced to jail for contempt of court.[22] Though we do not know the personal reaction of this individual to the incident, I spoke with one U.S. attorney who found himself in similar circumstances. A judge granted the defense attorney's motion to examine FBI investigative reports linking his client to an alleged crime. Since U.S. attorneys are strictly forbidden to let these reports out of their offices, the respondent called the department, informing them that he could be jailed for contempt if he refused to comply. "And the guy said, 'That's fine! Fine! We need somebody to go to jail now. We need a scapegoat because we've got some pending legislation about this very thing and it would relieve us.' 'You mean to tell me, you lousy son-of-a-bitch, that you really want me to go to jail?' And the guy said, 'Yeah.'"[23]

## THE ORIGINS OF CONFLICT

The interaction between specialized divisions in the department and generalists in U.S. attorneys' offices provides a specific example of a widespread phenomenon. James Fesler noted it a quarter of a century ago.

A problem that is ever with us... is the contrast between the specialized competence of the Washington Office and the more generalized orientation of regional and district offices. The central headquarters can generally slice its functional responsibility more finely than can the field offices.... Such specialization by groups of employees cannot be wholly reproduced at regional and district offices.... The administrative officer has to encompass all phases of administrative management.... The Washington office, then, is a complex of specialities, while the field office is much more generalized in function and personnel.[24]

The functional specialists in the department's divisions exercise nationwide responsibility for litigation. Moreover, career attorneys often further specialize in a specific category or type of case within the division's general responsibilities. A U.S. attorney's office handling such a case cannot normally assess its relationship or importance relative to other litigation on the same subject elsewhere, but the department, as one official stressed, "has *got* to see the whole picture." The picture as viewed by a specialized division in Washington, however, appears narrowly framed to a U.S. attorney. The division attorneys know nothing of important pending cases in other subject areas in the office. An assistant discussing a department attorney who handled Interstate Commerce Commission matters described this difference well. "The ICC is all he knows. He knows it backwards and forwards but he works in a very specialized area. He works on a pinhead. And the Department is a collection of specialized areas. You know everything in a very tight area. Here, it's different. You're out in the field. It's a shotgun approach. You do a little of everything and you don't get a chance to concentrate on anything."

The U.S. attorney, unlike anyone in the department outside of the attorney general and deputy attorney general, performs an aggregating function. Because he must seek favorable dispositions on a wide variety of both criminal and civil matters, he may find it necessary to sacrifice national policy in one case or to downgrade the priority given a specific matter in order to maintain his overall effectiveness. Thus, the need to try an Indian murder case in his eyes justifies pulling an assistant off tax work. But when he makes such decisions, those in the department who devote their full energies to the sacrificed area naturally object.

The inevitable conflicts that arise between area generalists and functional specialists at headquarters do not fully explain the tension between U.S. attorneys and the department. United States attorneys adhering to the "autonomous" rather than "field officer" conception

of their position in the department experience more tension and conflict. Divergence in career ambitions, already alluded to, also contributes. United States attorneys and assistants rarely desire to make a
career of their job. They regard the position as a steppingstone and
training ground, and seek trial experience and favorable evaluations
from those who can affect their future career prospects. Usually,
these people are located in the district. Boy scout-like obedience to the
department is not likely to enhance their local stature. At the lower
levels of the department, career prospects depend on the impressions
made on superiors. Advancement within the department (or even a
top-notch recommendation to a private law firm) does not come by
acquiescing in every action of men in the field and letting others try
the difficult and complicated cases. Differences in the strategic environment of men in the field and in Washington also explain the
existence of tension. United States attorneys interact daily with
judges, witnesses, defendants and plaintiffs, juries, private attorneys,
and the department. Most headquarters attorneys, however, deal with
a narrower range of individuals—U.S. attorneys and assistants, their
superiors and subordinates, and an occasional representative of
another government agency. A greater proportion of their time is
consumed by matters directly involving men in the field.

The strategic environment of supervisory personnel in the department, particularly the political appointees, rivals U.S. attorneys' in
complexity, but its components differ markedly. Political demands
regarding the direction and effectiveness of federal law enforcement,
whether generated by Congress, the president, the bureaucracy, the
press, interest groups, or some combination of these are directed
toward the attorney general and his subordinates. These pressures
affect behavior both on important, visible cases and policy areas and
on low visibility matters. The comments of a department lawyer regarding their policy in a relatively insignificant area illustrate the
latter point. If an indicted defendant is found mentally incapable of
standing trial, the department seeks to have the U.S. attorney insure
he remains in custody until arrangements for his hospitalization can
be made. "If he is let free and he commits a crime in another district,
the U.S. attorney is o.k. But we are to blame. We are letting murder-
ers and rapists loose on society." Department officials must project the
image that their organization effectively fights crime, particularly
since "law and order" has become a major theme in national politics.[25]
Since the department's performance in such politically sensitive areas
depends heavily on the activities of U.S. attorneys, the incentives to
control their behavior are especially compelling. Finally, department
officials feel directly the pressures generated by the congressional

appropriations process. The department's tightfistedness, with respect to expenditures for travel, office equipment, and the like, that arouses the ire of many U.S. attorneys stems directly from budgetary constraints imposed by Congress. At least some of the behavior denounced as "bureaucratic" by men in the field—the preparation of numerous reports and the emphasis on workload and output figures—results from demands for information from the House Appropriations Committee. From the late 1940s until the end of 1974, department officials had to face Congressman John J. Rooney of New York, the chairman of the House Appropriations subcommittee that handled the department's budget. His notorious reputation as a hard-nosed, abusive, and aggressive questioner was well-deserved.[26] Since the subcommittee evaluated the department on the basis of statistical measures at budget time, and since they had to submit detailed information on workload and expenditures, departmental officials understandably adopted a similar outlook and passed it on to their subordinates.[27] Preparing numerous reports and striving to keep the number of convictions and the conviction rate up without regard to the substantive significance of the cases may be a bureaucratic nuisance to U.S. attorneys, but to the department, it is a compelling necessity.[28]

# CHAPTER 5

# The Dynamics of Interaction: Strategies and Tactics of Control and Autonomy

The preceeding chapter established that while some U.S. attorneys embrace the concept of central control, others have deep reservations. Simply knowing a U.S. attorney's feelings about his relationship with the department, however, reveals little about his actual behavior. Those proclaiming their independence may in fact acquiesce to the department, while colleagues who pay lip service to Washington's prerogatives fight tenaciously to maintain effective autonomy. Furthermore, a U.S. attorney fighting to establish and maintain independence may fail. Similar considerations apply to the department. Belief in the principle of central control does not guarantee attempts will be made to implement it. Attempts to implement do not necessarily insure success.

Interactions between the department and U.S. attorneys fall into two distinct categories: those characterized by cooperation, negotiation, and influence, which clearly predominate, and a minority which involve overt conflict, confrontation, and influence through coercion and resistance. Although infrequent, the conflict mode of interaction significantly determines the frequency and content of cooperative encounters. The ability of either side to persuade the other depends on the expectations held about what the consequences of failure to reach agreement will be. These expectations in turn rest on memories of what happened in the past when overt conflict broke out.

Several distinctions are useful in analyzing both types of interaction. *Strategies* refer to general policies and modes of behavior designed to affect outcomes in a variety of situations over an extended period of time. *Tactics* refer to behavior designed to affect the outcome of a single interaction, regardless of whether it has long-range implications or general application. For example, a series of moves by the department seeking to improve the quality of information received from the field is a strategy. Dispatching an attorney to a district in order to get first-hand information about a particularly important case is a tactic. The choice of tactics is almost always a conscious one. Strategies often result from conscious calculations, but a series of actions, each undertaken without conscious reference to other actions or an overall plan, may produce the same results. For example, a U.S. attorney who fights the department in a sequence of disputes because the specific facts involved in each compel him to as a matter of principle may acquire a reputation in the department as a "fighter" just as surely as another man who consciously seeks to establish such a reputation by carefully choosing favorable issues on which to do battle. Both strategies and tactics may be either *overt* or *covert*. Outright disagreement and refusal is an overt tactic of resistance. Ostensible acquiescence accompanied by stalling and quiet subversion is a covert tactic. Finally, *offensive* strategies and tactics take the initiative, while *defensive* ones seek to counter and neutralize another's offensive moves.

## CONFRONTATION, CONFLICT, AND RESISTANCE

### U.S. *Attorneys' Strategies of Resistance*

Students of situations that involve mixtures of cooperation, conflict, and bargaining emphasize the significance of the reputations of the contending parties in shaping outcomes.[1] A department official explicitly acknowledged its importance for a U.S. attorney's independence. "The reputation you get in the divisions is very important. The career service people become afraid if a man is known as tough and right." Department attorneys consciously assess U.S. attorneys. "You'll find that there are good U.S. attorneys and bad U.S. attorneys," observed one, "and you work with the bad ones more closely." Department officials also evaluate U.S. attorneys, and they use the assessment to determine whether to seek their advice, let them handle a case, or accept their recommendations.

United States attorneys develop reputations then, on two general attributes: their own legal competence, integrity, and diligence and that of their assistants, and their propensity to argue with the department, to appeal adverse decisions to superiors and to win such appeals. Every U.S. attorney who serves for any length of time inevitably acquires a reputation on these attributes in the department's divisions.

The techniques for affecting the assessment of an office's legal competence are quite limited. Most U.S. attorneys work hard, strive for legal excellence, and try to improve as a matter of course. If neither the U.S. attorney nor his staff are capable, little can be done to prevent the development of a poor image in Washington. Offices staffed by competent attorneys become known as strong offices. However, U.S. attorneys can utilize several conscious strategies to shape perceptions of competence. Although they all recognize the importance of getting good assistants, some devote considerable effort to both the recruitment and retention of outstanding assistants.[2] United States attorneys skilled in courtroom advocacy can take time from their administrative duties to try crucial cases themselves. The U.S. attorney who competently tries cases himself enhances his office's reputation and may prompt the department to delegate cases to him that it would handle itself in other districts. Some U.S. attorneys exercise tight supervision over their staffs to protect the office's reputation. An assistant in one of the most independent offices noted that his boss was so concerned with the reputation of the office that he personally reviewed all proposed dismissals before they were forwarded to Washington for approval, resulting in a more stringent policy on dismissals than the department's.

United States attorneys enjoy greater flexibility in establishing a reputation for appealing headquarter's directives. A U.S. attorney in a small office described a strategy mentioned by several respondents. "Either the U.S. attorney runs his office or the Justice Department will. He'll meet them head-on early, and you've got to stand up. And usually the U.S. attorney will win. . . . It didn't take long for the word to spread around the Department to leave us alone."

Usually the strategy of taking an early stand is offensive in nature. However, newly appointed U.S. attorneys in districts with a tradition of autonomy may resort to it as a defensive measure to preserve the status quo. Shortly after he assumed office, one such individual discovered attorneys from the Civil Division attempting to usurp his office's traditional right to handle appeals. He interpreted it as a deliberate effort to erode the previous autonomy of the office. "They tried to jap us. I did battle and I did battle royally." "Doing battle" involved several trips to Washington to speak with the assistant attorney general and ultimately a meeting with the deputy attorney general. "The deputy attorney general deferred to me. The reason was that the assistant attorney general misrepresented this district's position to the deputy attorney general. As far as the Civil Division was concerned, they learned not to do it again."

Most U.S. attorneys conscious of the importance of their reputations for "toughness" concentrate in only a few areas. One respondent indicated he did not object to department attorneys trying "department cases," but that he invariably appealed an adverse ruling on a recommended compromise settlement. A few, however, pursue the time-consuming strategy of appealing whenever a disagreement arises in any area. An assistant attorney general reflected a common headquarter's perception of one such individual. "He makes it very unpleasant for you to try to influence how a case in his office is handled. You have to do battle with him."

If reputation is a crucial concept to students of conflict and bargaining, the communication of information is at least as important to students of organizational behavior. In their book on public administration, Simon, Smithburg, and Thompson observe that human cooperation rests on communication and that the exercise of authority in particular depends upon communication.[3] It is not the process of communication per se that is important, but the information that is transmitted. March and Simon in their book, *Organizations*, make an assertion about the communication of information that is particularly relevant to department—U.S. attorney authority structures:

... the person who summarizes and assesses his own direct perceptions and transmits them to the rest of the organization becomes an important source of informational premises for organizational action. The "facts" he communicates can be disbelieved, but they can only rarely be checked. Hence, by the very nature and limits of the communication system, a great deal of discretion and influence is exercised by those persons who are in direct contact with some part of the "reality" that is of concern to the organization.[4]

United States attorneys, obviously, transmit much of the information about "reality" required by the department to control its field offices. They communicate general intelligence about criminal activity in the district, reaction to department policies in the press and among the public, special problems with judges or investigative agencies, and information about specific cases. The latter is particularly significant. Referring to department attorneys, an assistant observed that because they are not in the district, "they don't know the ability of the lawyer on the other side. The file might refer to Dr. Jones. They don't know who Dr. Jones is. We might know that he's a big phony." Assistants possess a near monopoly over other information pertinent to the intelligent handling of a case, including the probable reactions of judges and juries and the quality of witnesses. Although the department possesses more information about cases than people in the field realize, perceptive headquarters officials recognize that they do not have as much knowledge about a particular case as an assistant does and find it a significant problem in supervising them.

United States attorneys pursue several strategies to enhance the advantage superior information confers on them. One is to restrict

the information communicated to the department. Some U.S. attorneys order their assistants to limit their communication with
Washington; some even require all contact with the department to be
routed through them. "I told my assistants not to call the Justice
Department unless you check with me first," one adherent of this
strategy observed. "We want to be as autonomous as we can be."
Another way to restrict information is to manipulate the case-
reporting systems developed by the department. By 1965 the department had developed a rather elaborate IBM marked sense card
reporting system designed to keep track of the tremendous volume of
cases. This permitted it to pinpoint cases in areas where it was supposed to exercise tight supervision, revealed cases that had been
pending too long, and recorded the degree of success achieved in
collection cases. Although the system appeared to work moderately
well, not all U.S. attorneys cooperated fully. "The statistics aren't very
good," commented a department official. "Many U.S. attorneys have
their own policy on statistics. They decide what they will fill out and
what they won't." United States attorneys used categories that revealed little about what was being done (especially the "060" code—
"other stage of proceedings not specified"), and arbitrarily assigned a
different code to a case to prevent its being tagged as "inactive."[5] The
department has continued its efforts to improve the quantity and
quality of information available, investing considerable sums in the
development of a computer-based "automated caseload system"
scheduled for completion in 1977. Subtler strategies to manipulate
information available to the department are also employed. In allocat-
ing authorized assistant positions among the districts, the department
relied (at least in part) on caseload. United States attorneys who assigned assistants to time-consuming significant cases instead of less
significant but rapidly handled matters faced the possibility of a drop
in caseload and a cut (or at least no increase) in staff. A former U.S.
attorney candidly outlined his response in this situation: "Now I can
admit this. We deliberately kept crap on the docket as a backlog. We
were playing a numbers game with the Department. I always said I
had $X$ percent of the pending cases. Not $X$ percent of the actual cases
tried or convictions but $X$ percent of the *pending* cases. And I used this
as justification for maintaining my staff."

This suggests a third general strategy pursued by U.S. attorneys—
cultivating alternative sources of support to call upon during disputes
with the department. Independent-minded U.S. attorneys especially
require a hard-working and loyal staff. An assistant who regards the
department rather than the U.S. attorney as his primary boss can
seriously undermine efforts to remain independent.[6] Consequently,

some U.S. attorneys seek to develop a cohesive and loyal group of assistants, particularly by backing them vigorously in disputes with the department. In one district, assistants told me that the U.S. attorney supports their decisions no matter how much he personally disagrees with them. Most assistants interviewed in such districts expressed a distrust of the department, but praised the U.S. attorney warmly.

United States attorneys greatly value the support of judges in disputes with the department, though the desire to win such support constitutes only one of a number of reasons to cultivate good relations with them. A department official related an incident that illustrates how judges can assist in disputes with the department. He had sent two of his attorneys to observe the trial of a very important case and to relay instructions from Washington directly to the trial assistant on how to conduct it. But, he observed, "the judge backed us down. . . . We found the case suffered from divided command. The assistants were young and inexperienced." I asked just what the judge did. "He told our attorneys to get out of the courtroom." The department recognizes clearly the support judges render U.S. attorneys. "Many of the judges are the strongest proponents of U.S. attorney autonomy," observed a Democratic official. "A lot of them are ex-U.S. attorneys. They feel it is best in the long run for them to have autonomy." But the department can do little about such support or U.S. attorneys' efforts to cultivate it.

Investigative agencies can also provide useful support. United States attorneys earn such support by establishing good working relationships with investigative agencies, but they can also coerce cooperation from these agencies in some instances. An official in the department's organized crime section, which at the time was arguing with a U.S. attorney over the conduct of the section's organized crime strike force in his district, described what the U.S. attorney told one agency. "If you take a case to the organized crime people, I will not take another case of yours in this jurisdiction."

## U.S. Attorneys' Tactics of Resistance

The strategies just described enhance the general capability of a U.S. attorney to exercise autonomy and effectively resist department attempts to exert control. The *tactics* employed in specific instances of conflict take a variety of forms.

One of the most interesting and dramatic is outright defiance and refusal to obey headquarters. Among the many such instances related to me by U.S. attorneys, one stands out as particularly useful in illustrating many of the elements typically found in their confrontations.

It involved a holdover Democratic U.S. attorney at the start of the Nixon administration. A conference of black leaders from all over the country was being held in his city. It attracted the attention of the national press, the FBI, and a number of congressmen. The dispute centered on whether to conduct a grand jury investigation of the conference (including issuing subpoenas to some of the participants) and, more importantly, when to commence such an investigation. The department, under considerable pressure from some congressmen, wanted to begin on Thursday, when the conference would still be in session. The U.S. attorney, who strongly opposed commencing the proceeding while the conference was in session, informed the department that he would be attending a judicial conference that Thursday and Friday but would be happy to begin the next Monday. The department replied that that was unacceptable. He would have to begin on Thursday. The U.S. attorney replied he could not do it then. The department responded that it would issue written instructions ordering him to begin on Thursday. The U.S. attorney indicated he would refuse to acknowledge or obey those instructions. As the U.S. attorney related the story, the department then said:

> "You are part of the Department of Justice and we are ordering you to do it." I replied, "I have been appointed by the President and this is my district and I'm not going to do it." They said, "We will have to take up the matter with the attorney general." I replied, "Well, I will have to take the matter up with the chief judge. I want you to call up the judge and discuss the matter with him and if he thinks I should not go to the judicial conference, then I'll change my mind." Of course, they knew that I would get down to the judge before they had a chance to call him.

The grand jury was not convened until the following week.

A second example of outright defiance involved a case being handled by a Republican toward the end of the Eisenhower administration. Though it occurred some time ago, the dynamics of such confrontations that it illustrates remain valid. The case involved a fairly small fraud penalty the department wanted to impose on a veteran for falsely claiming he could not pay for an operation at a Veterans Administration hospital. Since the department had instructed him to reverse the decision not to prosecute, the assistant on the case asked the U.S. attorney what to do. The attitude of the U.S. attorney toward the department in this case is demonstrated by his reported reply: "Tell 'em to go to hell!" Whatever the assistant's wording of his continued refusal to prosecute, it prompted another letter from the department telling him to proceed as instructed. This time the U.S. attorney himself replied to the department. "I wrote back and told them the matter had been referred to me—that I felt the assistant was correct. But they wrote back again. And I told them that somebody up there was being an ass-head, and that further correspondence would be of little value." From the reports of other respondents, an adamant refusal to prosecute, though it may prompt a wearying exchange of letters, usually causes the department to drop the matter. In this case, however, determined department attorneys summoned the respondent to a meeting during the U.S. Attorney's Conference. "Here were all these people sitting around on this little case. And they went and explained to me that this was fraud by law, and that's the way it is. And there was a previous case in Ohio which was very similar, and this should be prosecuted. And I told them that the case in Ohio was different" [and outlined his reasons]. Someone in the meeting explained that he "worked for so-and-so who worked for so-and-so who worked for the attorney general." This was enough to set the respondent off: "I'm a presidential appointee. And I don't care what you say about what should be done in this case. You can go to the devil! I just came from a conference on a far more important matter than this that was left up to my discretion. And I'm not going to prosecute. If you want to take it up with the attorney general, then go right ahead." The respondent described the parting scene with obvious relish: "Then I walked out, and as I was walking out, I heard the pitter-patter of little feet along side of me, and they said, 'Well, gee, we didn't realize that you felt so strongly about it.' Subsequently, they wrote a letter to us saying they'd reconsidered and changed their minds."

Such confrontations often involve relatively minor matters. Typically, the field attorney openly refuses to obey the department. In the series of exchanges that follows, the department stresses the formal authority of the attorney general. United States attorneys emphasize their status as presidential appointees and their responsibility for running their districts. They may rely upon others for support, resort to legal and practical arguments, or both. Sheer bluster and bravado on the part of the U.S. attorney are also common features. United States attorneys do not invariably prevail, but if their objections are not frivolous, very often they do.

The most dramatic strategy of resistance, resorted to only infrequently, involves expanding the arena of conflict by bringing the dispute into the open through the press. As a last resort, a U.S. attorney can threaten to resign and criticize the department publicly. However, they generally employ subtler tactics. One is to "reinterpret" department regulations. "If a regulation in the Justice Department ever conflicted with common sense," a former U.S. attorney recalled, "I told my assistants to come to me; and I told them I'd construe the regulation so that common sense would come out on top." Another is "inadvertently" to overlook a regulation entirely. An assistant handling lands cases complained of the delay in getting settlements approved, and added: "You don't have *time* to mess around two or three weeks, and I don't feel it merits a phone call. So I'll just go ahead and make the settlement . . . and I'll get a letter from them saying, 'We draw your attention to such-and-such a page of the *Manual* which requires that you get approval.' And I write them back and say I'm sorry I overlooked it." As long as this ploy is not used too frequently and the settlements are reasonable few problems arise. A much more common form of indirect resistance is stalling. Because there is no constitutional requirement for a speedy trial in civil cases, U.S. attorneys find sitting on cases very effective. A former U.S. attorney, lamenting the difficulty he had in getting acquiring agencies to approve settlements in lands cases, observed that if he delayed trying the case, the land would remain unavailable. Stalling is also possible on criminal cases before the defendant is indicted. Asked what could be done if the department wanted a poor case prosecuted, a former U.S. attorney replied: "There's lots. Just inertia. Just drag your damn feet a bit on handling a case." This appears to be a favorite technique. It also must be quite frustrating to the department. Asked how he "sat on" a case, a chief assistant replied: "Well, we write them (the department) letters all the time. We tell them we're going to get around to it." Although rarely employed, U.S. attorneys can indirectly resist the department by devoting less than full attention to cases brought at Washington's insistence. It is only natural that lack of enthusiasm for a case will effect the amount of preparation and the vigor of the presentation, and the department recognizes this. Consequently, indicating lack of enthusiasm for a case may deter the department from insisting on bringing it.[7]

The department sometimes counters such resistance by dispatching one of its headquarters' attorneys to take over a case. However, this does not always end resistance. In several districts, the U.S. attorney's office attempts to supervise closely department attorneys' preparations for trial. In one district, the chief of the local office's civil division tore up a paper a department attorney was about to file and threw it back at him. Sometimes, U.S. attorneys request the department to recall attorneys who become too haughty or overbearing. Complete lack of cooperation and outright harassment of headquarters' attorneys is unusual but not unknown. A former department lawyer described this strategy as follows: "As a visiting attorney, you need space, facilities, some secretarial time. You need someone who knows his way around town. They could do a lot in advance of your coming for you. And if they didn't do that, you had to spend two or three days doing the stuff yourself. . . . You'd get the cold treatment. They'd tell you there was no room for you."

Finally, U.S. attorneys' offices claim that though they would like to comply with orders from Washington, they cannot. An assistant attorney general described how U.S. attorneys use the grand jury in one version of their tactics. "It has been our experience that if the U.S. attorney wants to he can dog a case and he can make a presentation to the grand jury without ever saying 'don't indict' and they won't indict. And you know, you can get the indictment on the skimpiest of evidence as well."[8] Of course, if the U.S. attorney reports that the grand jury will not indict, a department attorney can be dispatched to present the case to the grand jury again. But if the grand jurors have already refused to indict, they may do so again. If the department waits until a new grand jury is empaneled, the case ages in the interim and may decay in quality. United States attorneys also blame judges for failures to comply with Washington's directives. For instance, the department instructs U.S. attorneys to oppose nolo contendere pleas. Judges learn quite rapidly when such opposition is genuine and when it is merely pro forma. The same is true with respect to the requirement that the prosecutor recommend jail sentences in tax cases if the judge asks for his opinion. In both instances, the U.S. attorney can report that he followed headquarters' official policy to the letter, but a nolo plea or sentence of probation nevertheless results. Although such outcomes result from tacit cooperation between a U.S. attorney and a judge, sometimes they cooperate explicitly. This tactic obviates the need to get department approval to dismiss an indictment. "I had one case that I wanted to dismiss," a federal prosecutor told me, "But I knew it would be hard to justify to the Department. . . . So I talked to the judge, and he dismissed it."[9] Similar collusive tactics can circumvent the department's disapproval of a U.S. attorney's settlement recommendation in civil cases. A U.S. attorney described how his judge would work out a stipulation of the facts in the pretrial conference that favored the other side. He would then use the stipulation to go back to the department again with his proposed settlement.[10]

## The Strategies of the Department of Justice

The strategies the Department of Justice pursues to cope with the confrontation, conflict, and resistance the emanates from the field fall into the same general categories as the U.S. attorneys' strategies just discussed. Members of the department seek to establish strong reputations, increase the information available to them, consolidate their support in the department while eroding or circumventing U.S. attorneys' alternative sources of support, and restrict their ability to take effective action in areas not under their control.

The techniques for establishing strong reputations with U.S. attorneys are fairly obvious. Recruiting and holding competent attorneys promotes an image of expertise.[11] Some divisions and sections enjoy an added inherent advantage in this regard. Most assistants with minimal courtroom experience usually feel capable of trying cases within the jurisdiction of the Criminal Division. This is hardly true with respect to tax or admiralty cases. A department attorney can acquire a reputation for firmness by vigorous opposition to resistance from the field, especially if he prevails when disputes with U.S. attorneys go to departmental superiors for resolution.[12] Thus, the incentives for section chiefs, and even assistant attorneys general, to maintain the respect and backing of the deputy attorney general and attorney general stem in part from the recognition of the importance such support has in shaping their reputations with the field offices. Like U.S. attorneys, section chiefs and assistant attorneys general find it advantageous to have a competent and loyal home base of support when engaged in such disputes. Supervisory personnel consequently like to back up subordinates in disputes with men in the field and to fight for good cases for their subordinates to try.

The department recognizes the crucial importance of information in controlling U.S. attorneys as much as U.S. attorneys do. Part of its strategy is to increase the degree U.S. attorneys cooperate with existing information-gathering systems. In 1965 the major part of one day's proceedings at the Annual Conference of U.S. Attorneys was devoted to a series of speeches exhorting, begging, convincing, and telling them to adhere faithfully to then existing information-gathering procedures.[13] Since then, new information-gathering procedures have been adopted. The four attorneys who head the regional branches of the Executive Office for U.S. Attorneys provide general intelligence about the functioning of the offices in their region. The department's automated caseload and collection system represents an effort to upgrade previous systems. By training the civil service clerical employees to fill out the forms routinely and by indoctrinating them into the necessity for doing so through orientation and training sessions held for them in Washington, the department may be able to limit U.S. attorneys' ability to undermine the new system.

The department relies on several strategies to reduce the desire for autonomy of U.S. attorneys and their assistants. It brings all new U.S. attorneys to Washington to meet its key personnel. According to one U.S. attorney, "This is a great thing. You're on a first name basis with the people that you're on the phone with. The indoctrination is very helpful." The conference of U.S. attorneys held each year continues this indoctrination. Some members of the department do not wait for U.S. attorneys to visit them. A highly placed career attorney indicated he occasionally traveled to the bigger districts to get acquainted with the personnel and bragged that he knew all of the U.S. attorneys by their first names. In recent years, the department has increased the number of face-to-face meetings. Both the Johnson and Nixon administrations conducted regional conferences to which they sent high-ranking department officials to meet men from the field, plan strategy on pending litigation, and discuss department policies. The Ford administration established the Attorney General's Advocacy Institute, which runs two-week trial advocacy training sessions and holds regional seminars on a number of specialized topics.[14] The department evidently finds it advantageous to develop personal relationships between headquarters and field personnel. To the extent such contacts reduce the desire of U.S. attorneys to be independent and erode the loyalties of assistants, they contribute to greater central control.[15]

Another technique for increasing the responsiveness of men in the field is to assign attorneys recruited in Washington to a specific district or a regional office charged with handling specialized cases for extended periods of time.[16] Sometimes these men are designated as assistants under the supervision of the local U.S. attorney.[17] Their primary loyalties, however, remain with their "home division" in Washington. The organized crime strike forces, consisting of teams of attorneys dispatched to eighteen cities, constituted the department's most extensive use of this technique.

Another strategy for reducing the ability of U.S. attorneys to resist Washington is to erode their standing and support in the district. If the department consistently pulls "end-runs" around a U.S. attorney, dealing directly with private attorneys opposing the government in negotiating settlements or speaking directly with judges about problems in the office, it harms the U.S. attorney's reputation and weakens his ability to win local support in disputes with headquarters. The department may also consciously bring cases itself that it knows will cause the judges' wrath to fall upon the local office. One assistant attorney general expressed his willingness to send his own men to the field to try cases the local U.S. attorney refused to bring because of judicial opposition. He wanted to assert his right to control what cases went to court, even if it proved costly.

By indicating a personal interest in his U.S. attorneys, an attorney general may establish personal loyalties that can be translated into a willingness to adhere to basic policies and programs of the department. Interviews with a number of men who served under Robert Kennedy indicate that he was fairly successful in this regard. One former U.S. attorney expressed the feelings of many: "I was impressed with the way Robert Kennedy handled the U.S. attorneys. He built a real team-rapport. He and his wife were at all of the Conferences, and they were very cordial. They made you feel like you were part of the Administration. They would have confidential briefings for us. In fact, right before the Cuban missile crisis, they gave us a briefing to tell us what was going on."[18] While this feeling did not result in unquestioning adherence to directives of lower officials (indeed, it encouraged appeals in some instances), it did guarantee cooperation and compliance in instances where Attorney General Kennedy had indicated a personal interest. Deputy Attorney General (and later attorney general) Kleindienst, in the Nixon administration, made a conscious effort to build a similar rapport with U.S. attorneys.[19]

The department pursues several strategies designed to limit the ability of U.S. attorneys to take independent effective action. The most important one attempts to regulate most of their activities by setting forth in detail the procedures and policies to be followed. The *U.S. Attorneys Manual* outlines policies to be followed in the enforcement of specific laws,[20] specifies the forms and reports that must be submitted, and contains a number of suggestions distilled from previous experience.[21] More significantly, the *Manual* removes discretion from the field and lodges it in Washington in a number of areas. No indictment can be dismissed without explicit approval from Washington. Settlements in civil cases above a specified dollar amount must be authorized by a department official. Nolo contendere pleas are to be invariably opposed. The department forbids field personnel from handling certain categories of criminal cases (for example, immigration and naturalization, purchase and sale of public office, and contempt of Congress) relying instead on its own attorneys to try them. Prosecution under newly enacted statutes frequently requires prior approval from Washington.

The department seeks more control over civil litigation, particularly during the pretrial stage. A "counterpart" attorney in Washington checks the trial assistant's wording of pleadings and motions, approves any requests for delays, and oversees other preliminary matters. The department's divisions supervise especially closely tax refund cases, admiralty cases, and antitrust suits in their preliminary stages and send their own attorneys to most districts when their cases are ready for settlement or trial.

As noted previously, tight control over expenditures is maintained by Washington. The hiring of new clerical personnel, their promotions and salary increases, the purchase of furniture, equipment, and supplies, and the authorization of travel funds, witness fees, and other expenses incurred in litigation all require approval from Washington.

The department employs several long-range strategies that can result in a reduction of U.S. attorney's autonomy. Because a strong U.S. attorney who exercises a measure of independence from the department often can defend encroachments on his autonomy successfully, divisions wishing to gain control of cases handled by such offices seldom challenge an entrenched incumbent. Instead, they wait until the incumbent leaves and a new U.S. attorney replaces him. The new man needs to learn how to deal with the department and maintain independence. He may not know just what degree of autonomy his predecessor managed to win. Consequently, he is vulnerable, and one or more divisions may test their ability to take control over cases away from the field office. Other divisions carefully watch the outcome. This strategy prompts U.S. attorneys to employ the defensive counterstrategy described earlier in this chapter. The department's divisions display considerable perseverance, because the predecessor of the U.S. attorney described earlier independently described the same sequence of events.[22]

A more general long-range strategy seeks to remove one of the principal resources of U.S. attorneys—the political support the appointment process gives them and the independence that accompanies the attorney general's inability to fire them.[23] Ramsey Clark, the last attorney general in the Johnson administration, proposed legislation to make U.S. marshals career civil service appointees. He wanted to pave the way for the removal of U.S. attorneys from presidential appointment. Some department officials serving under Johnson and Kennedy expressed the desire to convert the position of assistant to a career basis. They felt by basing advancement on their evaluation by the department, and by rotating them from office to office, problems stemming from limited loyalty, inexperience, and career flexibility could be eliminated. Though some proponents were unsophisticated in their assessments of the political difficulties involved in getting it adopted, others were not. One of the more sophisticated acknowledged changes would probably come only after a big scandal involving assistants. Officials in the Nixon administration expressed less interest in changing the appointment process, though an attempt was made to ease the task of removing U.S. attorneys by seeking to obtain a moral commitment from prospective appointees to resign if requested to do so. Proponents of fundamental changes failed to convince a special committee of the American Bar Association to endorse abolition of the president's power to appoint U.S. attorneys.[24]

A relatively recent stragegy poses perhaps the greatest long-range threat to the continuation of the existing level of autonomy of U.S. attorneys. The department has begun to remove whole categories of cases from the control of their offices and assign them to centrally dispatched attorneys who operate in the districts. They handle all matters pertaining to such cases. Thus, when President Nixon announced a drive on heroin pushers, the department created a special office with its own group of prosecutors to handle drug cases.[25] Even more significant was the establishment of organized crime strike forces in eighteen cities. All investigations and prosecutions relating to organized crime in these cities, regardless of the specific statute involved, were to be handled by the strike force, not the local U.S. attorney. A fascinating book could be written describing the conflicts between the strike forces and U.S. attorneys' offices when the program was being implemented.[26] Preliminary research suggests that in some districts, determined and strong U.S. attorneys were able to resist successfully the encroachment of the strike force, but that in others the U.S. attorney's authority and power were significantly eroded. The strike forces operated only in eighteen cities, though some encompass more than one district. While many districts remained unaffected by the strike forces, the program included many of the more important offices. The strike forces by themselves did not cause a permanent decline in the relative authority of U.S. attorneys, but the strategy of identifying certain categories of cases as "emergency" situations to justify the control of headquarters over them could be a very effective one for the department.

### The Department's Tactics

Department attorneys try many cases, even when no conflict whatsoever exists between headquarters and field. Though criteria vary from division to division, the department takes control when a case is difficult and complex, produces effective pressures on the local man, contains issues whose resolution can have nationwide and lasting impact on a number of other cases, or falls into an area of special concern to current department policy priorities. In addition, U.S. attorneys sometimes request the department's intervention. When U.S. attorneys ignore instructions, reject suggestions, or refuse outright to obey direct orders, however, taking over the case provides the department with a direct, simple, and effective remedy. The headquarters' attorney travels to the district and assumes control of the case. He may be treated shabbily by the U.S. attorney, secretaries, judges, and, indeed, by everyone in the district. The U.S. attorney may complain loudly to the attorney general. But the department handles the case.

Several other tactics, short of actually taking over cases, are employed. One is to dispatch an attorney from headquarters to the field solely to gather information about a case that otherwise could not be obtained from the U.S. attorney's office. One official reported sending a trusted subordinate to listen to the presentation to the grand jury of a doubtful case resting on oral testimony so his man could assess the quality of the witnesses. The presence of an observer in the grand jury room reduces the likelihood that an assistant will try to elicit a "no bill" when he is reluctant to prosecute. The department also dispatches attorneys to observe the pretrial negotiations or actual trial of important cases. Another tactic involves issuing direct orders to the field on how to proceed when persuasion and suggestion have failed.[27] When an assistant equivocates, the department can write a letter and ask for his decision, forcing him to commit himself on paper.

The efficacy of these techniques, particularly the issuing of orders, ultimately depends not only on the power to take over cases but also the ability to remove field personnel from office. Only the president can fire a U.S. attorney, and it generally becomes a painful, time-consuming, and delicate matter, particularly when there is no misconduct alleged. Nevertheless, as officials in recent Democratic and Republican administrations acknowledge, firings and forced resignations occur.[28] Assistants must worry more about being fired for insubordination because the attorney general can do so without going to the president.[29]

A final tactic, though used infrequently, is worth mentioning. Occasionally, holdover U.S. attorneys from a previous administration do not resign and cannot be fired immediately without creating embarrassing political repercussions.[30] But, by exercising its powers of control over budgetary matters and appointments, the department can create serious problems for the holdover. In one such instance, the department imposed a freeze on salary raises, permitted no appointments to fill vacant assistant positions, and even refused to authorize the purchase of note pads, paper clips, and other supplies. Furthermore, the clearer the department's intention to rid itself of this U.S. attorney became, the more difficult it was for him to deal effectively with others in his district.

## THE EXECUTIVE OFFICE FOR U.S. ATTORNEYS:
## IN THE MIDDLE

Although some officials in the Executive Office for U.S. Attorneys felt it had the potential to serve a mediating role between field attorneys and operating divisions within the department, its precarious strategic position makes it very difficult to do so. A former director of the office summed up the dilemma quite well:

I found that the office did play the role of advocate [for U.S. attorneys] but I felt strongly that it must always be aware of the danger of becoming known within the Department as strictly the advocate of the U.S. attorney. I felt that there was a fine line that we had to march between losing all credibility with the rest of the Department and losing credibility with the U.S. attorneys. Because they feel, "Well, what's the use of having these people in Washington if they don't do anything for us."

The "fine line" between the two may not exist in fact. The Executive Office possesses no sanctions it can invoke against the various divisions within the department. It can use its control of administrative and budgetary operations in the field offices to punish or reward U.S. attorneys. But a strong-willed U.S. attorney in the midst of a dispute with Washington over a matter of importance to him is unlikely to be swayed by such considerations. Consequently, the Executive Office acts at best as a mediator in disputes between headquarters and field. Its effectiveness in playing a mediating role varies, depending on the personality and status of the director. When the director is a forceful individual, is not interested in making a career in the department, and has the backing and confidence of the attorney and deputy attorney general, he can make his presence felt in specific disputes. Most directors, however, do not possess these qualities, and their effectiveness, though not negligible, is sharply limited.

The field research confirmed this gloomy assessment of the role of the Executive Office. In the course of my many interviews in Washington and the field, no one (with the exception of those actually in the Executive Office) mentioned it as a significant force in shaping headquarters–field relations. When I asked specifically about its role, men in the field typically responded as a former U.S. attorney did. "Those guys—I never understood their function. They generally did not understand the problems of the U.S. attorney." Even men in the Executive Office itself recognize the obstacles to its playing a significant role. A former director assessed the office in the following way.

I viewed the Executive Office as playing three roles and maybe they are so inconsistent that it was an impossible task. I viewed the Executive Office as being a mediator in disputes and having the confidence to be able to look at it from the Department's standpoint and being able to look at it from the U.S. attorney's standpoint. And also as being a supervisor in the sense of watching the U.S. attorney. And by the means of the pay and the travel and all the budgetary things having some influence over it.... I think that we were moderately successful in being a supervisor. I think that we were modestly successful in bringing some input from the field. And I think we never were able to get to the point of acting as a mediator in disputes.

## FACTORS LIMITING CONFLICT AND CONFRONTATION

The foregoing description of the relationship between the department and U.S. attorneys' offices presents a somewhat paradoxical situation. On the one hand, there is substantial evidence of an undercurrent of tension and hostility. Furthermore, both parties have the incentives to resist encroachments, the resources to engage in overt and covert resistance, and strategies available to pursue such resistance. On the other hand, I have emphasized that relations between them are typically marked by cooperation, negotiation, mutual accommodation, compromise, and a polite, often even friendly, atmosphere.

The seemingly paradoxical coexistence of underlying tension and day-to-day harmony can be explained by examining those factors which tend to raise the costs of open conflict and reduce incentives to engage in it. The conflict-dampening factors described below provide fairly compelling reasons to keep open conflict a relatively rare phenomenon.

Many U.S. attorneys appreciate the help headquarters provides them. Offices with heavy caseloads find the department's ability to dispatch additional manpower to try routine cases extremely useful. This is particularly true in very small offices, where the loss of an experienced assistant, a delay in filling a vacancy, or the simultaneous appearance of several lengthy trials can result in an impossible burden of work. The department can also lighten the workload substantially by preparing appeal briefs. The writing of a brief is a time-consuming task which a small office usually happily turns over to the department. The specialization within the department, plus the accumulated experience of tenured appointees at the lower levels, provide the department with an expertise that many U.S. attorneys and assistants rely upon. Although U.S. attorneys occasionally resist the department's attempts to take over complicated and specialized cases, more often they welcome them. As one U.S. attorney put it, "In most

cases, it's not a question of superseding. It's a question of the case
being very specialized—a speciality." Most districts have neither the
manpower nor the skill to try complicated civil tax cases, medical
malpractice suits, or tort actions arising from plane crashes (and involving potentially tremendous damages). United States attorneys
and assistants also utilize the department's expertise in handling their
own cases:[31] "I don't call on them often. But it's nice to know they are
there. If something comes up in court. . . I can go out and telephone
them right in the middle of a trial, and they'll work on it and call
back. . . . We do use them." The excellent library and reseaearch
facilities of the department are rarely matched in a U.S. attorney's
office. The department also has ready access to and knowledge of
earlier cases in the same area. Although assessments of the quality of
the assistance the various divisions provide differ widely, many U.S.
attorneys and assistants appreciate and rely upon the availability of
such help.

The department can also serve as a "heat shield" by taking over
cases which generate intense local pressure on the U.S. attorneys.
"You may be surprised at this," one southern U.S. attorney remarked,
"but we're not reluctant to have them come down from the Civil
Rights division." A colleague, who impressed me as unsympathetic
both to the department and to civil rights noted, "Civil rights is one
area where I'm happy with the department. I'm glad they handle
things. . . . It really takes the pressure off."[32] United States attorneys
welcome the relief from local pressures brought by turning over other
types of cases to the department, including prosecution of politically
and racially prominent individuals or investigative agents with whom
the office had worked closely in the past.

The department also serves as a "heat shield" when a local office
blames Washington for decisions unpopular locally. One U.S. attorney used this technique when local pressures to decline prosecution of
criminal cases arose. "You can just tell them that this is a Department
policy—that you need their approval. And this takes the heat off you
locally." The department will even issue formal instructions to a U.S.
attorney when he wishes to attribute a local decision to Washington.
Washington also protects offices from incurring the hostility of the
local press by issuing limitations on the information they can make
available on newsworthy cases.[33] Finally, the department can be used
to share the risks inherent in making difficult decisions. An assistant
put it this way: "I have judgment enough, in cases involving controversy or a new area, to call them in and ask them. I have no
hesitancy to do it. They have a saying—it's sort of pulling them into
bed with you. And I do."

The department earns the gratitude of U.S. attorneys in other ways. One is by refusing to entertain initiatives by litigants to bypass the local office. A U.S. attorney who exhibited considerable independence from the department nevertheless appreciated its support. "I always felt that when somebody tried to end run me and go to the Department with a complaint, they got nowhere." Another is to support the U.S. attorney in conflicts with others in his district by interceding with a judge giving his office a hard time or backing his position in disputes with investigative agencies.

Some U.S. attorneys recognize that the department can play an important role in frustrating or furthering career ambitions. This was particularly salient to one man: "I don't know how many times they told us this at the U.S. Attorneys' Conferences. They said, 'You'll be coming back to the Department many times after you go into private practice. And since you are a former U.S. attorney, even if the same people are no longer here. . . . you will start with the door open.' People will be more receptive to your problems." The department can also provide the U.S. attorney with invaluable experience in specialized fields of law.[34] Its support can be helpful to those men who wish to become federal district judges. Political careers can also be assisted in small but deeply appreciated ways. The campaign literature of a former U.S. attorney running for the state supreme court contained complimentary statements from the attorney general and deputy attorney general; another official was the featured speaker at a testimonial dinner for the candidate.

The department utilizes its opportunities to assist U.S. attorneys in all of the ways just described. As a result, U.S. attorneys develop a certain degree of loyalty toward and appreciation of the department that reduces the impetus to act independently and increases their susceptibility to persuasion. United States attorneys recognize that if they adopt a posture of conflict with the department, the cooperation and help they depend upon may cease. Men known as troublemakers can expect a less friendly reception when they deal with the department as private practicioners in the future. If they aspire to the federal bench, they may find their chances dashed by the department's vigorous opposition. Even the possibility of being fired, though remote, must enter into the calculations of any U.S. attorney contemplating vigorous combat with Washington.

One other factor operates to restrict sharply the frequency with which U.S. attorneys battle the department. Such disputes require tremendous time, energy, and resources. Furthermore, these efforts must be undertaken in addition to the normal workload. Thus, U.S. attorneys must pick and choose carefully among the many occasions when they might fight the department. An independent-minded U.S. attorney summarized many of these considerations when he explained why he did not insist on the department's appealing some of his cases. "We could have. But you're caught up in a great flood of litigation. We just didn't want to get involved. You get involved in your job and just have to go along." The combination of limited resources, battle weariness, and the pressure of other work make sustained and frequent conflict unappealing.[35]

Many of the same factors operate to limit the desire, ability, and incentive of the department to battle constantly with U.S. attorneys' offices. The volume of work handled by U.S. attorneys' offices is so great, and the manpower of headquarters so limited in comparison, that it cannot even oversee every area all of the time. Although the department employs explicit criteria for deciding what to supervise,[36] it inevitably passes over important areas and cases. A former assistant attorney general of the Criminal Division lamented the fact that his manpower shortage was so severe that his division could not even review briefs of appeals filed in circuit court before they were submitted. Given these constraints, the prospect of engaging in frequent, time-consuming, and acrimonious conflict with field attorneys appeals to few in Washington. The difficulty of obtaining vital information even from cooperative U.S. attorneys places attorneys in Washington at a disadvantage in arguments over how to handle a case. Furthermore, even if a trial attorney agrees to follow instructions, the supervising attorney in Washington cannot anticipate all choice situations that arise in the course of a lawsuit. Without a detailed knowledge of the facts and circumstances of a criminal case (strength of evidence, characteristics of the judge, skill of the defense attorney), it is difficult even to second guess the decisions made during plea bargaining, much less supervise them. Furthermore, the department's internal structure makes coherent supervision of the field difficult.

The specialized divisions within the department compete with each other for the time of assistant U.S. attorneys. The assistant U.S. attorney who wants to drop work on a tax case to handle an Indian murder case may win the gratitude and support of a counterpart attorney in the Criminal Division. Thus, a division or section's attempts to force compliance with its directives may bring it into conflict with other units within the department. Career attorneys also hesitate to engage in confrontations because they dislike bothering superiors with such conflicts. A career official in the frauds section expressed the feeling that if a career official pushes for a confrontation, he is likely to lose. Political appointees are not immune from such calculations. The top officials of the department may come to question the performance of a division that is constantly engaged in disputes with U.S. attorneys' offices.

The gratitude and appreciation of department personnel for the efforts in the field reduce incentives to do battle with U.S. attorneys. Sometimes, U.S. attorneys can provide manpower to other districts when the department encounters problems. "By the way, that's one of the prices I paid Justice to leave me alone," interjected a U.S. attorney. "There's been a murder down at —— penitentiary and [an incompetent U.S. attorney in another district in the state] will screw it all up. Will you send one of your guys down? 'Well,' I'd say, 'I can't spare him but I'll send him down.'"

Finally, the department finds it costly to invoke formal powers of control. When asked why he dispatched an attorney from Washington to take over a case rather than ordering the U.S. attorney to try it, an assistant attorney general replied, "They might just walk in and throw it. I'm not saying they would, but it is a possibility. So we send our own man." But manpower limitations sharply restrict the number of cases that can be handled by headquarters' attorneys. Limitations on the ability to fire U.S. attorneys and assistants inhibit conflict and limit the department's ability to control them even more. The value of the removal power as a deterrent to resistance from the field depends on the perceived seriousness of the sanction. Most assistants intend to stay only two or three years anyway. Observing that he sometimes ignored procedures in handling cases, one assistant asked, "So what are they going to do, fire me? So, I'll go back into private practice." United States attorneys whose career ambitions do not depend upon the department's support share this perspective. Many know they can return to lucrative private practices with their old law firms at any time. Although the attorney general can fire assistants on his own initiative, he customarily seeks the approval of the U.S. attorney. If the U.S. attorney opposes the removal, it creates difficulties. Firing a U.S. attorney becomes even more involved. A perceptive career attorney described what happened when the department encounters an obstreperous U.S. attorney:

[The deputy attorney general] says, "Goddam it. I got this guy's resignation [in an undated letter signed when he was appointed]. If he doesn't do what we say, we'll get rid of him!" And I can't say, "——, I've been around here 25 years and I know that's a lot of crap!" First of all, the statement's too general. I mean there are some we can get rid of .... But you get some other guy who's leaking information to a political friend who may be the subject of an investigation, you know, then you have to question. Well, can we get rid of him? Do you really want to bite that bullet? Does he want to take on that senator? And if he can win, do we want to pay the cost? Does he even want to face the problem?[37]

Asked if he had fired any U.S. attorneys, a former attorney general replied that he removed several. "We kept some we wouldn't have kept just because we couldn't take the pressure from the senator. Nine times out of ten the U.S. attorney gets backing from the senators. It's a costly move to fire them."[38]

Three processes operate on both U.S. attorneys and the department to inhibit conflict, reduce tension, and promote cooperation and mutual accommodation. The first is a simple psychologically based desire to avoid unpleasant confrontations and disagreeable situations. The chief of the civil division in one district pointed out that "showdowns" with people in the department are not only a black mark for everyone but also jeopardize future relations. Both know they will have to work together again. Thus, both make concessions in order to avoid such situations. Since much of the professional activity of lawyers involves negotiation and compromise, they are hardly strangers to it. Second, both parties recognize their dependence upon one another, and both realize each will suffer from strained relations. A department official summarized the feelings of many when he observed: "We can't do our job without them, and they can't do nearly as well without us." An assistant attorney general indicated how this outlook justified giving in to one U.S. attorney who was often adamant about his autonomy. "We have to cooperate with [him] on a lot of other things. He has a highly qualified staff. They do a good job on 90 percent of the cases, so if they don't do such a good job on 10 percent it is worth it for the 90 percent that they do a good job on. We let the 10 percent go by." Third, the personal friendship and mutual respect that sometimes develops between U.S. attorneys and department officials make clashes more distasteful and less likely. A very independent U.S. attorney in a large district described how he became close friends with the assistant attorney general in charge of the Criminal Division. He went on to describe the tenor of their conversations: "I called you to let you know what I'm going to do. Don't tell me I can't because I know god damn well I can." "What are you going to do?" and I'd tell him. "Uhh, sounds like a pretty good idea. You're a crazy son-of-a-bitch. You're going to get your tits in the wringer." Because we understood each other."

## THE STRATEGY AND TACTICS OF PERSUASION

Some strategies that the department and U.S. attorneys employ to enhance their capability to engage in conflict also serve to bolster their ability to persuade. Strategies designed to build friendships with counterparts and to establish reputations for competence, expertise, and helpfulness have already been described.[39] In addition, both consciously attempt to reduce existing sources of tension and hostility. For instance, officials in the Executive Office for U.S. Attorneys came to recognize that assistant U.S. attorneys deeply resented the discrepancy between their salaries and the salaries of men with similar tenure and rank in the department. The Executive Office undertook vigorous (and eventually successful) efforts to reduce the discrepency, partly in the hope that resistance to and resentment of the department would diminish.[40] A U.S. attorney whose predecessor had engaged in violent controversy with the Tax Division committed additional personnel to tax work in order to clear up the backlog of cases in this area and hired a former member of the department's Tax Division to head his office's tax work. These actions, he felt, removed the Tax Division's legitimate complaints about the office.

The tactics of persuasion are fairly straightforward and can be described briefly. Arguing about the legal merits of the question at hand defines the dispute as a disagreement between professionals and opens the possibility of relying upon statute and precedent. Being "right" in a legal sense and arguing the point well is the most effective (and probably most frequently employed) persuasion tactic. Both parties often claim to possess information unavailable to the other. When U.S. attorneys, closer to the facts and personalities that shape the outcome of cases, claim a case cannot be won because of poor witnesses, an unfriendly jury atmosphere, or an outstanding opposing lawyer, department attorneys find it difficult to challenge them. Superior information about the collectability of civil claims also permits effective persuasion. "Sometimes the DJ would compromise when the case was uncollectable," explained a former U.S. attorney. "And often, I was very generous in determining just what was uncollectable." United States attorneys also exploit the widespread recognition in the department that the men in the field must maintain satisfactory relations with judges and other key participants in the district court community by asserting that their position will be undermined if they adopt the department's position. Department attorneys counter with the claim that the dictates of national policy support their position and that failure to abide by it will jeopardize its implementation. They also have access to information about similar cases in other districts that lend weight to their argument. Finally, both appeal to authority. United States attorneys call upon their authority as presidential appointees, particularly when dealing with career attorneys. But when a U.S. attorney or an assistant deals with higher officials, especially the attorney general or his deputy, the claim of authority may run in the opposite direction. Both refer to department policy in supporting their arguments, particularly when it is set forth in the *U.S. Attorneys Manual*. Most often, it is the department attorney who refers field personnel to the provisions of the *Manual*. But occasionally, U.S. attorneys are delighted to find in it justification for their position. With obvious glee, one recounted an argument he had with a Tax Division attorney over whether a weak case should be prosecuted. When the division lawyer admitted that they wanted to proceed to deter similar violations, the U.S. attorney refused, quoting a portion of the *Manual* prohibiting such prosecutions.

CHAPTER 6

# Patterns of Interaction: A Summary of Department– U.S. Attorney Relations

The preceding two chapters provide a foundation for understanding the complexities and dynamics of relations between U.S. attorneys and the Department of Justice, but the most difficult and significant questions remain. What generalizations can be made about the relative degree of central control versus field autonomy? In what ways can individual districts stray from the typical pattern? What factors are associated with this variation? How does the relationship between the department and U.S. attorneys compare to other headquarters–field relationships in the federal government? This chapter seeks to provide the answers to these questions.

## CLASSIFYING PATTERNS OF INTERACTION

The field research revealed a fascinating and intricate set of patterns in the relationship between U.S. attorneys' offices and the department. Summarizing them poses a challenge, particularly if the underlying similarities in all districts' relations with Washington are to be conveyed without either over-dramatizing the differences or obscuring those that are important.

### The Dimensions of Variation

Two critical dimensions along which U.S. attorneys and the department differ in their approach to one another determine in large part the nature of the relationship: (1) the U.S. attorney's willingness to resist or propensity to accept the department's efforts at control; and (2) the intensity of the department's efforts to exert control. As the preceding two chapters indicate, U.S. attorneys differ both in their desire to resist department control and in the tenacity and skill

Table 6.1. Schematic Representation of Patterns of U.S. Attorney–
Department Interaction

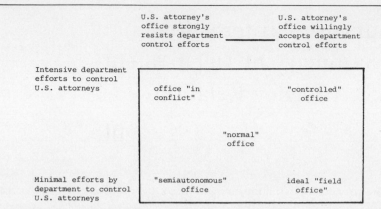

they employ in seeking autonomy. Similarly, the vigor of the department's efforts to oversee and control the work of its field offices varies from district to district. The interaction of these two dimensions affects both the ratio of overt conflict to cooperation found and the locus of effective decision-making (i.e., the ratio of central control to field autonomy). Table 6.1 summarizes the patterns of interaction that result from various combinations of efforts to exert central control and achieve autonomy in the field. The solid lines surrounding the diagram represent schematically the fact that powerful incentives operate to dampen both the department's efforts to control and the U.S. attorney's to resist. Likewise, the impossibility of knowing what the department "wants" in every instance limits the extent to which a U.S. attorney can carry out the department's wishes, and the department's commitment to establishing and maintaining national policies and standards restricts the amount of discretion it can delegate to the field. Thus, variation both in the amount of conflict and the degree of imbalance of decision-making between headquarters and field is limited. As Table 6.1 suggests, however, variation exists within these boundaries. Essentially, the hypothesis underlying Table 6.1 states that knowing the department's efforts to exert control and the U.S. attorney's efforts to resist such control allows prediction of two basic characteristics of their interaction: how much conflict there is and the balance between central control and field autonomy.

### The "Normal" District

The interaction of relatively moderate efforts of the department to control and U.S. attorneys to resist control produces the "normal" relationship, the pattern most frequently encountered in the field research.[1] Two propositions summarize the level of conflict and overt hostility found in the "normal" relationship.

*Proposition 1.* The level of overt conflict and disagreement is low.

This proposition recapitulates a major theme of the preceding chapter. Both the department and U.S. attorneys generally applaud their relationship and do not feel threatened by each other. The department typically asserts control in areas the U.S. attorney concedes to it anyway. United States attorneys insist on exercising discretion in areas the department finds impossible and unnecessary to handle itself. Both recognize the strategic situation of mutual dependence. As a result, they deal with one another in a way designed to maintain an atmosphere of cooperation. Both generally shun commitments from which they cannot back down and they rarely issue ultimata. Both are open-minded and willing to be convinced by the merits of the other's arguments. However, the relationship cannot normally be described as "close."[2] A Nixon appointee's response to a question asking if he felt relations with the department resembled more of a "team spirit" or "detached" atmosphere probably represents the views of most U.S. attorneys: "Oh, I would say it is a detached thing. I think they work on a schedule and a set of rules with a set of schedules that just fit into a slot. They've got the answers for what you need, with statistics. And I think it is a very detached thing. You have some friendships in the Executive Office but generally it is simply a matter of routine with everybody."

*Proposition 2.* When inevitable disputes do arise they are usually resolved through muted and polite give-and-take discussion.

When a disagreement arises, a "talking through" of the problem usually produces an acceptable accommodation. "It's very seldom that any areas develop where the positions of you and the department are diametrically opposed," observed a senior assistant U.S. attorney. "It's unusual when you can't get one or the other of the sides to be convinced."

United States attorneys seldom resort to strategies of outright defiance, and the department rarely invokes its power to issue direct orders. According to one assistant, "It's not that tight a control. Most of the direction is in the form of suggestion. It's worded so it is not a direct order."[3] "What kind of working relationship do you have if someone has to order you to do something?" another assistant asked. "This is what you want to avoid. . . . Every problem can be worked out if you sit down." Disagreements occur, but, as one assistant put it, "It's not really fighting that occurs."

Summarizing the balance between central control and field autonomy poses more problems than assessing the level of conflict and overt hostility. The amount of discretion an office exercises at any given time varies depending both on the type of case and on who in the office handles it. An office may enjoy considerable autonomy in tort cases, but find its handling of tax evasion tightly controlled. The department gives a free hand in almost any case to some assistants but scrutinizes others closely. Furthermore, an office's autonomy may change substantially over time. Consequently, attempts to generalize about an office's relations across the whole range of cases and personnel inevitably produces some oversimplification and distortion. Nevertheless, several useful and valid general propositions concerning autonomy and control in "normal" districts emerged from the research.

*Proposition 3.* United States attorneys have a large amount of discretion in the day-to-day execution of their duties.

Men at headquarters and in the field recognize this fact and accept its desirability. The statement of an official in the Criminal Division during the Johnson administration summarizes the view of headquarters. "Unless a statute has really been abused, we leave them alone. In the long run, we feel it is better if the U.S. attorneys are on their own." An assistant described the discretion that results: "The Department doesn't bother me. I have a wonderful relationship. . . . I'm more my own boss and still working for somebody else than I could be anywhere else."

The department delegates such day-to-day discretion by choice. But U.S. attorneys in "normal" districts also fight for and win autonomy in some circumstances. Specifically:

*Proposition 4.* United States attorneys often prevail in disputes which do not involve major areas of policy.

The observations of a political appointee in the Civil Division during the Nixon administration provide strong support for this proposition. During a discussion of the heated disputes that arise over whether headquarters or field attorneys will try attractive cases, he summarized how such disputes were resolved. "I would say generally that the U.S. attorney's office will win a lot of those cases unless we decide it is really a national case and has national ramifications." When U.S. attorneys devote the time and attention required to back up adamant stands on specific issues that the department does not regard to be of major importance, the department generally changes its mind or acquiesces. The next proposition outlines the significant limits on U.S. attorneys' abilities to prevail in disputes in the "normal" relationship.

*Proposition 5.* The department can prevail on matters which do not involve major areas of policy when it so desires.

If it feels strongly enough, it can control such things as whether a settlement in a civil case is accepted. The addition of the qualifying "when it so desires" is crucial. As noted in the previous chapter, the department's limited resources prevent it from imposing its will on every point of disagreement.

*Proposition 6.* The Department of Justice nearly always prevails on matters involving major areas of policy.

United States attorneys normally voluntarily comply with the important general policies set by the department. When they do not, the department can almost force adherence. However, it is more difficult to force U.S. attorneys to take positive action (e.g., increase collection efforts on debts owed the government) than to insure that they refrain from prohibited ones (e.g., not trying tax refund cases themselves).

The evolving policy of the department on the prosecution of violations of the Dyer Act (interstate transportation of a stolen motor vehicle) and the response of U.S. attorneys to it provides a useful illustration of Proposition 6. For a number of years, the department left to the field decisions on whether routine car thefts (many of which involved juveniles) would be prosecuted. A U.S. attorney in a large district expresses the view shared by many toward such cases. "The FBI likes to report how many stolen cars they recovered.... It's all bullshit." Strong-willed U.S. attorneys like this man sharply restricted prosecution of Dyer Act cases to those that involved an interstate theft ring. Some U.S. attorneys in smaller districts refrained from bringing them in response to pressure from judges who regarded routine cases as "junk." But FBI agents generally pressured U.S. attorneys and assistants to authorize prosecution, and they often succeeded. In the mid 1960s, between 16 percent and 17 percent of all criminal cases terminated were Dyer Act violations. Toward the end of the Johnson administration, the department attempted to reduce such prosecutions, particularly when they involved teenagers. As one official put it, "Most of your big offices were just delighted to have an excuse not to handle some of the junky Dyer Act cases." But he acknowledged that in many districts, particularly in the South, U.S. attorneys ignored the guidelines. He felt the policy made some difference, an assessment borne out by the slight decline in prosecution in fiscal 1964 reported in Table 6.2. But, he added, the department did little when an office refused to follow the guidelines. Though the department expressed concern over Dyer Act prosecutions, it failed to devote serious efforts to enforcing the new guidelines, and these cases

Table 6.2.   Dyer Act Prosecutions: Fiscal Years 1964–1975[a]

| Year | Total number Dyer Act cases terminated | Total number all criminal cases terminated | Dyer Act as percent of all criminal cases terminated |
|------|------|------|------|
| 1964 | 5,083 | 31,186 | 16.2 |
| 1965 | 5,222 | 31,175 | 16.7 |
| 1966 | 5,190 | 30,428 | 17.0 |
| 1967 | 4,996 | 29,923 | 16.6 |
| 1968 | 4,432 | 27,394 | 16.1 |
| 1969 | 4,414 | 31,317 | 14.0 |
| 1970 | 4,440 | 34,748 | 12.7 |
| 1971 | 3,127 | 39,748 | 7.8 |
| 1972 | 2,809 | 47,933 | 5.8 |
| 1973 | 2,479 | 44,518 | 5.6 |
| 1974 | 2,199 | 43,572 | 5.0 |
| 1975 | 1,922 | 45,217 | 4.3 |

[a]Figures for each year are taken from the *Annual Report of the Attorney General* (Washington, D.C.: U.S. Government Printing Office, 1965–76).

continued to account for a substantial proportion of all criminal cases. The new administration escalated the importance of securing adherence to the new guidelines. The attorney general decided to downgrade (but not eliminate) prosecution of "non-ring" cases (i.e., where no organized car theft ring was involved). The Executive Office not only monitored prosecutions under the Dyer Act, but (in the words of a member of the Executive Office) "indicate[d] to them that this is what is expected in terms of change and there should be no differentiations [among districts] in this area." The department's efforts began to pay off, as a U.S. attorney in a small district revealed. He claimed the new policy was "the only thing which has changed my attitude." The figures in Table 6.2 support the impressionistic evidence. As the department elevated its concern and increased its efforts, it effected a decrease in these prosecutions.

These six propositions about the characteristics of the "normal" district's relations with the department provide the outlines of a composite view. Any given district will exhibit some variation in specific details. These differences, however, are not substantial enough to invalidate the usefulness of designating them as "normal." Some districts, however, differ significantly enough from the "normal" pattern that they assume a qualitatively separate character. These differences result from large deviations from the central region on one or both of the two dimensions in Table 6.1 (department efforts to control, and U.S. attorney efforts to resist such control).

*The "Controlled" and "Field Office" Patterns*

In some districts, the U.S. attorney and his assistants seldom resist department efforts to control their behavior. In fact, they make conscious efforts to adhere to the department's policies and directives. Personnel in such districts exhibit most of the following characteristics:

1. They acknowledge the office is part of the department and rightfully subject to headquarters control.
2. They make no sharp distinctions about who in the department has the authority to direct the field staff.
3. They think attaining and adhering to uniform national policy is very important.
4. They regard the U.S. *Attorneys Manual* with reverence, as a source of behavioral guidelines that must be followed.
5. The U.S. attorney appeals decisions or instructions to higher-ups in the department only rarely and reluctantly.
6. The U.S. attorney dislikes disagreement and conflict, and is neither aware of nor skilled in the subtleties of bargaining and arguing with the department.
7. The U.S. attorney values the friendship of members of the department highly, and feels honored when they regard him similarly.
8. The U.S. attorney's career ambitions depend on the support or at least neutrality of the department.
9. The U.S. attorney has no policy goal he feels are of overriding importance.

In both the "field office" and "controlled" districts, the level of conflict is even lower than in "normal" districts. Disputes arise less often because the U.S. attorney's office seeks to avoid them. When they do arise, they are short-lived because the office accepts headquarter's views. Consequently, there is less give and take.

The difference between these two patterns results from the extent of the department's efforts to oversee the activities of an office. When headquarters lacks confidence in the legal competence (or even integrity) of a U.S. attorney and his staff, or when a number of important cases originate in the district, the "controlled" pattern results. When the local office has a good reputation, the day-to-day discretion found in the "normal" pattern is exercised in the "field office" as well. But such discretion is exercised against a background of sincere effort to follow department policy religiously.

### The "Office in Conflict"

This pattern results when a U.S. attorney seeks to resist department efforts to control him, but the department displays no corresponding willingness to accede to the U.S. attorney. The U.S. attorney wants to be independent, but the department does not want him to be. United States attorneys' beliefs concerning the proper relationship between the department and the field conform to the "autonomous" position as depicted in Chapter 4. The field office matches the department's increased efforts to supervise with vigorous efforts to retain discretion. The overall level of discretion equals or even exceeds slightly that found in the "normal" district, since the department neither desires to nor can fight continuously. What is unusual is the level of conflict. Bitter arguments, confrontation, and the use of strategies to evade or control replace persuasion. Indeed, the ability to persuade declines on both sides as the level of conflict increases. The U.S. attorney's office in conflict pays a high price for whatever gains in autonomy it achieves, however, both in terms of the energy expended and the inability to prevail in matters the department considers very important.

Even districts in conflict with Washington enjoy tranquil and mutually agreeable relationships with specific sections and even whole divisions in the department. Nevertheless, those aspects of the relationship where conflict rages generate considerable hostility, and it tends to affect the relationship across the board. At times, conflict escalates into public disagreement and recriminations. This occurred in June 1966, when the department and the U.S. attorney in Chicago publically exchanged mutual criticism.[4] The private exchanges between the department and the U.S. attorney prior to the emergence of the conflict in the press must have been heated.

### The "Semi-Autonomous" District

The Southern District of New York handles a significant portion of the caseload of the department and an even higher proportion of the more important cases. Its symbolic significance is perhaps even greater, for it serves as a constant reminder to the department that its field offices can achieve a position of semiautonomy and it provides other U.S. attorneys with a model of how much independence is possible. As Table 6.1 suggests, its semiautonomy results from a strong desire to resist control from Washington, coupled with the department's willingness to forego strenuous efforts to exert such control. The resistance to departmental control rests on a strongly entrenched tradition of autonomy bolstered by short-run incentives to continue the tradition. The comments of a federal judge and former U.S. attorney in this district suggest the content of this tradition: "It [the office] has an historical background.... Men of the calibre of Henry L. Stimson took the position. They won't take the position if they couldn't handle cases themselves. They set a standard or status and all succeeding U.S. attorneys have to follow it.... I don't remember any U.S. attorney not able to have the attorney general keep the Department of Justice out of here."

An assistant holding an executive position in the office gave me an example of how the tradition of independence found expression: "I've had the Chief Judge of the Court of Appeals, Judge Lumbard, say to me: 'You have to watch those Washington people. I saw a couple of strange faces around court today.' It's a type of parochialism you might say. We all work and practice here. It's a tradition of the New York bar."[5]

The office's "alumni" in private practice also support the traditions, as the comments of a former head of the civil division (a member of a large Wall Street firm) reveal: "I never belonged to a college fraternity. But that's the kind of way I feel about that office. It's just the best place I ever was and I feel that way about it and the people who are there. And I try to find out who's there and what they are doing."[6]

Part of the tradition requires the substitution of "excellence" for "politics" in the hiring of assistants. Most assistants throughout the country depart when there is a change in administration. But traditionally, assistants hired by one's predecessor in the Southern District of New York stay on when a new U.S. attorney of the other party assumes office.[7] As a result, even members of the Department of Justice who wince at the office's autonomy acknowledge the legal competence of its assistants. The desire to maintain this "excellence" provides one incentive for the U.S. attorney in the Southern District to maintain the autonomy of the office. One man who headed the office explained why he insisted on maintaining jurisdiction over cases the department wanted to handle. "We want to hire the best men that we can. The salaries for assistants are very bad. Miserable. The way to keep good people is by giving them good cases and good experience." The office handles most cases on appeal to the Circuit Court of Appeals and Federal Trade Commission litigation as well, cases department attorneys try in most districts. The fact that this office handles such important cases inevitably gives it more influence in the shaping of policy than offices falling into any of the other four patterns.

That the Southern District of New York resists department efforts at control is not difficult to explain. Understanding why the department does not generally seek to exert control is somewhat more complicated. The answer rests in a complex combination of motives—a begrudging respect for the ability of the office to handle cases competently, a resignation based on the knowledge of past failures to exert control, and deterrence based on the anticipation of fierce resistance to any new efforts to encroach upon what the Southern District regards as its prerogatives.

The comments of officials about Robert M. Morgenthau, the Democratic U.S. attorney who served from 1961 to 1970, capture something of the flavor of department attitudes toward the office. A former attorney general observed, "Morgenthau is an example of someone not affected by political considerations. . . . He was very able and effective. He became an institution." A career official in the Criminal Division did not entirely agree about "political" considerations, but the rest of his comment speaks volumes. "Morgenthau had a political bias. Morgenthau was very difficult to deal with. Morgenthau was very uncooperative. He was also a very effective man."

The outstanding battle during Morgenthau's tenure concerned the handling of civil tax refund cases. The obviously frustrated official who sought to win the right of the department's Tax Division to handle these cases described what happened when he went to New York to announce the new policy. "I was confronted by a solid phalanx of former U.S. attorneys. They informed me that the Department was generally corrupt and that the Southern District of New York was clean and upstanding. They said they had handled these cases and it was a continuing thirty-year tradition." The vigorous attempts to assert control were an admitted failure. "I had a terrible time with those fellows." Interviews with men in the Southern District confirmed this assessment. Conflict was extremely bitter for a time. "We were going to the brink every day." Morgenthau's ultimate threat was that he would take disputes to the attorney general. One of his assistants noted that he had a close personal relationship with the attorney general, "at least as good as the relationship of the assistant attorney general with the attorney general." Consequently, all concerned knew he stood a good chance of winning arguments before the attorney general.

With the passage of time and a change in a few personnel who had obvious personality conflicts with one another, the level of conflict with the Tax Division diminished. Interestingly, a top official in the Southern District believed that by and large the office had good relations with the department in most other areas. But the low level of overt conflict masked continuing hostility and suspicion. During the mid 1960s, there was widespread suspicion of the department and a feeling that schemes to erode the office's autonomy were continuously being contemplated in Washington. Said one official, "We try and maintain good relations, but not at the expense of surrendering our autonomy." He used the expression of the "wolf at the door" and observed "They are always trying to take cases. We don't let them."

The difference between the Southern District of New York and other districts can be summarized by referring to propositions five and six regarding the department's control of "normal districts." The department did not prevail in some disputes over what it regarded as major policy. Of course, sometimes the department did win. An organized crime strike force began operations in the district over Morgenthau's bitter objection. But its inability always to win is noteworthy. With respect to less important matters, the department avoided trying to exert control because it knew inevitable and bitter struggles, the outcomes of which were in doubt, would result. Although the personal style of Morgenthau's Republican successor was less combative, on the basis of interviews with members of his staff and with critically oriented members of his predecessor's office, it appears that he preserved the basic "semiautonomous" pattern during the first term of the Nixon administration.[8]

## STABILITY AND CHANGE IN INTERACTION PATTERNS

In his book on the exercise of authority in organizations, Robert Peabody observes that temporal dimensions of authority relations are generally ignored.[9] The point is well taken. The five patterns of interaction just presented can be used to describe department–U.S. attorney relations at any given point in time. But these relations are dynamic, not static.

Peabody identifies two sources of variation over time: organizational change and growth and changes in the level of crisis faced by the organization.[10] The impact of both on department–U.S. attorney relations will be examined later in this chapter. But there is a third source of change not mentioned by Peabody. The cyclical nature of American politics, timed to the ebb and flow of the cycle of presidential elections, affects the interactions of U.S. attorneys and the department. When a new national administration takes office, virtually all U.S. attorneys, an overwhelming majority of assistants, and the entire politically appointed leadership of the department resign. Their replacements all start fresh and must develop relationships with each other from scratch. These relationships change as the newly appointed U.S. attorneys mature in office and the leadership of the department simultaneously gains experience. Occasionally, substantial changes in relations with a given district change when a new U.S. attorney takes office.

The most volatile period comes in the first year or so following a change in national administration. The new political leadership in the department characteristically displays a vigor and enthusiasm that leads to attempts to institute new policies with relatively little regard to preexisting headquarters–field relationships.[11] The corps of new U.S. attorneys, many of whom recognize that their appointment stems at least in part from the favorable action of the department's new leadership, generally share their enthusiasm. Consequently, newly appointed U.S. attorneys exhibit little resistance to department initiatives. United States attorneys know relatively little about their prerogatives and display little skill in asserting them. Although the leaders of the department also lack experience, they have the advantage of a corps of civil service employees who are both experienced and anxious to reduce the autonomy of field offices.

At the outset of a new administration, then, the level of conflict is likely to be relatively low and authority may shift somewhat to headquarters. Things soon begin to change, however. The inevitable conflicts between headquarters and field described in the two preceeding chapters begin to manifest themselves once the routine work of the field offices begins. As newly appointed assistants gain experience, their confidence and ability increase. They learn how to deal with the department,[12] and they begin to talk to and learn from each other. One independent-minded U.S. attorney reeled off a list of like-minded brother U.S. attorneys for whom he had high regard, and commented, "And believe me, *none* of them took any shit from Washington. I've been with them. We had discussions." At the same time, the initial impetus and vigor of the department's leadership wanes as it confronts the task of routine administration and experiences the frustration of dealing with skillful and tenacious resistance from the field. An official in the Kennedy–Johnson administration summarized the changes that occurred: "By . . . 1966, the bloom was off the rose. Very strong patterns developed. . . . Some of the strong U.S. attorneys were taking on positions. One U.S. attorney would say, 'This is my area of interest and they can't tell me what to do.'" After the initial period of increased central control and little conflict, the level of conflict increases and a shift toward somewhat greater field autonomy occurs. Eventually, stable patterns develop and, as mutual expectations about the probable outcome of potential disputes develop, the level of conflict once again moderates.

Another factor possibly associated with the electoral cycle that affects relations between the department and its field staff is the party of the administration in power. The specific policies pursued by both headquarters and field may differ substantially in form and substance from a Republican to a Democratic administration.[13] The successive regimes of Ramsey Clark and John Mitchell offer a sharp contrast.[14] There may even be some relationship between these policies and the dominant ideologies of the two parties and their leading elected officials. But, with a few exceptions, these changes have little bearing on the relative balance struck between central control and field autonomy. Furthermore, the changes in relations found at the beginning of a new administration stem from its newness rather than from its partisan coloration.

To the extent the parties really disagree in their basic approach to the question of "big government" and "centralization," however, we would expect the GOP to grant more autonomy to U.S. attorneys. Certainly this would conform to President Nixon's rhetoric about creating a "new federalism." There is sketchy evidence to support this view. A Republican political appointee in the Civil Division agreed with my statement that historically the trend has been toward centralization, but then added, "Certainly under President Nixon the emphasis has been in the other direction." However, when pressed, he could offer no specific examples, stating, "It is just a feeling that if there are any situations where it [decentralization] can develop that it should be developed." A superior did give an example in the criminal area: the granting to U.S. attorneys the authority to handle civil rights and desegregation cases. In addition, as already noted, the Nixon administration made no effort to put assistants on a career basis or to change the method of appointing U.S. attorneys, both potential means for enhancing headquarter's control. Some evidence even suggests that control from Washington increased in certain areas. Several career officials observed that the new administration removed more assistants and career people associated with the previous administration than the Kennedy administration did in 1961. The efforts made during the appointment process to insure the loyalty and responsiveness of new field personnel have already been described. Finally, the most serious threat to existing U.S. attorney authority and discretion—the organized crime strike forces—were expanded and emphasized by the Nixon administration. Thus, if differences in the balance struck between central control and field autonomy exist between recent Democratic and Republican administrations, they are not great enough to be significant.

As suggested earlier, changes in the individual who occupies the position of U.S. attorney also produce shifts in relations between the department and a given district. Constant factors, such as the size of the office and the nature of pressures generated by the local federal court community, restrict the magnitude of such changes. Nevertheless, four important variables can change when a new U.S. attorney takes office: the department's assessment of the legal competence and integrity of the office's personnel; the U.S. attorney's attitude toward departmental control; his willingness and ability to resist headquarter's control; and the political support he is perceived to have. Depending on the direction of the changes on these four dimensions, shifts in the U.S. attorney's willingness to resist and the department's efforts to exert control can be great enough to change the fundamental pattern of interaction.

## EXPLAINING VARIATION

Why does any given U.S. attorney's office fall into one of the five patterns of interaction and not another? As the foregoing discussion suggests, the answer depends in part on the life cycle of an administration and the length of time the U.S. attorney has been in office. A more satisfying answer, however, must examine the factors that determine how willing to resist the department the U.S. attorney is and how vigorously the department seeks to control him. Three such factors can be identified: the personal characteristics and goals of the U.S. attorney and key department personnel; the degree and nature of support each has from other key participants in the federal legal and political processes; and the size of the district. Although analytically distinct, these three factors display some interrelationship.

Anyone talking with U.S. attorneys, assistants, and department personnel cannot avoid detecting significant differences in the forcefulness of their personalities, their sense of self-esteem, the degree to which they shy away from or welcome conflict, and the balance between the drive to dominate and the need to be dominated. Likewise, commitments to specific policies (rendering "justice," alleviating racial injustice, smashing organized crime) strongly motivate some, and they base their behavior in dealing with headquarters on calculations designed to achieve these goals. Others worry most about how their behavior will affect their future careers. And some appear to be most concerned with "getting along" (muddling through), responding primarily to the daily pressures generated by events, personalities, and office routine. These personal characteristics help account for the attitudes of both headquarters and field men toward the proper balance between field discretion and central control and their behavior in dealing with one another. The field research left me with the impression that the egotistical, strong-willed, policy-oriented U.S. attorneys are most likely to try to resist department control. Similarly constituted officials in Washington are disturbed by field autonomy and do not shrink from efforts to curb it.

One of the most fascinating aspects of U.S. attorney–department relations is the impact that relations with third parties have on their interaction. This is particularly true with respect to U.S. senators and other important political figures in the district. Senators sometimes participate directly. "I was head of the Lands Division," observed a former high department official. "The senators became involved in these cases. They sometimes know the farmers involved intimately. They would contact the U.S. attorney regarding the compromises on these cases." Although most senators know nothing about the overwhelming majority of cases, their participation in a few arouses the concern of the department. Senators and other local political officials more often indirectly affect a U.S. attorney's relationship with the department. An astute career official in Washington identified the crucial component when he observed that a U.S. attorney's ties to senators and local political figures gave him a sense of independence. The president also appoints assistant attorneys general, but they have no political base upon which to anchor independence from the attorney general. When the department sought to establish an organized crime strike force in a Democratic U.S. attorney's district, he asserted he wouldn't let them come into the district. I asked if he had any choice in the matter. His reply suggests the importance he attributed to his relations with the senators in dealing with Washington. "When your party is in power—your party is President of the United States—and your two senators are Democrats and those people ask you over your objections to take the office, and you say in advance, 'I am going to run it the way I want to run it, under those conditions I will take it. Without those conditions being there, I won't take it,' you are in a pretty good bargaining position."

A U.S. attorney's relations with members of the local federal court community also contribute to his ability to resist the department. In the Southern District of New York, assaults on autonomy are resisted not only by a number of judges, but by "alumni" of the office in private practice. Such people support the U.S. attorney in other districts. When asked why the department could not have dispatched an "acting" U.S. attorney from Washington following his predecessor's resignation, one respondent explained: "Well, I doubt very much that that ever would happen, that they could have got away with that in [this town]. I mean, after all, [this] is a pretty sophisticated town. . . .

Because there is no question that the courts in the big city are *very* resentful of the 'school boys' [Department attorneys] as they say." He too was able to prevent the organized crime strike force from taking any significant action. "The judges wouldn't put up with anybody trying a case unless I said the guy was a capable trial lawyer," he recalled, "And I wasn't going to." What would happen, I asked, if the strike force went ahead and brought a case anyway? "They'd cut your balls off. You'd lose your case." The local branch offices of federal investigative agencies also can support the U.S. attorney. This particular U.S. attorney reported an extremely good relationship with the special agent in charge of the FBI in his district. It proved helpful when the department established a strike force. "I just told the Bureau to bring the cases to me and we decided the case. So the strike force just sat around shuffling many papers around."[15] Finally, the U.S. attorney's relationships with his assistants shapes his ability to resist the department. A dedicated and loyal staff provides an essential foundation for sustained resistance. A divided, bickering staff, some of whom turn to the department for support in their disputes with other members of the office, can cripple efforts to maintain autonomy.

The same considerations apply to the relationship between an attorney general and his key personnel. Without a cohesive and loyal group of top administrators, an attorney general cannot successfully make any sustained effort to increase control over the field offices. His relationship with the president is also important. United States attorneys correctly perceive a Robert Kennedy or John Mitchell to have the strong support of the president. United States attorneys disposed to support the president are likely to respect the wishes and follow the orders of such an attorney general. Even U.S. attorneys with strong backing in their district and from senators exercise caution before engaging in a confrontation with an attorney general known to have the president's ear. On the other hand, the ability of the attorney general to prevail, and consequently his ability to influence the behavior of his field staff, suffers when it is known that the president's support for him is limited. United States attorneys who aspire to a federal judicial appointment (as many do) may rightly speculate that a strong attorney general could persuade the president not to nominate them. A weak attorney general may be unable to do so, making defiance of him less costly.

The size of the office provides the best single indication of the relationship between a U.S. attorney and the department. The larger the office, the more likely it is to be found toward the lower left ("semiautonomous") portion of Table 6.1. The smallest offices tend to cluster in the "field office" and "controlled" patterns.[16] Part of the reason is because larger offices often have incumbents whose personal characteristics and goals dispose them to pursue autonomy vigorously. Moreover, as office size increases, the U.S. attorney must forego handling his own cases and concentrate on administrative duties. As the daily activities of a U.S. attorney shift from those of a trial attorney to those of an administrator, it inevitably shapes his perspectives and behavior. He becomes more conscious of his office's prerogatives, more concerned with establishing favorable patterns of interaction with Washington, and more experienced and skillful in doing so. Because large districts tend to generate more important cases, and these cases are likely to attract the attention of the department, the department regards U.S. attorneys in the larger districts as important. It is only natural that they come to think of themselves as important as well. Thus, U.S. attorneys in large offices demand greater discretion in order to achieve the flexibility required to deal with administrative problems, acquire a self-image that supports such demands, and gain the experience and skill needed to fight the department.

United States attorneys in larger offices also enjoy greater support from other participants. Because interesting and important cases regularly arise in the larger districts, U.S. attorneys can recruit competent assistants seeking good experience. These assistants render enthusiastic support to the U.S. attorney's efforts to resist encroachment by the department and display high morale and loyalty. United States attorneys in multi-judge districts depend less on each judge than their colleagues in a district with one or two judges, making their position vis-à-vis the local court stronger. Since most judges share the local court culture, which in large districts often includes a tradition of independence from Washington, judges in large districts frequently will back the U.S. attorney in disputes with Washington. Finally, local political sponsors in large districts possess more potent political resources. The backing of the mayor of Philadelphia or Chicago (if he is of the president's party) carries more weight than that of the mayor of Asheville or Billings.[17]

A U.S. attorney in a larger district possesses resources with which to pursue an independent course. As the size of his staff increases, the occasions when he must depend upon the department for extra manpower and expertise decline. His assistants can specialize, and the expertise they develop in tax, tort, and other complicated cases can be used to justify opposition to the assignment of such cases to attorneys from Washington. As the complexity of the internal organization of an office increases, the department encounters difficulty in determining lines of authority and responsibility. By referring requests and demands up and down the organizational hierarchy of his office, a U.S. attorney can frustrate department efforts at control.

## U.S. ATTORNEY–DEPARTMENT RELATIONS AS A CASE STUDY OF DECENTRALIZATION

How do the relationships between the department and its field offices compare to other headquarters–field interactions in the federal government? Few studies of the dynamics of headquarters–field relations exist, and none seek to make explicit comparisons.[18] Furthermore, the theoretical problems encountered are formidable and cannot be dealt with systematically within the confines of this study. However, a few impressionistic and tentative conclusions about how one might compare agencies and the placement of the Department of Justice in such a comparison can be presented, in the hope that they will make some modest contribution to the development of a theory of decentralization.

### The Meaning of Decentralization

Bernard Baum's summary of previous studies of decentralization led him to conclude that the literature in this area suffered from vagueness, ambiguity, a nonstandard nomenclature, and a lack of adequate concepts.[19] The description of U.S. attorney–department relations suggests that one way to begin the process of developing useful and unambiguous concepts is to pose the question: Decentralization with respect to what? Two analytically distinct but related answers are suggested by the research. The first involves where decisions about what will be done are effectively *made*. The second concerns who actually *implements* the decisions. Decentralization, as it is commonly used, usually refers to the first. When field personnel make important discretionary decisions affecting an organizational policy, it seems reasonable to describe the organization as "decentralized."[20] The second classifies an agency as decentralized to the extent that field personnel actually perform the organization's administrative tasks. Although this second notion provides an intuitively less satisfactory definition, it appears to be a necessary addition to the concept of decentralization. Ultimately, an adequate conceptualization requires using both concepts.

An organization with no field staff cannot be decentralized using either conception. But if an organization does have a field staff, knowing what tasks headquarters and field perform helps determine where decisions are actually made, if the organization has enunciated no clear general policies. Selective Service headquarters, for example, evidently provided few guidelines to state headquarters and local boards on who should be deferred and who should be drafted.[21] Agencies may fail to establish such policies deliberately, in the face of uncertainty or political conflict. Alternatively, genuine efforts to adopt policies may fail because of ambiguity in their wording or communication. Sometimes the lack of policies results from internal splits in the agency that make it impossible to identify which of a number of contradictory policies enunciated by various elements in headquarters should be followed. Regardless of cause, however, in such organizations the question of who actually implements decisions answers the question of who effectively makes them. If headquarters' men administer programs from Washington (or travel to the field to try cases) in areas where no central policy exists, leaving only routine housekeeping chores to the field, decision-making is centralized. If field personnel make decisions in these matters, however, decision-making is decentralized. The fact that local Selective Service boards performed the procedural tasks of classification and deferring registrants meant that these decisions were decentralized.

Where headquarters establishes general policies and seeks to enforce them, knowing that field personnel implement decisions does not by itself reveal where effective control is lodged. Instead, it is necessary to determine if the field's implementation coincides with what headquarters would have done. When it does not, headquarter's control is ineffective and field personnel make decisions, again, producing a decentralized decision-making pattern.

When field personnel's decisions implementing centrally established policies coincide with what headquarters would have done, the question of who effectively makes the decision is not easily answered. It is reasonable to expect that a semiautonomous office will frequently decide to do on its own what its headquarters' policy dictates. Although it is unlikely that the question can be answered completely, Kaufman's study of the Forest Service provides a partial answer. The explanation for the high correlation between headquarters' policy and the behavior of forest rangers rests in part on the fundamental similarity in outlook, a similarity produced by conscious headquarters' strategies in the recruitment, training, rotation, and promotion of rangers. Such "induced conformity" can reasonably be assigned to the "centralized" category.

Obviously, "induced conformity" through these techniques cannot account for conformity to headquarters' policy in U.S. attorneys' offices. Here the answer to the question of where decisions are made lies in examining conflict. The resolution of such conflict (even if it arises only rarely) reveals whether field personnel follow department policy because it is department policy or because they merely happen to agree with it. If the field loses such conflicts, it alters the propensity to stray from headquarters' policy. If the field prevails, headquarters cannot be said to have effective control over decisions.

Utilizing the two dimensions of where decisions are *made* and who *implements* them produces a richer descriptive scheme than the traditional unidimensional measure of "centralized-decentralized" and permits classification of agencies with field staffs in the same conceptual field as administrative agencies without them. Table 6.3 presents the resulting scheme. The extent and nature of decentralization depends on the location of an administrative agency in the diagram. The traditional model of the ideal field service is found in the lower left of the table. Headquarters makes all of the significant decisions about what will be done and the field staff does the leg work. Unitary agencies with no field staff are found in the upper left. For them, no questions of centralization arise. The closer an agency is located to the lower right-hand corner, the more "decentralized" it is. At the extreme lower right are "agencies" with all field staff and no headquarters. Before the establishment of the Department of Justice in 1870, the activities of the various U.S. attorneys very closely approached this situation. In "participatory agencies," policy is wholly made by field units but carried out by a responsive central organization.

### Comparing the Department of Justice with Other Agencies

Table 6.4 locates several federal agencies in the centralization–decentralization field defined in Table 6.3. The most interesting contrasts are found among the four federal agencies with a field service

Table 6.3. Locus of Effective Decision-making Concerning What Will Be Done (*Where* Decisions Are *Made*)

| Who Performs the Tasks of Implementing Decisions | HEADQUARTERS----------------FIELD | | |
|---|---|---|---|
| | HEADQUARTERS PERSONNEL | UNITARY AGENCIES (No field staff) | "PARTICIPATORY" AGENCIES |
| | FIELD PERSONNEL | "RESPONSIVE FIELD SERVICE" AGENCIES | ANARCHIC "NON-AGENCIES" |

Table 6.4.  Location of Selected Federal Agencies on the Two Dimensions of
Centralization–Decentralization

Locus of Effective Decision–making Concerning What Will Be Done

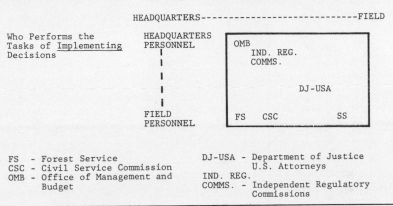

```
                        HEADQUARTERS---------------------------FIELD

Who Performs the        HEADQUARTERS    ┌──────────────────────────────┐
Tasks of Implementing   PERSONNEL       │ OMB                          │
Decisions                       ¦       │       IND. REG.              │
                                ¦       │       COMMS.                 │
                                ¦       │                              │
                                ¦       │                   DJ-USA     │
                                ¦       │                              │
                        FIELD           │ FS    CSC              SS    │
                        PERSONNEL       └──────────────────────────────┘
```

```
FS  - Forest Service              DJ-USA - Department of Justice
CSC - Civil Service Commission             U.S. Attorneys
OMB - Office of Management and    IND. REG.
      Budget                      COMMS. - Independent Regulatory
                                           Commissions
```

about which we have some data: the Department of Justice, the Forest
Service, the Civil Service Commission, and Selective Service.
Department–U.S. attorney relations display a distinctive combination.
The field makes a fairly significant portion of decisions, while headquarters and field share the implementation of decisions. The department stands out among federal agencies because it sometimes
asks headquarters personnel to perform precisely the same chores
that its field personnel do. The proportion of decisions made in the
field for the Department of Justice exceeds that found in most agencies, although Selective Service showed even more decentralization.

Agencies with field services can be compared on somewhat less
sweeping grounds by modifying Table 6.1. By locating the degree to
which headquarters seeks to control each field office and the degree
to which each field office resists or accepts such control, we can produce a schematic summary of the quality of headquarters–field relations. United States attorney–Department of Justice patterns are distinctive among the agencies plotted (and probably among all federal
agencies) on two grounds: First, there is substantial variation in relations with individual field offices. Other agencies tend to cluster in
one region of the diagram. Second, the "center of gravity" of relations
with all field offices tends to fall further to the left, that is, there is on
balance greater resistance to headquarters (Table 6.5).

Several other distinctive characteristics of U.S. attorney-depart-
ment relations deserve brief comment. The heads of field units in
other agencies probably seldom match the motivation of U.S. at-

Table 6.5. Comparison of Department of Justice–U.S. Attorney Relations
with Headquarters–Field Relations for Selected Other Agencies*

```
                          Field office strongly      Field office willingly
                          resists headquarters       accepts headquarters
                          efforts to control         control efforts

Intensive headquarters    1  1                              2    2
efforts to control        1                              1 2   1    1 2
field units                                                 2    2      2
                                         4 41  4      1 2
                                       1 4  44 4
                                       44  141422        212
Minimal headquarters              1    1 4        2  2     2
efforts to control           1         1 411 44   2  2
field units                1          1  4  4  14 3  3 3  3  3  3
                         1  1                   1 3 1 3 1 3 1 3 1
                                                3 3  3
                                                   3
```

*Each number in the diagram symbolically represents the location of
field offices.

1 - Department--U.S. attorney        3 - Selective Service
2 - Forest Service                   4 - Civil Service Commission

torneys to resist headquarters. The resources they utilize in resisting
central control are unusually plentiful. The degree to which the
amount of decentralization found changes over time is also noteworthy. Relationships not only change over time, but change with the ebb
and flow of politics generated by tides of the presidential electoral
cycle. This fact, coupled with the unusually high proportion of key
officials in headquarters and field who are politically appointed, produce a relationship between U.S. attorneys and the department more
responsive to the larger political system than most federal administrative agencies.

## THE FUTURE OF DEPARTMENT–U.S. ATTORNEY RELATIONS

Over the past one hundred years, the result of organizational
change and growth in the department (one of the two sources of
temporal change identified by Peabody) has moved it very strongly
toward centralization. The same forces that produced the growth of
the federal government and necessitated the establishment of field
offices generally, also changed the structure of federal justice. Even
the federal judiciary, which is composed of notoriously independent
individuals, has shown signs of some degree of centralization in administrative and procedural matters.[22]

It is impossible, of course, to predict future developments with any certainty. In part, the department's relations with U.S. attorneys will depend on whether the national trend toward centralization continues, or whether the Nixon administration's rhetoric about "returning power to the states" generates sustained support. But several crucial characteristics of the organizational structure and procedures in the department will strongly influence future developments, regardless of the general direction in the locus of decision-making in the United States.

Perhaps the most important is the method of appointment. As long as U.S. attorneys require Senate confirmation and can be removed only by the president, and as long as assistants continue to be noncareer, young attorneys chosen for all practical purposes by U.S. attorneys, the department will fail to achieve the control that most headquarters have over the field. As noted in Chapter 5, some department officials sought to bring about changes in the appointment and removal process for U.S. attorneys. These efforts failed, and the likelihood of success in the future remains in doubt because of the political support U.S. attorneys can mobilize from senators and local political figures. Only a strong president's vigorous support for such change stands much chance. Converting assistants to a career basis is somewhat less difficult, but such a proposal would undoubtedly mobilize opposition from U.S. attorneys, the corps of former U.S. and assistant U.S. attorneys scattered throughout the country, and their political allies and supporters.

The department's ability to dispatch attorneys from Washington to handle specific cases or categories of cases provides the potential for another technique to reduce permanently the discretion and influence of U.S. attorneys' offices. The ability of these offices to shape policy and resist department control ultimately rests in the fact that they handle cases. By systematically removing whole categories of cases from their jurisdiction and turning them over to centrally dispatched "trial teams," the fundamental source of U.S. attorney influence with the department could be eroded. The establishment of the organized crime strike forces, described earlier, represents the most significant use of this strategy to date. Although individual U.S. attorneys managed to cripple the operations of the strike forces in their districts, they were generally not successful in preventing them from being established. Frequently, their successors either did not care to continue the resistance or were not able to do so successfully.

Whether the strike forces serve as the forerunner of a number of other specialized task forces dispatched from Washington which reduce U.S. attorneys' jurisdiction, or whether they represent a passing fad depends on what the Carter administration ultimately decides to do with them. If it accepts proposals made in the waning months of the Ford administration to integrate them into U.S. attorneys' offices, it is less likely that the department will dispatch prosecution teams from Washington to take over other areas. If the strike forces continue, the department may try to establish similar operations for other categories of crime. Two factors limit how far such a movement could progress. First, as the number of task forces in each district increases, demands for "coordination" of their efforts will arise, and U.S. attorneys are the logical people to provide it. Second, the pool of attorneys available in Washington to staff such task forces is limited.

This suggests another long-range trend that will shape the balance struck between headquarters and field—the allocation of additional manpower. If Congress authorizes increases in the number of attorneys based in Washington, they can be used to create task forces, step up supervision of field personnel, or take more cases away from the field on an ad hoc basis. If Congress authorizes additional personnel for the field, U.S. attorney autonomy will be enhanced, because as the size of a U.S. attorney's office increases, so does its ability to resist the department. Although there is no guarantee that the trends of the immediate past will continue, recent decisions on the allocation of personnel have benefited U.S. attorneys. Between 1969 and 1973, 559 new positions (attorneys and supporting clerical personnel) were authorized in Washington in areas relevant to the work of U.S. attorneys.[23] During this same period, 845 new assistants and supporting personnel were authorized. These figures represent a 32.6 percent increase in the number of authorized personnel in these units of the department and a 41 percent increase in field personnel. Recent increases in the allocation of new attorneys reveal a continuation of this pattern. Between fiscal year 1975 and 1976, the number of attorneys authorized in Washington (including administrative personnel and antitrust attorneys) increased by 139 (8.3 percent), while U.S. attorneys' strength rose by 137 (9.2 percent).[24]

Peabody identifies crisis as the second source of organizational change. Both career and political department personnel told me that they were waiting "for a big scandal" involving assistants so they could launch a campaign to put all assistants on a career basis. However, crisis and scandal do not inevitably work to the advantage of headquarters. Charges of political interference in the handling of cases by the department during the Watergate era (including the antitrust suit brought against International Telephone and Telegraph) came at a time when U.S. attorneys had performed in an apolitical fashion in highly publicized cases. Vice-President Agnew, for example, resigned as the result of an investigation conducted by the Republican U.S. attorney in the vice-president's home state. These events encouraged criticism of the department on the grounds that its top personnel succumbed to political pressures and reduced the impetus for changing the status of U.S. attorneys.[25]

Future developments in U.S. attorney–department relations depend to some extent on the nature and timing of such crises. If future scandals involve gross misbehavior by U.S. attorneys, a career service might result. On the other hand, if scandal again rocks the department's leadership when an experienced corps of U.S. attorneys know their power and are in communication with one another, the intriguing possibility arises that they might seize additional autonomy. In the period between the resignation of Elliot Richardson in the fall of 1973 and the appointment of Attorney General Saxbe, Solicitor General Bork was "acting attorney general." He had been solicitor general only a few months, had no real base of political power, and was not close to the president. He had neither the political support nor the incentive to ask the president to remove a well-backed but independent U.S. attorney. Periods like this permit U.S. attorneys to act with greater independence.

Although predictions about the precise development of headquarters-field relationships in the Department of Justice cannot be made with much assurance, several underlying features of their interaction suggest that the rapid centralization and increase in headquarters control characterizing the past seven decades will slow significantly. The highly professional and discretionary tasks litigation requires guarantee that field personnel will continue to shape how the mass of cases litigated in the district courts will be handled. United States attorneys and their supporters possess enough political strength to resist complete domination by the department. Fewer and fewer offices suffer from the strategic weakness of having few assistants, and more enjoy the flexibility, prestige, and resources for resisting the department that accrue to those with fifteen or more assistants. As the number of assistants authorized increases, then, the ability of offices to resist the department increases. Furthermore, the quantum leaps in the department's ability to communicate with its field offices and to send men to the field that accompanied the development of telecommunications and air travel will not continue. United States attorneys probably will not regain the degree of independence they enjoyed in the past. Thus, something of a permanent stalemate is likely, suggesting that the fascinating and perhaps unique interactions between headquarters and field in the Department of Justice, described in this chapter, will continue for some time.

# CHAPTER 7

# U.S. Attorneys and Judges

I asked a Republican U.S. attorney in a small district to reflect on the factors that shaped how he made his decisions, with special reference to the importance of judges. "I like to think that I make my own decisions," he replied. "I never really considered it other than that." Several minutes later he revealed he had not prosecuted a case after the judge suggested it be dropped. When asked why, he answered: "To move cases, to get the workload done, you want to have a cooperative judge. You want to have a judge that wants to move cases too. I feel that I should and I do take the attitude that the judge is the boss and I am not going to quarrel with the judge. Whatever, right or wrong, he is right and I am going to go along with what he is going to do and I am going to bend to that in the operation of my office."

The coexistence of the desire to make one's own decisions with the recognition of the necessity to accommodate judges illustrates in capsule form the nature of U.S. attorney–judge relationships. Judges have a significant impact on the most important aspects of a U.S. attorney's work. The ability of U.S. attorneys to affect the worklife of judges significantly is by comparison rather slight. Yet variety and complexity characterize relations between U.S. attorneys and the judges before whom they practice. Many factors shape this relationship, and the patterns that result do not always conform to the image conveyed by the man quoted above. In this chapter, I will explore the sources of influence of judges and U.S. attorneys upon each other, the dynamics of their interaction, the patterns that result, and the factors that account for these patterns.

## THE SOURCES OF INFLUENCE

Without convictions and meaningful sentences in criminal cases and favorable verdicts in civil cases, a U.S. attorney's office fails in its most fundamental tasks. The ability of federal district judges to affect the outcome of cases provides their most potent source of influence over U.S. attorneys.

126

Judges affect case outcomes in a number of ways. Judges' decisions on pretrial motions for discovery and to suppress evidence significantly affect the chances of winning a case at trial. One former assistant, who alleged that a judge ruled against him on such motions when he did not like the case, expressed his frustration and displeasure. "He disposes of them contrary to every precedent, and he knows it too." In nonjury trials, judges alone render the verdict, subject only to possible reversal on appeal. Usually, appellate courts confine their scrutiny to questions of law and procedure. If serious procedural errors are made, reversal may come. But appeals courts give trial judges wide latitude on their findings of the facts. The finding of the facts must be "clearly erroneous" to be reversed. In practice, U.S. Courts of Appeal rarely reach this conclusion. In jury trials, the judge shares his decision-making power with the jury, and the jury renders the actual verdict. But the judge can prevent the issue from reaching the jury by directing a verdict for either the plaintiff or defendant in a civil case or by directing a verdict of acquittal in a criminal case. The double jeopardy provision of the U.S. Constitution prevents the government from appealing a directed verdict of acquittal.[1] A variety of judicial actions influence jury verdicts. Commenting on the evidence and charging the jury offer judges substantial opportunities to affect case outcomes.[2] Judges enjoy wide discretion in ruling on motions and the admissibility of evidence. The standing of the attorneys in the eyes of the jury can be affected by the trial judge's treatment of them. Judges can intervene directly at crucial points in the proceedings by asking questions of witnesses themselves or suggesting to an attorney how he should proceed.

United States attorneys want to "win" their cases. "Winning" depends in part upon the sentence imposed in a criminal case or the dollar amount of the verdict in a civil action. In nonjury civil cases, the judge determines the amount of the verdict. In criminal cases, whether jury or nonjury, the judge imposes sentence. It is not difficult to imagine the reaction of an assistant who found himself being publicly rebuked for what the judge felt was a minor offense. After pronouncing the defendant guilty, the judge imposed a sentence of a one dollar fine.

Judges significantly affect the speed and manner in which cases proceed through the federal courts. They decide when to set cases for action, the order in which they are heard, and the time when litigants' attorneys must submit briefs, motions, and answers (once the statutory minimum has elapsed). United States attorneys repeatedly expressed their recognition of the power these decisions gave judges.[3] A judge's refusal to grant a few extra days to turn in a brief can throw a whole office into an uproar. "The judge can hurt you by assigning cases," one respondent explained to me. "'I'm hearing U.S. vs. Jones on Tuesday, and if the government is not ready, it's too bad.' This is a weapon, a big weapon." Judges help or hurt U.S. attorneys when they set the sequence in which jury trials are heard. If "open-and-shut" trials are scheduled first, U.S. attorneys believe the guilty verdicts reached dispose jurors to convict on subsequent (and weaker) cases. In some districts, the judges delegate to U.S. attorneys the task of determining the sequence of trials.

Unlike most attorneys in the United States, assistants spend a substantial amount of time in the courtroom. Their behavior there is subject to the general supervision of judges, and the sanctions that judges can impose are potent indeed. The power to hold an attorney in contempt of court gives judges their most terrifying weapon. Though seldom invoked (even threats of contempt are infrequent), the mere recognition of their ability to issue contempt citations impinges on the attorneys' consciousness. "He can lock you up for no reason at all!" exclaimed one federal attorney. "He'll just tell the Marshal, 'Marshal, lock that man up!' And you'll sit in jail until the Court of Appeals lets you out." In the spring of 1974, the potential sanctions available to judges became reality for a U.S. attorney and four of his assistants. A district judge summarily disbarred them, forcing them to obtain a temporary stay in the execution of the disbarment order from the Court of Appeals via telephone.[4] Informal banishment from a single courtroom cannot be voided by a formal appeal to a higher court. One judge revealed that a colleague in another district had banned an assistant from ever coming into his courtroom again after the assistant mouthed "S.O.B." following an adverse ruling. The existence of such sanctions, accompanied by the trappings of judicial power (the robes, the raised dias, the formal rising ceremonies at the entrance and departure of His Honor from the courtroom, the deferential forms of address), produce deference, respect, and a certain amount of underlying fearful caution that condition the way in which assistants approach their dealings with trial judges.[5]

If the awesome powers of contempt, disbarment, and banishment exert a constant, indirect, and subtle influence, mundane judicial powers operate more directly and openly (though no less constantly). No one likes to spend his days working in an unpleasant atmosphere. If they so choose, judges can make life miserable for an assistant. One described what happens when a particular judge feels a case is not worthy of prosecution. "He'd say the government should never have

brought this case. . . . Generally, he's got you wishing you were dead
by the time you finish these cases. It's embarrassing to be in court and
in front of a jury and have the judge criticize you and make fun of
your efforts." On the other hand, judges can make life much easier in
the courtroom. By intervening in a proceeding (asking questions of
witnesses, clarifying proceedings for the jury) they can help or hinder
an inexperienced attorney in the conduct of his case. "They could say
that you've overlooked something, perhaps a question that you could
have asked. I've seen the judges ask the witnesses questions. The
judge *could* just sit back and say nothing, and then give a directed
verdict." Since assistants are usually more inexperienced than their
opponents, judicial assistance in the presentation of a case helps the
U.S. attorney's office more than opposing counsel.

Judges' sources of influence extend beyond their control over courtroom behavior and outcomes, however. "In a small district, the judge
can be a recommendation for you, an excellent recommendation,"
observed an assistant. "A lawyer comes into the judge and says,
'Judge, do you know a good young man? We have an opening.' And
the Judge answers, 'Well, so-and-so in the U.S. attorney's office is a
good man.' . . . The opinion of the judge means a lot." If the private
bar knows that a judge has banished an assistant from his courtroom,
firms looking for federal trial specialists, particularly in jurisdictions
with only a few judges, will hesitate to offer him a position. In addition, because of their knowledge of federal law and procedure, judges
can give valuable advice and training to inexperienced attorneys. "If
you're willing to learn and pay attention," said one assistant, "they'll
make a good lawyer out of you."

Judges clearly dominate their interactions with members of the U.S.
attorney's office. But U.S. attorneys possess some resources that permit them to influence judges in marginal ways. The most significant is
their ability to affect the condition of the docket. In the past fifty
years, the pressures exerted on district judges to keep their dockets
current has grown substantially. Senior circuit judges attending the
annual Judicial Conference in the 1920s began to report on the quantity and quality of the output of the district courts in their circuit.[6] In
the 1930s, the conference began to issue recommendations to trial
judges designed to expedite the flow of judicial business.[7] Later, the
chief judges of the various districts within each circuit reported on
problems of congestion at circuit conferences.[8] Recently, these pressures have accelerated. In 1967 the Federal Judicial Center was established. Its first director, retired Supreme Court Justice Tom Clark,
not only felt the center should be concerned about dockets but also

expressed his willingness to pressure those judges whose dockets were not current. In testimony before the Senate Appropriations Committee in 1969, Clark observed, "When in town I might say: 'Well, the bar association invited me to speak here and I plan to make a little speech on the docket.' That needles him."[9] The center conducts training seminars for new judges and stresses the importance of current dockets, along with administrative techniques for achieving them. Finally, Chief Justice Burger regards the condition of dockets in federal courts as an area of major concern.[10] It would take an unusually dim-witted or strong-willed judge to fail to get the message and take action to keep the case backlog down.[11]

Because the U.S. attorney conducts more business in federal court than any other single litigant, his policies and procedures significantly affect the condition of the docket. By exercising discretion on what cases to prosecute, he reduces the criminal caseload. An effective U.S. attorney encourages federal agencies to reach out-of-court compromises, thereby reducing the potential civil caseload. Compromise settlements sharply reduce the time it takes to dispose of docketed cases. The bargaining skill of the U.S. attorney's office, its willingness to compromise, and its reputation with opposing attorneys on how well it can try cases all help to determine how many cases are settled through compromise, without a time consuming trial.[12] Merely keeping the court informed of developments aids judges in managing their dockets. Accurate estimates of the probable length of upcoming jury trials permit scheduling so that a minimum of time is lost. Immediate notification when defendants scheduled for trial decide to offer a plea also facilitates efficient scheduling. Finally, an attorney's techniques can reduce the time cases that do go to trial take to complete.[13] "For instance, when you are qualifying a jury for trial, you can ask endless and meaningless questions or you can't," an older assistant explained to me. "Another thing. You can dismiss a number of jurors just because you don't like their looks. I don't do that. On cross-examination, you get right to the point."

Judges confront several major sources of uncertainty in their work. They are expected to make legally "correct" decisions on a variety of questions, and they know their performance will be evaluated by people whose approval they desire—fellow district judges, the members of the federal bar, and appellate judges.[14] But it is sometimes difficult to ascertain what a "correct" decision is. No judge can keep himself informed on the myriad of questions upon which he is called to rule. The fact that he must often render a decision instantaneously compounds the dilemma. Even when he has time to consider a decision carefully, he must choose between articulate and persuasive arguments presented by each side, with only ambiguous guidelines from the court of appeals. A judge must also maintain control over his courtroom and the behavior of those who appear in it. The less predictable the behavior of the participants, the more uncertain becomes his ability to retain control. Ill-prepared or incompetent attorneys contribute to this uncertainty. One judge commented that when an assistant doesn't know what the law is it "makes us feel uncomfortable during the trial." When attorneys break local court rules and customs, a judge must decide whether to ignore the infraction or try to enforce compliance. Thus, inexperienced attorneys, unfamiliar with the court and the judge, create a variety of uncertainties—the unpredictability of behavior (including possible incompetence), the possibility of leading him into reversible error, and the prospect of having to deal with infractions of court customs. The uncertainties judges face produce a certain amount of anxiety,[15] and U.S. attorneys' abilities to reduce it elicit favorable reactions from judges. Although no one can eliminate their uncertainty, U.S. attorneys can lessen it somewhat. The ways they do this are described below as one of the strategies U.S. attorneys pursue in dealing with judges.

United States attorneys possess several other resources. They defend judges under mandamus and those being sued by convicted defendants. United States attorneys sometimes accommodate a judge by appointing a favorite clerk as an assistant or doing "small favors" for him. As one of them pointed out, "Occasionally, there is some kind of a favor the judge wants done. I come from the city administration, and very frequently I can help him." Such favors could conceivably extend to the treatment of cases. Though probably extremely rare, it is not entirely unknown. As assistant told me, "Judge 'Smith' had a friend against whom we had a (small) collection case, and he came in, really in fear, and asked that it be compromised. And it was." Finally, U.S. attorneys and assistants can embarrass the judge by being unprepared or behaving in an unprofessional manner in the courtroom. "If, say, you came into his court drunk, or if you took a contemptuous attitude, you put him on the spot so he has to take some action. And this is embarrassing to him. . . . There is an identification. You're working with him all the time. I've had people tell me, 'Oh, you work over with Judge "Jones" don't you?' . . . What an assistant does influences, has an effect on the judge." Though such "negative resources" cannot be readily employed, they have some significance. For instance, the potential embarrassment a judge might feel if the government were woefully unprepared might make him more responsive to requests for extensions or continuances.

## THE DYNAMICS OF INTERACTION

### Mutual Influence on Behavior

The patterns of interaction between U.S. attorneys and judges faithfully reflect the obvious asymmetry in their sources of influence. Judges significantly influence the behavior of U.S. attorneys' offices, while U.S. attorneys only marginally affect them.

Judicial influence over U.S. attorneys' decisions to prosecute belie the conventional belief that American prosecutors exercise unfettered discretion in this area.[16] The field research suggests that U.S. attorneys modify prosecutive decisions both in response to direct initiatives of judges and through anticipation of judicial reactions.[17] Direct initiatives make lasting impressions on assistants.[18] Several days after an assistant declined to prosecute a stolen or forged draft card case (he couldn't remember which), a judge summoned him to chambers. "When I walked in, there was the General in charge of Selective Service in the area. The judge said, 'I think the case is a good one for prosecution.'" A former U.S. attorney described how his judge discouraged continuation of a case he had already authorized for prosecution. "He called me in and said, 'Why don't you *dismiss* this case?' And in effect, he told me I was going to lose the case."

It is through indirect influence, however, that judges most often affect the decision to prosecute. Interviews with both prosecutors and judges indicate that judges enjoy hearing some cases and dread others. Those labeled "technical violations," "minor matters," or "police court cases" annoy judges with a crowded docket.[19] Some judges abhor cases they find difficult and tedious to try. An assistant confronted with a case falling into one of these categories encounters incentives to decline prosecution. For one thing, the judge may make the trial of such a case difficult. A former assistant observed that when one judge "doesn't like a case, he's completely merciless and takes it out on the lawyer." This same judge confirmed this. "Now, I get on the U.S. attorney if he is bringing in too many nickel and dime cases." In addition, the case may be lost. "If you go down there and get your hands burned on one sort of case," commented a U.S. attorney, "you're not going to come back again with the same kind." Even if a conviction is obtained, a paltry sentence can effectively discourage future prosecution of similar cases.[20] As an assistant suggested, "There is some predilection on the part of assistants not to push a case when the judges won't work hard on it and the individual won't get much of a sentence." Judges often find it unnecessary to chastise the prosecutor, belittle the significance of the case, or hand down a ridiculously light sentence to discourage prosecution. The desire to maintain good relations with the judges suffices in many instances. Asked if he was influenced by judges' attitudes in deciding to prosecute, a U.S. attorney responded: "It definitely has some bearing on it. For example, we know that our judges feel the court is degraded if we bring people in on mail fraud amounting to a few dollars. . . . Consequently, we screen them out fairly carefully." Just as certain types of cases are not prosecuted due to the cool reception they elicit from judges, so too are others pushed vigorously because of obvious judicial interest in them. In one district, a veteran judge learned from acquaintances in the trucking business of a raft of thefts from interstate truck shipments. His general inquiries to the U.S. attorney's office about the problem were treated as an expression of a desire to see some prosecutions.[21]

Judicial influence extends substantially beyond the decision to prosecute. The form of indictments is sometimes affected. "In this district, there was a time when they had 20 or 39 counts in an indictment. *Our* practice is to charge with one-half that number of counts or even less. This is a matter of brainwashing on the part of the judges, and they finally succeeded."

In preparing and presenting cases, assistants inevitably shape their behavior to conform to the predilections of the judge hearing the case. The form of pleadings, the type of briefs submitted (if indeed any are submitted), the amount of time spent in preparation, the lawyer's demeanor in the courtroom and etiquette in questioning witnesses, and the strategies employed in oral argument all vary according to which judge hears the case. The following sampling of statements from U.S. attorneys and assistants suggests the variety and scope of such influence.

Judge "Roberts" just doesn't like long-winded pleadings. . . . He likes it short and concise, presenting the facts—as it should be. I wouldn't do this anyway, but I wouldn't do it especially because he would be unhappy about it.

He's for the underdog. And I'm always careful, in the presentation of the case, that I don't put the defendant in the position of an underdog.

One time, I said that the Supreme Court had decided something on such and such a case. And he said, "I don't care what the Court said. *I'm* the judge here." . . . It's helpful to know that when you go into his courtroom. You have to use more pragmatic arguments.

Some judges influence the internal administration of a U.S. attorney's office. They occasionally recommend candidates for appointment as assistant U.S. attorney, and U.S. attorneys give these recommendations serious consideration. Judges sometimes take an active interest in the preparation of a case for trial, even to the point of intervening in the conduct of the investigation. They also influence the assignment of assistants to cases and courtrooms. When a judge banishes an assistant from his courtroom, the U.S. attorney must juggle assignments to insure that the assistant goes elsewhere. More often, the U.S. attorney's office anticipates problems arising from personality clashes between assistants and judges and separates them before the judge indicates his displeasure.

Judges occupy such a strategic position in the federal judicial process that they even affect interactions between U.S. attorneys and other significant participants. In several districts with a tradition of U.S. attorney independence from the department, the judges participated in the "socialization" of new members of the office into the district tradition. We have already seen the central importance judicial support can play in a U.S. attorney's struggle to resist department domination. Reliance on the support of judges offers one of the most effective tactics in resisting the department. Judges also shape relations with private attorneys. Judges can affect the work life of private attorneys appearing before them almost as much as assistant U.S. attorneys. Consequently, private attorneys also modify their behavior in anticipation of judicial reactions. Inevitably, these anticipations influence the interaction between opposing attorneys in pretrial negotiations. "The judges here are rather conservative in their approach to tort claims," observed one private attorney. "This gives the U.S. attorney some boldness. He can bring this out in negotiations." Although few federal judges participate in plea bargaining in criminal cases, defense attorneys who practice regularly before them learn to predict what sentences they will likely impose. Which judge hears the case therefore affects the content and outcome of plea bargaining between prosecution and defense. A mutual desire to work out a plea encourages the attorneys to collaborate in "shopping" for a reasonable judge. The interactions between U.S. attorneys and investigative agents, described in the following chapter, also reflect the presence of judges. If judges display hostility to certain kinds of cases, assistants often discourage agents from submitting them for a prosecutive decision.

The influence exerted by U.S. attorneys over judges can be summarized briefly. Like any litigating attorney, a U.S. attorney seeks to influence judicial decisions on the admission of evidence, the granting or denial of various motions, objections to his opponent's questions and witnesses' answers, verdicts, and sentences. But such influence flows primarily from his status as an advocate and is independent of his role as government attorney. Requests for additional time to file a brief, postponement of a trial date, addition of another trial or arraignment day for the government's cases, and the selection or extension of a grand jury's life, however, may receive some extra degree of favorable consideration, due to the resources of the U.S. attorney's office (and particularly its responsibility for such a large portion of the docket). The limited scope of judicial behavior over which U.S. attorneys seek influence provides an unreliable guide to its significance, however. Failure to influence judges on these matters is extremely serious, and success is important to fulfilling the fundamental objectives of U.S. attorneys.

### U.S. Attorneys' Strategies and Tactics

United States attorneys' dependence on their ability to influence judges structures the content of their goals in dealing with them. The most compelling and fundamental objective is to avoid, if at all possible, an open break with the judge. Very few judges would use the full power of their position to oppose a U.S. attorney's every move in a personal vendetta. But even intermittent and partial opposition has serious consequences for an office's success and tranquillity, and merely avoiding an open break hardly suffices. To be effective, an office requires some minimal "access" to its judges—the ability to obtain fair consideration of its views on close questions of law and a sympathetic hearing of its administrative problems that can be ameliorated by judicial decision. "If you have a good relationship," explained an assistant, "the judge is willing to listen to you present your arguments. He may beat you, but at least he's willing to listen to you."

Some offices seek to go beyond attaining such access to establish a close working relationship with the judges. If attained, such a relationship provides the office flexibility in scheduling cases and help during trials. United States attorneys and assistants with a close relationship to the judges also benefit from frequent informal chats, which increase rapport, make the judges more sympathetic to the office's problems, and broaden the U.S. attorney's knowledge of the judge's modes of thought. One U.S. attorney found the informal discussions of the law he had with a judge very helpful. "It gives me a notion of the law. It's a guiding light. It would be very difficult in this district if the relationship wasn't like this." These chats also provide a U.S. attorney with an opportunity to influence judges that private attorneys do not enjoy. "For instance, the judge might say, 'I don't quite get what you were driving at in court the other day.' This gives you an opportunity to explain again in congenial surroundings. This is an opportunity to persuade."

Because they have practically no effective means of exerting influence on judges through coercion or threats, U.S. attorneys must depend upon influence through persuasion. The overwhelming majority of U.S. attorneys and assistants interviewed sought to establish a fund of credit and good will with the judges as a central component of their behavior. They are particularly adept at exploiting opportunities to comply with a judge's wishes and to earn his gratitude and respect. A number of assistants stressed the importance of acquiring a reputation for credibility. An assistant in a large district noted that in most cases the judge would not know the opposing counsel. "If the judge believes what you say, you've got a leg way up." Assistants follow a number of rules to enhance their ability to persuade judges, including not prosecuting cases the judges dislike and prosecuting those they do, conforming to the judge's wishes regarding courtroom demeanor and the form of questions asked of witnesses, speeding the movement of cases, informing the judge when he has been inadvertently misled by revealing relevant information, being certain that "when you prosecute . . . people are guilty," and showing respect for the judge, the jury, and the opposition.

A related set of tactics reduces the anxiety that judges confront. Performing competently is an important aspect of reducing anxiety. Commenting on the incompetence of some inexperienced assistants, one judge observed: "It makes the judge's job much more difficult. Trying the case is a breeze if there are competent lawyers." If a judge feels confidence in the assistant, he need not worry about whether ex-parte orders are drawn up properly, whether the prosecutor is trying to slip inadmissible evidence past him, or whether innocent men are knowingly indicted. The anxiety produced by the appearance of strange attorneys can be minimized by keeping department attorneys out of the district or schooling them in local rules and procedures when they cannot be prevented from appearing.[22] Diplomatic suggestions to help judges avoid error also reduce anxiety: "The judge really appreciates your taking care of him. He has to shoot from the hip—make a lot of decisions from the bench. You want to call his attention to any errors he makes, especially with all of the new rules."

New U.S. attorneys possess few viable strategies that do not involve increasing their ability to persuade. Although outright defiance of a judge on all matters is a highly unusual, drastic, and generally disastrous course, many judges respect an attorney who occasionally stands up and battles vigorously (but with decorum) for a position with a sound legal basis. Several strategies utilizing various forms of manipulation exist. Sometimes U.S. attorneys can depict the department as the source of behavior that antagonizes the judges, when in fact the U.S. attorney himself has chosen that behavior. Some judges misperceive the control exerted over U.S. attorneys by the department, and the U.S. attorney need only avoid dispelling such impressions.[23] Where possible, U.S. attorneys seek to manipulate case assignment procedures to either "shop" for a judge likely to be favorably disposed to the government's position, or (as is more often the case) to *avoid* an unfavorably disposed judge. But despite the astounding ingenuity attorneys show in devising ways to obtain or avoid a particular individual, the judges in most districts have established blind draw or random case assignment procedures that thwart them.

Most of the strategies U.S. attorneys pursue, then, seek to improve their ability to persuade. The techniques described can be divided into three categories: enhancing credibility; demonstrating expertise; and presenting themselves as cooperative, deferential, and likeable people. One tough-minded U.S. attorney expressed many of the themes just discussed in a brief statement, and his comments make an excellent summary.

Well, you go into the office with the full realization that those judges down there have a great influence on the success or failure of your office. You make up your mind that you are going to get along with them or you are going to give up wanting to run a good office. By getting along with them, this means that you prepare the cases well, that you get your briefs in on time, that you do not embarrass the judges by having them pull your irons out of the fire or apologize for some assistant who doesn't know what he is doing. . . . This is the only thing you have to do to get along with them.

### Judges' Strategies and Tactics

Analyzing judges' strategies and tactics in influencing U.S. attorneys requires examining entirely different questions. Judges possess an impressive array of resources that they can mobilize to influence U.S. attorneys and assistants. Furthermore, few external restraints operate to prevent exploitation of their advantages.[24] Nor must judges devise subtle strategies. Often, they need only indicate their preferences to elicit an accommodating response. If this fails, imposing a light sentence, making a critical comment, or formulating an explicit request usually accomplishes a judge's objective. Generally speaking, once a judge decides he wants to affect a U.S. attorney's behavior, he encounters few obstacles in doing so.

Three preconditions exist to the conscious exertion of influence by judges. First, a judge must perceive a need to intervene. Second, he must feel that it is proper for him to do so. Finally, he must believe that his attempt will be successful and that it will not require more effort than a successful outcome would merit. Although this last condition is usually met, there are some interesting exceptions that will be described below.

The relationship between U.S. attorneys and judges exhibits a pronounced asymmetry. With the exception of partial control over their caseload and the condition of their docket, U.S. attorneys influence judges only to the extent that they can persuade them. Judges can usually reject U.S. attorneys' influence attempts with little fear of the consequences, and they have little incentive or inclination to modify their behavior to conform with the wishes of the U.S. attorneys. Judges, on the other hand, profoundly affect the most central aspects of the U.S. attorneys' work life. They exert influence through the exercise of authority. Actual or implied threats, backed by the capacity to carry them out, are so effective that they are rarely necessary. United States attorneys eagerly anticipate judges' commands and wishes and seek to avoid the necessity of confronting actual threats.

## PATTERNS OF INTERACTION

Judges will always significantly influence the way in which attorneys who litigate in their courtrooms conduct themselves. But the manner and the extent to which assistants modify their courtroom behavior before individual judges and the overall impact judges have on the policies of the U.S. attorney's office varies substantially. The patterns of this variation take the same general form as patterns of relations with the Department of Justice. They result from the interaction of two variables: the degree to which judges seek to influence the office and its representatives who appear in their courtrooms; and the extent to which members of the office accommodate or resist the judges' efforts to shape their behavior.[25] Their interaction produces the five patterns summarized in Table 7.1. The five patterns located in Table 7.1 display differences in three areas: the atmosphere characterizing interactions between U.S. attorneys and the judge; the relative influence exerted; and the level of conflict. None of the districts studied displayed the "conflict" pattern, though a number of respondents referred to several districts which exhibited its characteristics. "I know of some districts," observed one U.S. attorney, "where the U.S. attorney and the judge aren't even on speaking terms with one another." I encountered examples of the other patterns during the research,

Table 7.1. Schematic Representation of Patterns of U.S. Attorney–Judge
Interaction

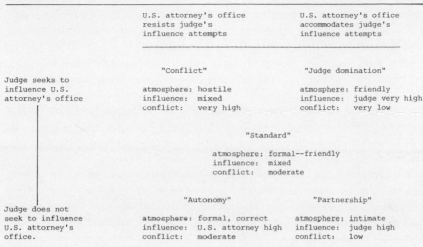

| | U.S. attorney's office resists judge's influence attempts | U.S. attorney's office accommodates judge's influence attempts |
|---|---|---|
| Judge seeks to influence U.S. attorney's office | "Conflict" <br> atmosphere: hostile <br> influence: mixed <br> conflict: very high | "Judge domination" <br> atmosphere: friendly <br> influence: judge very high <br> conflict: very low |
| | "Standard" <br> atmosphere: formal--friendly <br> influence: mixed <br> conflict: moderate | |
| Judge does not seek to influence U.S. attorney's office. | "Autonomy" <br> atmosphere: formal, correct <br> influence: U.S. attorney high <br> conflict: moderate | "Partnership" <br> atmosphere: intimate <br> influence: judge high <br> conflict: low |

however, and a brief description of several will explicate their chief
characteristics.

A former U.S. attorney in a one-judge district established a
"partnership" during his tenure in office. He repeatedly described his
relationship with the judge in glowing terms, using such adjectives as
"topflight," "excellent," "the finest." "In fact, after the judge had
made up his mind, he would tell me how he was going to decide the
case. We'd write an opinion for him. We'd do all the work, and he'd
just sign it. All our dealings were straight across the board. We handled more damn stuff when we were in there. Even now, he says to me,
'When we were in there, we really got a lot of business done.'" The
judge participated indirectly in plea bargaining by indicating to the
U.S. attorney whether he would impose a prison sentence or grant
probation in cases possibly requiring long trials. The judge and the
U.S. attorney even discussed the length of prison sentences (sentence
bargaining) on an informal basis, an unusual occurrence in the federal court system.[26] Cooperation also extended to other fields. Rather
than go through the usual process of getting departmental approval
to dismiss a case, "I'd go to the judge and discuss it with him . . . and
the judge would dismiss it. They can't argue with the judge. . . . I
never went through the department." They also discussed various
problems that came up in the trial of a case. "We didn't collaborate on
the case, and he didn't tell me what he was going to do. We kept a sort
of arms-length relationship there. But if any unusual question came

up, I'd have no hesitation to discuss it with him." Limits on the intimacy of their dealings existed. "By the way, he called me by my first
name, but I was not on a first name basis with him. I kept a respectful
attitude at all times. . . . When the judge puts his robes on, he's a
special person and you keep that distance."

The fact remains, however, that most respondents would hardly
consider the relationship described as being at "arms-length." One
final attribute of the relationship in this district deserves special mention. The respondent indicated that he was extremely sensitive to the
judge's preferences and quirks and made conscious efforts to adapt
his behavior accordingly. The judge exerted substantial influence
through anticipated reactions.

The incentives of the U.S. attorney's office to accommodate judges
increase as the determination of judges to exert influence intensifies,
since such judges more readily employ the resources of their position
to gain compliance. The behavior a judge seeks to influence can be
narrow or extensive in scope. If it is confined to one or two aspects of
the U.S. attorney's activity, the relationship will resemble the "standard" pattern in most respects. For instance, one assistant acknowledged that his judges did not care about the decision to prosecute. But
once a case is filed, he reported, "They treat us as if we are an arm of
the court. . . . They're interested in keeping it moving."

When judges express concern about a broad range of the U.S.
attorney's activities, however, the district may become dominated by
them in a number of important respects. United States attorneys
faced with such judges must be particularly skillful if they are to avoid
domination without slipping into a pattern of conflict. In the district
that most exhibited the characteristics of judge domination, substantial agreement existed among a number of respondents on the role
played by its judges, and particularly the chief judge. An experienced
assistant in this office expressed the conclusion of most people I interviewed in this district.[27]

The judges go beyond themselves in overseeing the office. They don't say we
shouldn't bring certain categories of cases anymore. But they are concerned
with whether specific cases should be prosecuted. The chief judge will be in
the U.S. attorney's office all the time. They'll talk about the status of different
cases and the different investigations pending. That's where (the chief judge)
plays quite an important role. The judges feel like we are working for *them* to
some extent. And we are, but this can go too far.

The loss of autonomy the U.S. attorney experienced was compensated for in several ways. First, the judges actively helped the government in criminal trials. "There are and have been cases," a defense

attorney bitterly stated, "where the trial judge mixes with the U.S. attorney behind the scenes and tells him what to do." He claimed this applied to civil cases too. In a civil tax case, "The judge called down the U.S. attorney and told him to write a brief with certain points in it so he could adopt it. The reason I know about this is that an assistant told me." Second, by cooperating, the U.S. attorney avoided the harsh consequences that would have flowed from stormy relations. The difficult time one of the judges gave private attorneys he did not like provided a constant and vivid reminder of the consequences of poor relations. Finally, the judges were willing to help out when problems arose. A former U.S. attorney there observed: "They're on our side when you're in a real crack. If you go down there and say, 'Judge, I won't be able to be ready. I need an extension,' they'd give you an extension. Also, whenever your ethics would permit, you could go down there and they would give you advice on how to proceed."

Respondents in this district repeatedly referred to the strong personality and domineering character of the chief judge as the primary explanation for the patterns of interaction just described. But in some districts the judges make hardly any direct or indirect attempts to shape the behavior of the U.S. attorney's office. One such judge felt he should not be concerned with what sort of cases the U.S. attorney prosecuted. Unlike most of his colleagues elsewhere, he claimed to have no policies or practices which he liked to see the U.S. attorney's office follow, aside from the expectation that the office not be "partisan-minded" and strive for "justice." Furthermore, he did not feel it important for the U.S. attorney to have a good relationship with him. "Of course, having friendly relations is always better than having unfriendly ones, but, again, I don't see that it would make much of a difference if they were not friendly." He did not feel it proper for him to make life either difficult or easy for the U.S. attorney. "Who wants to make life easier? There's nothing to gain by intimacy. I try to remain on cordial but not intimate terms with the U.S. attorney.... It's not a good idea to hobnob." If he so desires, a U.S. attorney with such judges can enjoy considerable autonomy. But if he seeks nevertheless to accommodate the judge somewhat, the pattern of interaction would fall into the "standard" category.

In the "standard" pattern, the one I encountered most often,[28] most members of the U.S. attorney's office accommodate judges as a matter of necessity up to a point, but do not go to the extremes their colleagues in dominated and "partnership" districts do. The judges in standard districts display a moderate concern with the functioning of the office. Complex patterns of interaction result, particularly in multi-judge districts. Considerable variation is often found in relationships with individual judges. Aloof judges may sit on the same bench with men who actively seek to control the U.S. attorney's behavior. Intimate relations approaching the partnership model may characterize interactions in one courtroom, while the courtroom across the hall borders upon open conflict. Unless one of the four nonstandard patterns predominates, such districts are best classified in the "standard" category.

## THE SOURCES OF VARIATION

The pattern of interaction between judges and the U.S. attorney found in a district at any given time depends on many of the same factors that influence his relations with the department. Those U.S. attorneys who display forcefulness, independence, and a willingness to engage in conflict when dealing with the department exhibit the same characteristics in their dealings with judges. When asked if he might be inhibited from firing several career assistants because of possible adverse reaction from the judges, one such man replied emphatically: "You've got to start out right from the beginning that you are going to run your shop or the judges are going to run it. The judges don't have as much clout as they think they do because in the last analysis, they have to protect their own record." Men with unaggressive, submissive, and conflict-avoiding personalities, on the other hand, respond more readily to judicial pressure. Some extremely accommodating U.S. attorneys consider the judge to be their "boss." One graphically stated: "I got along fine with the judges. Whenever they said frog, I leaped. I really tried to anticipate their every need." Such men naturally challenge their judges directly only reluctantly. One responsive U.S. attorney failed to seek a writ of mandamus from the court of appeals, challenging a judge's decision to set aside a plea of guilty on his own initiative and dismiss criminal charges, despite the fact that the department thought it should be done. By contrast, a notoriously independent U.S. attorney did not hesitate to seek a writ of mandamus removing a judge from presiding over the retrial of a case that had resulted in a hung jury, and he did not even bother to seek the required departmental approval for such a step. Of course, the largest number of U.S. attorneys fall between these two extremes.

The nature of relationships between some U.S. attorneys and particular judges shapes their interaction. Sometimes these relationships predate their both assuming office, as the comments of a Nixon appointee reveal. "Bill and I grew up together. I've known him for about thirty-five years. We went to camp together, and my relations with him, of course, are quite good." He indicated that a second new judicial appointee was "a friend of mine politically. I'm extremely pleased to see him here because I like his attitude." Of course, in some districts a long-standing enmity exists between the U.S. attorney and one or more of the judges. But sometimes close relationships develop after the U.S. attorney takes office. This same man did not know the chief judge (a Democrat) well before becoming U.S. attorney, but he indicated that he was, "a very very profound admirer, very profoundly and emotionally pleased and attached to our chief judge."[29] A U.S. attorney who develops a heavy dependence on a judge's support in his disputes with the department finds it especially difficult to ignore the judge's suggestions and wishes.

Career goals also shape the willingness to accommodate the judges. A U.S. attorney young enough to anticipate a subsequent career with a leading local firm may find the judges' assessment of him crucial. His chief value to a firm lies primarily in his knowledge of and ability in federal court. If the judges dislike and disrespect him, this expertise loses much of its usefulness. A strong recommendation to a firm by a judge (particularly if the judge is a former partner) can be especially important. A U.S. attorney seeking a federal judgeship also recognizes the impact incumbent judges can have on his chances.[30] But if he already has established ties to a local firm to which he intends to return, if he is seeking elective office, if he plans to retire after leaving the U.S. attorneyship, or if he is motivated by strong policy goals (such as fighting organized crime), he may pay less attention to the judge's wishes.

A U.S. attorney's responsiveness to judges also depends on his beliefs about whether judges ought to provide guidance. The views expressed by a Democratic U.S. attorney reveal why he was willing to accept administrative oversight from his judges. "When the U.S. attorney's office is not an efficient, credible operation, they are concerned and justifiably so." His Republican successor explained why he generally acceded to the occasional recommendations that he dismiss certain cases. "Nine times out of ten they are usually right because they know more about it than I do. They have been here longer." But other U.S. attorneys do not share this view. When asked about judicial influence on the decision to prosecute, one replied, "They don't interfere. Everybody knows it would be improper if they did. . . . Oh, there may be some grumblings and grouchiness, but they're only human beings. We do not let this affect what cases we bring."

The extent to which judges implicitly or explicitly convey such "suggestions" to U.S. attorneys depends on a similar set of factors. Intervention in the form of suggestions requires recognition of a need to intervene, accompanied by the belief that such intervention is permissible. Although federal judges share similar views in a number of areas,[31] substantial differences exist in attitudes about what things merit intervention and whether it is proper for them to do so. Some feel it highly improper for them to try to affect the type of cases prosecuted. "It's none of my business what suits are brought," a federal judge stated. "I decide what happens to them after they are brought. . . . Any judge who concerns himself with this has the wrong idea about the function of a district judge." Others exhibit inconsistent beliefs. When asked if he would discourage prosecution of minor cases, such as shooting a robin with a bow and arrow, a judge replied, "It doesn't take long to fine the man five dollars. I don't tell him what to prosecute." But he then continued: "Many of our cases involve bootlegging. They know I'm in a better mood if they're higher-ups (in the bootlegging operation). They know our general attitude. If some are being prosecuted who shouldn't be, I'll make a comment like, 'There is a lot of trash in this Court.'" Though he considers direct attempts improper, he allows himself to indicate his general attitude with the expectation that the U.S. attorney will get the message. Some judges fail to comment on the propriety of exerting influence on what cases are prosecuted. They emphasize the U.S. attorney's obligation to be selective in his prosecutions. One felt the U.S. attorney "ought to screen his cases pretty carefully" so he only brings cases when he can get a conviction. Another "gets on" the U.S. attorney if too many minor cases are prosecuted. "He's got the discretion to prosecute or not. He should use it."

Judges with either strong progovernment or prodefendant biases often take an active interest in the outcome of criminal cases. A *New York Times* "Man in the News" profile of Julius Hoffman, the controversial judge in the "Chicago 7" trial, quoted one Chicago attorney's assessment of the man. "Hoffman regards himself as the embodiment of everything federal. So, in criminal cases, at least, he tends to see the defense and their attorneys as the enemies."[32] One proprosecution judge explained how he intervened in trials. "The young attorneys get to depend on the seasoned old judge to take them by the hand . . . I have to watch the defense attorney carefully because the assistant won't object properly." When the inexperienced prosecutor does not object, the judge does. Sometimes, prosecution-minded judges, particularly those who are former prosecutors themselves, find it impossible to resist the temptation to take over the case themselves. A former U.S. attorney claimed that the court of appeals found 1,200 prejudicial remarks made by his judge in the course of a two-week trial: "The judge was really the prosecutor. He believed that anyone who was brought in before the court was guilty. If the U.S. attorney wasn't nailing the defendant to the cross properly, then he would take over and do it for him." Defense-minded judges also intervene, but on behalf of defendants. One proudly stated that, "When a defense attorney does not make the proper motions, I make them and then sustain them. I get a great kick out of this." Most judges fall somewhere in between the proprosecution and prodefendant extremes just illustrated.

Personal attitudes about what a fair trial requires also lead to differences in the nature of judicial intervention. One judge interjects questions of his own to witnesses "when something has not been developed which is material . . . and there would be a miscarriage of justice if it weren't." Such men often believe that as an officer of the U.S. government, a federal prosecutor has, in the words of one judge, an "obligation to see that he [the defendant] gets everything he's entitled to. He's not only a prosecutor. He has a dual purpose to serve." They may intervene to ensure that the prosecutor meets this obligation. Other judges, however, regard criminal trials essentially as adversary proceedings. The role of the prosecutor for them is somewhat different. "He has a duty to protect the innocent, of course. But the proceeding is an adversary one. . . . Sometimes there is a close question, and in those instances, he has an obligation to represent the government." Understandably, such judges less often oversee the prosecutor's behavior, but they also infrequently intervene in behalf of the prosecution. "You can't help the prosecutor in trying his case without violating the rights of defendants," observed one such judge.

Judges also disagree about whether they have a duty to oversee the conduct of assistants for propriety and competence. Asked if he expected more from government attorneys than private attorneys, one judge replied: "I do, although I know I'm not supposed to say that. It's because a private lawyer has his own client to whom he is responsible, and it's the client's responsibility to see that he is doing a good job. The U.S. attorney . . . represents the government, which means everybody and also nobody. There is no one there so directly concerned as to watch like a client would. So it's partially my responsibility to see that the government attorney does a good job." Some judges who adopt this view believe part of their responsibility extends to insuring improvement in the quality of the performance of assistants in the courtroom. Explaining how he liked to "help young people to develop skills," a judge continued, "I invite these kids to come in and talk to me. They have access to my chambers. I usually have a critique session with a new assistant after he has tried a few cases before me." Others take the opposite position. When asked if he expected more from members of the U.S. attorney's office, a judge replied that an assistant "just represents a client" like any attorney. A like-minded colleague responded to a question asking if he helped break in new assistants with an abrupt "That's not my job."

Differences in judicial attitudes on a variety of other topics produce differences in the efforts made to shape U.S. attorneys' behavior. Judges concerned with their dockets tend to encourage the compromise of civil suits, bring the parties together for negotiations, make recommendations on their own initiative, and even coerce one or both sides into an agreement.[33] But not all judges worry about their dockets. Some do not care if cases are settled or tried. Many of the judges interviewed in 1965 did not even utilize the pretrial conference procedure. The field research also suggests that some judges hold strong "progovernment" or "antigovernment" views in civil suits which shape the likelihood and direction of intervention in the trial of damage suits against the government.[34]

Judges who feel there is little chance that an attempt to influence the U.S. attorney's office will be successful refrain from trying, even though they may feel it would be proper. If a judge believes the U.S. attorney's actions result from Department of Justice orders, he may conclude that efforts to induce change are fruitless. In the rare case where relations between the judge and the U.S. attorney have degenerated into open conflict, a judge may anticipate so much resistance to his attempts to influence that it is not worth the bother. Some judges, however, clearly understand the potency of their resources for coercing compliance from U.S. attorneys and appear to enjoy invoking them.[35] It was easier to get stipulations from the U.S. attorney than the defense in criminal cases, explained one judge. "You have a club on the U.S. attorneys and can force them to do these things. You can direct a verdict against them, exclude them from asking questions. . . . No matter what you do, the government can rarely get a mistrial. They have to take the judge's ruling. What he says goes."

## THE IMPACT OF DISTRICT SIZE

The previous chapter identified the size of a U.S. attorney's office (a measure based on the number of assistants authorized) as the characteristic that best indicates the nature of a U.S. attorney's relationship with the Department of Justice. It is also the best single piece of information available for predicting a U.S. attorney's relations with his judges.

Although the size of a district depends on the number of judges

and assistants, the peculiarities of federal court organization complicate the picture. As Beverly Blair Cook notes, some districts are tech-
nically multi-judge courts, but they assign individual judges permanently to designated city locations.[36] Typically, the organization of the
U.S. attorney's office follows the patterns of judicial assignment.
Branch offices of the main office, permanently staffed by one or more
assistants, handle litigation presided over by such geographically dispersed judges. Relations between these judges and assistants in small
branch offices by and large resemble those found in single-judge
districts.[37] In the dicussion that follows, relationships hypothesized
for "small districts" (those with less than eight assistants) are also
found in geographically dispersed "solitary" divisions of multi-judge
districts.

The largest districts cluster toward the "autonomous" corner of
Table 7.1; the smallest ones are likelly to be "judge-dominated"
(though some evolve into the "partnership" pattern). A variety of
factors account for the association between office size and the pattern
of U.S. attorney–judge interactions. As noted in the previous chapter,
U.S. attorneys in large districts exhibit personal characteristics and
goals which dispose them to seek autonomy. Growth in skills of leadership and administration which heading a large office encourages,
coupled with the added flexibility and expertise which the resources
found there make possible, provide the wherewithal to resist judicial
influence. Furthermore, as the number of judges increases, the proportion of time any given member of the office spends before each
judge decreases. The implacable hostility of a judge in a district with
three or fewer judges creates a major problem for an office. In a
ten-judge district it remains a problem, but one that can be tolerated.
Consequently, the dependence of the office on any given judge decreases as the number of judges increases.

Reduced frequency of interaction with any given judge inhibits the
development of close rapport. Large districts must institutionalize
procedures for scheduling cases and arranging the docket, cutting the
occasions for informal contact. A more formal atmosphere surrounds
trials. The cases are more important, the news media more attentive,
and opposing attorneys less likely to be well acquainted. This formality contributes to a lower incidence of the development of close relationships between U.S. attorneys and judges. Furthermore, both
judges and assistants have enough colleagues to develop friendships
with their peers, reducing the incentive to form close social relationships with each other. The physical proximity of judges and U.S.
attorneys in the courthouses in most small districts facilitates the development of a close rapport. As a U.S. attorney put it, "Here the

judges' chambers are right around the corner. There are many things to discuss with them—the progress of the calendar, signing papers, and so forth. There are a lot of excuses I have to go in there."

Even if a U.S. attorney wanted to cater to the preferences of his judges in a larger district, doing so presents formidable problems. Beverly Blair Cook's research on federal judges in the Seventh Circuit revealed that the larger districts tended to have judges with heterogeneous backgrounds.[38] The likelihood of finding a consensus among the judges in a large district about how the U.S. attorney's office ought to be run or what the role of judges should be in shaping its operation is low. Even if the judges in a large district could agree on how the U.S. attorney's office should be run, the size of its operation would make oversight extremely difficult. There is just too much going on for one judge to follow, and it is extremely difficult to share the task of oversight among several judges.

Judges in smaller districts appear more likely actively to seek influence over the operation of the U.S. attorney's office. The relative importance of judges vis-à-vis the U.S. attorney increases as the number of judges decreases. Furthermore, since the responsibility for the condition of the docket can be placed upon specific judges in a small district, they have more incentive to insure that cases assigned to them are moved expeditiously by the U.S. attorney's office. Finally, Cook's study of Seventh Circuit district judges found judges on solitary benches more likely to be intensely political types, more likely to have engaged in an all-out campaign to secure their positions, and more likely to believe they should take an active role in nonjury trials than their brethren on multi-judge courts.[39] Such men are also likely to initiate efforts to influence their U.S. attorney.

The limited effect of judges on prosecutive decisions in larger districts exemplifies their reduced influence in most areas of activity. In larger districts, prosecutive decisions are often centralized. The assistant handling a case before a judge exerts little or no influence on the original decision to prosecute. Furthermore, that assistant probably will not find himself before the same judge again soon. However, even large districts take judicial attitudes into account in prosecutive decisions. If a large office knows a case will annoy the judges, it thinks twice about presenting it. "Of course, a lot of judges bitch about the cases," an assistant in a large district told me. "Their needs are considered, but it doesn't deter us." Smaller districts often refrain in similar circumstances. "We could file on more cases than we do. We reject some to keep the judges from grumbling too damn much."

Of course, factors other than office size also influence the pattern of U.S. attorney–judge interaction. An office's location affects such relations in several ways. In some southern districts, judges regard the U.S. attorney somewhat the way a father regards his son. They desire to assist him, yet feel responsible for his conduct and entitled to have a strong voice in shaping it. The informal rural "folksy" atmosphere that abounds in many southern districts contributes to this tendency, and the unusually large number of very small districts in the South reinforces it. These factors encourage the development of judge-dominated relationships. In the South, parts of the West, and the rural Mid-West, members of the U.S. attorney's office, the judges and court personnel, and members of the local bar express considerable shared resentment and prejudice toward the stereotype of the self-assured, condescending Justice Department lawyer. Local people reveal their views through references to themselves in pseudoderogatory terms like "hay seeds" or "just country lawyers," and by anecdotes relating the stupidity or snobbishness of Justice Department attorneys. Even in some larger districts local personnel express resentment directed against "outsiders." Such attitudes increase feelings of "we-ness" and partnership between U.S. attorney and judge, particularly when the department can be thwarted by close cooperation between the two. One of the largest offices conformed to the "partnership" pattern on major questions of policy, particularly when the office was engaged in one of its frequent battles with Washington. The U.S. attorney and chief judge worked closely with another during these episodes, and their cooperation extended to other policy areas as well.

Relations between a U.S. attorney's office and judges exhibit the same instability over time that relations with the department display. Judge-dominated districts may revert to the standard pattern with a change in the person of the chief judge, U.S. attorney, or both. These temporal fluctuations are not as closely tied to the political cycle as relations with the department. However, as a U.S. attorney nears the end of his tenure in office, he may adopt the attitude of one man who observed, "Near the end there I didn't give a damn about what most of the judges thought anyhow." But changes also accompany shifts in the composition of the bench. One U.S. attorney observed in this connection: "With the next replacement we will have four of the judges, in effect, that are brand new judges . . . and it takes a judge a while before he starts throwing his weight around, at least insofar as outside offices are concerned."

# CHAPTER 8

# U.S. Attorneys, Their Clients, and Opposing Counsel

The nature of a U.S. attorney's interactions with the Department of Justice and federal district judges largely determines the dominant characteristics of the operations of his office. But relations with several other positions encountered in the strategic environment are also important. Patterns of interaction with several of the most significant will be described in this chapter.[1]

## RELATIONS WITH FEDERAL INVESTIGATIVE AGENCIES

Because the department exercises relatively loose supervision over criminal cases, U.S. attorneys enjoy substantial discretion in their interactions with the agencies that investigate and bring violations of federal criminal law to their offices for prosecution.[2] The discussion that follows first examines the interaction between agency personnel who conduct investigations and the assistant U.S. attorneys who authorize prosecutions and handle the cases. It then analyzes relations between administrative personnel, particularly those between the U.S. attorney and his administrative counterparts in charge of the various branch offices of federal investigative agencies located in his district.

### Assistant U.S. Attorney–Investigative Agent Relations

The most significant and frequent interaction between assistants and agents occurs when investigators bring cases to the U.S. attorney's office for prosecutive decisions.[3] Other occasions of formal contact include consultation on the progress of investigations prior to official submission for prosecutive decisions, the review of evidence and testimony in preparation for court appearances, and direct courtroom contact during trial.[4]

The decision to prosecute generates a web of mutual dependence that determines the basic character of assistant–agent interactions.

150

With few exceptions,[5] no federal investigative agent may make an arrest unless an assistant U.S. attorney authorizes it. Federal prosecutors enjoy a distinct advantage over their local counterparts in this respect. Local law enforcement agencies ordinarily do not require approval of the prosecutor's office before making arrests.[6] United States attorneys familiar with local criminal justice systems understand the significance of this difference.

When you're dealing with the FBI, they understand and you understand what a lot of people don't understand—and that is that the FBI does what the U.S. attorney *tells* him to do. The FBI can't make arrests without the authority of the U.S. attorney. You never get pressure at all from the investigative agencies as a U.S. attorney. But as a district attorney, they can make life miserable for you. They can give you a hard time, make a lot of publicity. It's your job to prosecute if some jackass goes out and makes a bad case for you. Sometimes it's very difficult to drop a bad case.

Both assistants and investigative agents recognize the crucial importance of prosecution to the agent's work. "We devote a lot of time to investigating an offense and then developing a case," explained one agent. "Then the prosecution is the culmination of it. If you don't get a prosecution, then your work is wasted." Agents face incentive structures within their organizations that emphasize results. "Our record is based on statistics," observed a postal inspector. "It's not the investigations completed or closed, but the results of the investigation that are important. . . . If I had 300 cases in a year, and all of them are closed with negative results, then that's no good. If I have 25 to 50 arrests and as many convictions, then that is important. My boss and the higher-ups, they look at the record."[7] Assistants repeatedly characterized the FBI as particularly "statistics happy." The power to authorize arrests assumes considerable significance for agents required to produce "statistics," as the explanation of an assistant suggests. "Every agency, particularly the FBI, has an awful lot of pressure to equal performance for the previous year in a particular category. Around this district, white slavery is negligible. . . . Well, one year we had three or four cases. So, for the next two or three years, they had to explain why white slavery cases were going down. They were interested in making cases in the white slavery category that really weren't good ones." To the extent that agencies evaluate their agents' performance on actual convictions, the agents depend upon the skill of assistants to obtain guilty pleas and win convictions when defendants go to trial.

Agents do not invariably want an assistant to authorize prosecutions on the cases they bring for a decision. Some agencies, the FBI included, require a formal written declination of prosecution for every matter investigated before the file can be closed. Postponing a final declination and requesting additional investigation results in files remaining open. Agents' supervisors look with disfavor on open files, and the paperwork open cases generate takes time that could be used to work on promising matters. Timely declinations also serve a protective function. An agency under pressure from aggrieved citizens (e.g., the parents of a girl receiving obscene mail) can pass the responsibility to the U.S. attorney's office. "When we close a case, it's giving a finality to the case," a perceptive assistant observed. "It's a way of getting it off their hands, and it protects them from questions later on. If someone says, 'Why didn't you do something on this case?' they can say, 'The U.S. attorney said not to do anything.'"

Agents depend on assistants in other ways. They can affect the careers of the agents they encounter by contacting superiors about their behavior. Agency supervisors view reports of lax performance by an agent from the U.S. attorney's office seriously. Complaints by a U.S. attorney reportedly have caused agents to be transferred to less desirable assignments and subjected them to investigation of their conduct. On the other hand, some assistants make it a point to write letters of commendation for agents who do superior work. The quality of an investigator's work life also depends heavily on his relations with assistants. He deals regularly with them about matters of the utmost importance to his work. Occasionally, he will interact intensively with an assistant during a protracted trial of one of his cases. The physical proximity of their offices produces frequent occasions for informal contact. Finally, assistants constitute the only audience, outside of fellow agents, with whom an agent can freely discuss his work without fear of compromising his investigations. If the frequent interactions with assistants are pleasant, it contributes substantially to making the agent's work life enjoyable.

The same is true for assistants, of course. Those assigned to criminal work spend a significant portion of their time interacting with agents. Numerous hostile and unpleasant encounters sour an assistant's entire work experience. But assistants' dependence upon investigators extends beyond influencing the conviviality of their work lives. Ultimately, an assistant's ability to win cases (i.e., secure convictions) requires cooperation from investigative agents.

The need to win cases constitutes the strongest incentive in the work environment of assistants. As John Kaplan, a former assistant U.S. attorney, observes, the standing of an assistant among his peers depends in part on his conviction record.[8] His record also determines his reputation among the judges and members of the private bar, and this reputation in turn affects the job opportunities available when he leaves. Furthermore, U.S. attorneys utilize conviction rates to assess the work of their assistants. Despite the problems with conviction rates, they provide U.S. attorneys with a means of comparing the performance of their assistants, judging the efficiency of manpower allocations, and demonstrating to "a rather ill-defined public constituency" demanding convictions that they are fulfilling their obligation.[9] A U.S. attorney's standing with the local judges depends upon his ability to facilitate movement of the docket, which in the criminal area requires maintaining a high guilty plea rate. Without a high conviction rate, the guilty plea system is jeopardized.[10] Furthermore, U.S. attorneys believe judges dislike devoting substantial portions of their limited courtroom time to presiding over acquittals. Finally, U.S. attorneys desiring high marks from the department recognize that conviction rates provide an obvious and convenient measure to compare the relative performance of various offices.

Congressional pressure reinforces the department's concern with conviction rates. The following exchange between the chairman of the House Appropriations Subcommittee for the Department of Justice, John Rooney, and the department's Will Wilson suggests the origins of its concern with the conviction rate.

*Mr. Rooney.* How do you account for these unusual figures at page 48 of these justifications? In the criminal cases in which section attorneys participated convictions were way off. To what is that due, indictments without being thorough-going enough or incompetent new help being recruited?

*Mr. Wilson.* You talk about the difference between the 813 and the 449.

*Mr. Rooney.* Yes. In the first half of 1970 you have 512 and you convicted only 136 where section attorneys participated. . . .

*Mr. Rooney.* Can you make a further defense of these pathetic figures, the difference between the number indicted and convicted as shown on page 48?[11]

The ability of assistants to obtain convictions depends initially on the quality of their prosecutive decisions. Strong incentives operate to encourage declination of poor cases rather than dismissals after charges have been filed. The department requires approval for dismissals and they create visible "nonconvictions." But the department rarely scrutinizes an initial declination. Assistants depend heavily on the quality of information provided by an investigative agent to decline probable losers and to win convictions when they authorize prosecution. Furthermore, inexperienced and less skillful assistants often rely on the advice and suggestions of experienced agents. "They know far more than I do," admitted a young assistant. "They know the mechanics, the procedures. . . . They know where we keep our own records here. They know the way in which you get into court on a case." Since most assistants stay only several years, veteran agents frequently encounter assistants to whom they can impart their experience. Even experienced prosecutors find agents' knowledge useful. "It's extremely invaluable to have the investigator's opinions, especially in matters of intent and design," observed one assistant. "There isn't anyone other than the investigator who has looked over *all* of the facts of a case." Another assistant noted that often only investigators have seen the witnesses and the defendant. "And sometimes demeanor is very important. What the defendant looks like or how he acts often comes as a surprise." He went on to explain how much of a surprise he got one December 24th, when he was prosecuting a number of cases against defendants who were duck hunting without having purchased duck stamps. One of the defendants, when his case was called, walked up in a Santa Claus uniform, his hands red with cold and Salvation Army bell in hand. He explained he had been trying to "save" the man he was arrested with. The judge dismissed the case.

The mutual dependence of prosecutors and investigators does not produce a complete identity of interest. Several basic characteristics of the strategic environment of each create some divergence in interest and outlook. In one broad respect, U.S. attorneys' interactions with investigative agencies resemble their relations with the department. In both situations, they are generalists dealing with people who are responsible for relatively restricted areas. The specialist knows his own area thoroughly, and understandably attaches great importance to it. The U.S. attorney's office performs an aggregating function. Considerations of time, manpower, policy goals, and strategy lead U.S. attorneys' offices to pick and choose among the cases presented to them. Inevitably, they decline to prosecute many cases that appear extremely serious to the enforcement agency. A U.S. attorney related an example of a conflict he had with Social Security that emanated from such differences in perspective. A widow who had remarried continued to receive survivor's benefits. "This is an offense. We determined it was not properly a prosecutive case. There was little jury appeal. The individual in the Social Security Administration is confined to that one little area of fact. He is not able to view the incident in the broad perspective of all criminal violations. He views this as a serious thing. . . . We did not agree with them that this should be prosecuted and we did not prosecute."

Differences in the basic responsibilities of prosecutor and investigator also produce divergent perspectives and even resentment. The prosecutor regards the investigation, while necessary, merely as a means to a conviction. The investigator seeks to identify the criminal, obtain evidence against him, and convince the U.S. attorney to prosecute. Securing his conviction is, of course, also important. But because he is less directly involved in getting it, an agent often feels he has essentially completed his task when he makes an arrest. As a result, investigative agents resent declinations when they know the defendant is guilty, feeling that the stigma of federal prosecution justifies an unsuccessful prosecution. They also regret the loss of cases inexperienced assistants should have won. They feel insulted when an assistant lacks interest in a case they feel is important. They regard assistants' requests for additional investigation as inconvenient and frequently unnecessary burdens. Experienced agents dealing with new assistants who may be twenty years younger than they feel twinges of discomfort, especially if the assistant adopts an insulting or superior attitude and then proceeds to botch the case.

For their part, "green" assistants may feel uncomfortable with their own inexperience, uncertainty, and lack of skill. They learn that many agents are insensitive to the problems encountered in obtaining convictions. When agents communicate their desire for prosecution of cases unlikely to result in conviction, many assistants become annoyed. They resent even more faulty investigative work that complicates and sometimes fatally injures cases. It is frustrating and annoying to assistants when agents are unwilling or unable to learn how to maximize the prospects of getting convictions. Sometimes relevant information has been gathered, but the agent fails to communicate it to the assistant. But this is less infuriating than when an agent's testimony in court fails to correspond with what he has led the assistant to believe it would be.

Finally, a different set of pressures impinges on each position. As we have seen, U.S. attorneys operate in a web of significant relationships that include the department and judges. They may be forced to decline cases the agency wants because of department policy or the hostility of judges to them. The investigative agent's world is less complex. He deals primarily with the U.S. attorney's office, his superiors, and that portion of the public encountered during investigations.

The existence of divergent interests and perspectives does not alter the fact that assistants and agents depend heavily upon one another to achieve goals important to each.[12] Assistants generally recognize the importance of investigative agents, but do not uniformly acknowledge their dependence on them explicitly. Investigative agents emphasize their dependence somewhat more. "We are so intertwined," observed an FBI agent as he twisted his fingers together, "that we cannot operate without each other." This difference in expressed recognition of dependence reflects the balance of influence in the relationship. Assistants hold the upper hand.

The U.S. attorney's office depends on each agency (and each agent) for only part of its investigative needs. Poor performance, hostility, and lack of cooperation are bothersome but not disastrous. Federal investigative agencies, however, normally must take all their cases to the U.S. attorney's office. There are many similarities in the relationships between investigative agents and assistants on the one hand and assistants and federal judges on the other. The assistant, so dependent on judges yet unable to influence them save through persuasion, finds himself in the superior position when dealing with investigative agents. Overall, however, his advantage over agents is less pronounced than the advantage judges enjoy over him. Both judges and assistants can influence the weaker party, because they make discretionary decisions in significant areas. Although judges encounter some restraints in making decisions affecting assistants, assistants are even more restricted in their decisions that affect investigators. The ability to decline prosecution provides assistants with their most potent discretionary power, but many of the cases presented leave little room for the exercise of discretion. Some are so trivial or so weak that prosecution would be ridiculous. Others are obvious choices for prosecution. Assistants want convictions. They normally do not let the opportunity to authorize a strong case (provided it reaches a minimum level of seriousness) pass. If they were to decline strong cases, they would face the possibility of an appeal by the investigative agency and review and rebuke by the U.S. attorney or the department. Finally, a consensus about what cases ought to be prosecuted develops in most offices,[13] and most assistants come to share it. In some districts, this consensus is molded by prosecutive criteria explicitly established by the U.S. attorney.

Of course, assistants retain significant discretion. Although they probably constitute only a small proportion of all matters referred for a prosecutive decision, some cases are "borderline" in the sense that the decision to prosecute can go either way. Investigative agencies, particularly those that have few cases to begin with, attach great symbolic significance to many of those borderline cases. In addition to the decision to prosecute, assistants exercise discretion in several other areas that investigative agents regard as important. Before the speedy trial act took effect, they determined how quickly cases moved. Delays in bringing a good case to trial frustrated agents and probably damaged the strength of the case. An assistant's enthusiasm and interest in a case still affects how much time he devotes to its preparation for trial. Of course, assistants do not deliberately lose cases in order to punish an investigative agency. Work habits and personal pride usually prevent deliberate slacking. The knowledge that his reputation among other attorneys and the judge depends on his courtroom performance also discourages it. Preparation that reflects a minimum degree of competence and attention to duty is required to avoid a directed verdict and reprimmand from most judges. But in close cases failure to make an extra effort can spell the difference between defeat and victory. Prosecutor effort can also affect whether the case is even authorized. Assistants can delay a declination to give the agent an opportunity to gather enough additional evidence to sustain prosecution. They can even take an active role in guiding the investigation.

Assistants exercise broad enough discretion to make it worthwhile to investigative agents to try to shape its exercise.[14] Similarly, assistants depend upon agents enough to try to influence how they perform their investigative function. The combination of bounded discretion and incentive to influence its exercise provides the preconditions for the interplay of strategies pursued by both positions in dealing with each other.

The primary strategy investigative agents employ resembles the one assistants use in dealing with judges—improving the ability to persuade. The three elements of this strategy described in the preceding chapter are also found in the behavior of agents; presenting themselves as cooperative, deferential, and likeable people; enhancing credibility; and demonstrating expertise.

An FBI agent succinctly described the dominant characteristic of investigators' style when dealing with assistants: "We curry their favor." Agents are deferential. They normally comply cheerfully with requests for additional investigation. Experienced agents willingly assist those new assistants who ask for help. The manner in which they prepare and present cases varies to conform to the perceived desires of assistants. "You try to present the reports in the investigations as the individual U.S. attorney may desire," one agent observed. "They're individuals like everyone else. Some like a long detailed report; others want a shorter report."

Credibility comes primarily through playing it "straight" with the assistant. The most effective way of achieving credibility is by giving "balanced" reports—presenting the strengths and weaknesses of the case, with particular emphasis on pitfalls that might be encountered in the courtroom. Dispassionate presentations enhance credibility more than a "gung-ho" prosecution-minded exhortation. Astute agents avoid enthusiastic presentation of cases likely to be declined, and even communicate their expectation. "Some who you learn to trust will say, 'Well, here's a lemon,'" reported an assistant. "They'll point out the fallible part of the case." Investigators from agencies which do not require decisions on all matters avoid having to present cases sure to be declined by not presenting them at all.[15] Past experience with similar cases in part prompts such prior screening, but sometimes feedback obtained from informal telephone consultation during the investigation's early stages deters bringing it for a formal prosecutive decision. In either event, as noted in Chapter 2, prosecutive decisions influence investigative agency allocations of resources.

Agents demonstrate expertise by doing a good investigative job and presenting strong cases. Individual agents and the entire contingent of investigators from a given agency acquire reputations among assistants. The comments of an assistant in charge of the criminal division in an office with less than a dozen attorneys suggest the type of judgments typically made, though they do not necessarily reflect most assistants' assessments of the agencies mentioned.

The FBI is the best and most efficient of them. . . . They take complete statements from everybody. The Secret Service men don't take full statements. . . . The same thing is true of the postal inspectors. You have to depend pretty much on the ability of the agent. . . . There are some postal inspectors I can rely on. There is one in particular, that if I'm busy and he says "I've got a case for you," I say go ahead and file it. But most postal inspectors will present it like it's the best case in the world and you will have to throw it out. Alcohol and tobacco tax agents are delightful persons. Everyone likes them very much. But they will investigate anything. When they bring a case, you don't know what the hell they've got.[16]

The combination of direct experience and office scuttlebut soon makes most assistants aware of the reputation of individual agents and their agencies.

Agents who have acquired some capacity to persuade employ several techniques to increase the chances of prosecution in borderline cases. One is to do an exhaustive investigative job. This enhances its attractiveness by making the case easier to prove, but it also exerts subtle but compelling pressure for an authorization, as an assistant explained. "Although there was something less than criminal about it [the offense in question], the investigator did an *exhaustive* report. . . . The guy worked his brains out. We prosecuted because we knew it was important to him and important to the agency. . . . You have to work with them day-to-day, and this is a matter of comity and good relations."

A related technique is to submit a written report rather than the oral presentation many agencies frequently use for minor offenses. The written report forces greater attention to the matter and requires a written reply. An offhand dismissal becomes more difficult. Agents also exert pressure in trying to "sell" a case by an enthusiastic oral presentation emphasizing the strengths of the case. Occasionally, an agent enjoying a very close working relationship with an assistant will even make an overt request for prosecution. Some assistants interviewed conveyed the impression that requests from such men were heeded, an impression confirmed by John Kaplan's recollections of his experiences as an assistant.[17] Assistants perceive frequent telephone calls asking about the progress of a case or offering to get additional information as a mild form of pressure. Agents sometimes describe to assistants the pressure being received from the "public" (usually aggrieved victims). Finally, agents may resubmit previously declined borderline cases with the claim that additional investigation has uncovered new evidence.

Investigative agents employ several strategies that do not depend upon their ability to persuade. The most prevalent is to obtain authorization for prosecution by "shopping" for a favorably disposed assistant. Most agents interviewed acknowledged that when they had a case they wanted prosecuted, they tried if possible to avoid assistants who had declined similar cases previously. Interesting offensive and defensive strategies emerge in the battle to prevent "shopping." Many offices have developed schemes for preventing it (for example, assigning one assistant to decide all cases involving a specified set of violations or centralizing all prosecutive decisions in the hands of a single man). Agents counter by ascertaining whether the man they wish to avoid is in his office. If he is not, they ask for him and are assigned to someone else. Or they may wait until his vacation time comes around. If an extremely important case can be prosecuted in more than one district, the agency may "forum shop" by taking the matter to the office most likely to authorize and do a good job of prosecution.[18]

Finally, investigators can appeal a negative decision. Usually, they appeal directly to the assistant who initially declined prosecution. Such "appeals" consist of reiterations of arguments for prosecution and requests for the reason the case is being declined. Even if the assistant remains firm, persistent and frequent appeals may cause him to hesitate before subjecting himself to the bothersome ordeal of defending his decision on similar cases in the future. Sometimes an agent will go to another assistant in the office with whom he has a close relationship to see if he will speak to the initial assistant about it.

Another option is to take the matter to the U.S. attorney or the first assistant. Many of the assistants interviewed indicated that the possibility of appeals shaped their decisions. "If it's a critical case, or there is a pattern of a number of similar cases which are being declined, they will appeal. They can lean pretty hard on us if they feel we are not giving them the attention they feel they deserve." The fact that such appeals sometimes succeed enhances the efficacy of agents' implicit threats to appeal.

An investigative agent or (as is more likely) his superior can appeal a declination to the Department of Justice. A postal inspector's comments about this tactic reveal why it is rarely used. "You may be disappointed on a case today, but you may have a case tomorrow that you want him to prosecute. And you can't get the U.S. attorney too hostile." Appeals to Washington require an agent to get the support of his superiors. The fact that most agents request such support reluctantly also inhibits the use of this strategy.

Assistants differ more among themselves in how they interact with agents than agents do in their encounters with assistants. Many of the differences flow from the assistant's view of what the investigator's role should be in the decision to prosecute. A few believe the investigator bears the primary responsibility, with the prosecutor merely checking over the case and handling the technical problem of securing a conviction. Referring to migratory bird cases, one assistant illustrated this viewpoint. "We sort of leave it up to investigative agents. If they think the case should be prosecuted, we go ahead and prosecute." A far more common view holds that the agent and prosecutor are partners, each with the information and skills necessary to achieve joint goals. The assistant leads the discussion, but solicits the opinions of the agent. "The agent came in [on a bank robbery case]," related a U.S. attorney adhering to this view. "He didn't think he had enough evidence, and I told the agent to keep working on it. He came up with a little more evidence and we sat down and decided that perhaps it was time for an indictment. We sort of work things out together like this." Explicit requests for prosecution from an agent to such a prosecutor do not insure an affirmative response, but neither are such requests thought to be inappropriate. A third view, however, regards such requests as quite out of place. "No one ever tried to say we ought to do this or that. No one gave an indication of what he thought. If he had, I'd have told him what his job was." For these assistants, investigators work for them, speaking only in reply to questions. "I really don't let them do much presenting," reported an experienced assistant holding this view. "I ask questions and, depending on their answers, I'll decide whether to prosecute or not." But the questions asked rarely involve matters regarded to be the prosecutor's responsibility (the quality of the evidence, the credibility of witnesses, the appropriate charges to file). "You have to remain a certain distance from someone when you are telling him what to do," said one. "I am not entirely candid with them." Unlike their colleagues, assistants holding this view do not develop close relationships with agents.

What produces these differences among assistants? One possibility is that U.S. attorneys' offices develop a distinct consensus among their assistants that varies from one district to another. Furthermore, its content can change when a new U.S. attorney takes office. A defense attorney compared the response of two U.S. attorneys in his district to borderline cases. "[The first] is a lot easier to work with. He's more practical. [The second] has more of a vengeance. He thinks there is such a thing as a bad boy.... He'll prosecute on almost anybody." This explanation fails to account, however, for why assistants in the same office hold very different views of the role of investigative agents and pursue different prosecutive policies. Apparently, personality traits and personal values about the seriousness of specific offenses help account for intraoffice differences. Some assistants seek to accommodate those with whom they interact, including investigative agents. "In this job, you can tend to be callous and not be sensitive to the needs and feelings of the investigative agents," explained one such assistant. "And, if you do, you become less effective. You should be more compassionate and try to see the other guy's viewpoint." Such men consciously seek to build rapport and win the friendship and admiration of agents. They authorize borderline cases when asked, put in overtime to go over important cases, soften declinations with a sympathetic comment, and strengthen egos by seeking agents' advice and treating them with respect. By contrast, other assistants worry little about their interpersonal relations. "I know none of them [agents] personally and I don't care," observed one assistant tartly.

Differences in assistants' conception of the criminal process also help account for variation in relations with agents. Those who regard themselves as "officers of the court" and adhere to a "due process" model rely more on their own legal judgments and less on the attitudes of agents, while men more eager for prosecution, who accept the "crime control" model, accord agents more say.[19] Finally, more experienced assistants appear to rely less on investigators. In part, this is *because* they are more experienced and do not need the information and advice agents can provide. But for some, experience produces disillusionment, as the statement of a seasoned assistant reveals.

When the FBI agent comes in, you're doing business with a man whose image is good. Whatever this good fellow says suits me. It takes a while to get down to a realistic picture. . . . It's sort of like when you see a really beautiful woman walking across the street. If you manage to go to bed with her and sleep with her, after a couple of days your image begins to change. You see her in the morning with her hair all down and frizzly, and you look at her a little differently. Now, that's the way it is with the FBI.

Consequently, a number of assistants approach encounters with investigative agents skeptically. "They'll always come in and make a pitch," observed one assistant. ". . . unless you know the agent well, it will have something sour in it."

Both assistants and agents usually describe their relationship in similar enthusiastic terms. The atmosphere is generally friendly and cooperative and frequently accompanied by close rapport. Investigative agents and assistants often come to know each other extremely well. They each learn how the other feels and thinks. With striking regularity assistants state that despite the strict adherence of FBI agents to a directive forbidding them to express their own opinions about cases, in the words of one assistant, "You can tell. You get the feel from his conversation what he feels about the case. This is never said explicitly; but you know how he feels about it just by knowing the man." Rapport implies mutual friendship as well as an ability to communicate implicitly. Though a few exceptions can be found in every district, assistants and agents regard each other as friends, often as very good friends. The fact that most cases brought to trial result in convictions bolsters perceptions of the quality of their relationship. Assistants have the added satisfaction of participating in a close relationship in which they are constantly deferred to and made to feel important by the other party. Investigative agents find that assistants positively evaluate their work,[20] frequently consult them, and sometimes prosecute borderline cases.

### The "Partnership" Pattern of Interaction

The balance of influence in the relationship definitely tilts toward assistants. Agents have little choice but to accept their inferior status. The level of overt conflict and tension is therefore typically quite low, primarily because most agents take pains to see that it is low. Asked what difficulties he encountered in his relations with assistants, an agent replied there were none. "He's our counselor. And if your attorney tells you to do something, why, you usually go ahead and do it." But as noted previously, most assistants lack experience, recognize the expertise of agents, and come to depend upon their help. Recognition of the stake of agents in their investigations and the feelings generated by rapport and friendship also lead assistants to consult investigators. Consequently, enough sharing of power occurs to characterize the typical relationship as a "partnership," although the assistant definitely acts as the senior partner.

Both prosecutors and agents stress the importance of maintaining a cordial, cooperative relationship, and this commitment produces significant effects on their behavior. Both parties refrain if possible from taking actions that may jeopardize the relationship. Agents, for example, realize that many prosecutors dislike declining prosecution. This knowledge provides them with an additional reason to refrain from bringing weak cases to an assistant or to preface their presentations with an apology. For their part, assistants readily detect the incipient disappointment that will follow the declination of a case that an agent wants prosecuted. Where a close relationship exists, this may be sufficient to cause him to authorize where he otherwise would decline. These factors result in a fascinating "game" of maneuver in which either can improve his chances of influencing the other by indicating that an unfavorable response will erode rapport and good will. The party that commits himself first has the advantage. Agents do this when they prepare exhaustive written reports on questionable cases or covertly communicate an eagerness to prosecute in their oral presentation. Assistants, of course, can and do play the game too. Requests for additional work on a case or special investigations may be subtly linked to maintaining good will. Requests that investigative procedures be changed or certain cases no longer be presented for authorization fall into the same category.

Several signficant implicit rules limit the way this "game" is played. First, ill-defined but nonetheless powerful norms of reciprocity operate. Neither can draw on the stock of good will in the relationship too much without replenishing it by doing something for the other party. Second, agents do not often play the "game" with cases likely to result in acquittals. Finally, neither party can commit himself too frequently without eroding the effectiveness of his play. Investigative agents in particular must be cautious because of their inferior strategic position. Even if reciprocity is maintained, they must exercise considerable restraint by picking only a few of many possible occasions for seeking to influence the prosecutor.

Despite the agreement of assistants and agents on the cordial and satisfying character of their relationship and the desirability of maintaining it, the relationship rests on a fragile foundation. Although overt conflict rarely breaks out, there are important differences in perspective and a number of sources of tension. Furthermore, an outbreak of overt conflict and a breakdown in cooperation would result in troublesome but not unlivable problems. As noted earlier, a number of factors limit assistants' discretion significantly. They cannot decline good cases or authorize on many trivial ones; they dare not deliberately slack off to the point where they lose cases they ought to win. They can complicate the work of agents, but they cannot incapacitate them. Similarly, investigators cannot stop bringing cases; nor can they deliberately conduct poor investigations that lead to declinations or acquittals.

I confirmed the limited effects of overt conflict during an interview with a U.S. attorney in a small district. We were interrupted by a phone call from the special agent in charge of the local FBI office. The agent wanted the U.S. attorney to authorize prosecution of a federal prisoner who stabbed another inmate. The U.S. attorney brusquely asked why phone authorization was required before the written report was submitted. A heated five minute exchange ensued, laced with hostility and anger directed toward the agent. Later, the U.S. attorney said that he "wouldn't break his neck" or go out of his way for the agent, but he added that they would continue to work together and that he would do what he had to do.

Thus, no matter what relations are like, most cases will be investigated and tried well enough to maintain a high rate of conviction. The expectations of other significant actors and personally held standards of conduct structure the strategic environment of investigator and prosecutor to insure that federal law enforcement will not be drastically hampered by their minimal cooperation and mutual dislike. In the words of an FBI agent, "We have certain defined duties, and they have them. And they have to be done. They'll be done, regardless of what kind of relationship you have." Similar restraints operate to prevent too close a relationship from developing. The U.S. attorney's office cannot dominate completely investigative agents or their agencies. The self-respect and pride of investigators militate against it. Pressures from within the agency effectively limit the extent to which agents modify behavior to conform to the wishes of the U.S. attorney's office.

Given the narrow scope of the actual degree of mutual dependence, what accounts for the importance attached to maintaining a close, cooperative relationship? Part of the answer lies in the nature of the perceptions of both parties. Neither stops to analyze the general picture. Both focus on how poor relations would make life difficult when contrasted to the cooperative, friendly situation good relations produce. Assistants emphasize the few difficult cases that can be won with the enthusiastic cooperation of investigators, the painstaking review and questioning of investigative reports that would be necessary if relations were bad and the embarrassing courtroom scenes and cases lost that would result if agents failed to cooperate fully. Agents deeply appreciate it when assistants win difficult cases and authorize prosecution on a few minor cases to improve statistics. Finally, and perhaps most significantly, both regard the psychological costs of substituting hostile and tense relations for friendly, cooperative ones to be very high.

### Other Patterns of Assistant–Investigative Agent Interaction

The pattern of assistant–agent interaction described as "partnership" appears to be the most common by far, but several other patterns exist. The most interesting resembles the typical pattern in atmosphere, but exhibits a more even balance of influence. The description of an assistant indicates the influence agents sometimes achieve. "Sometimes they say whether you should authorize or decline as they are presenting the case. Some of them are pretty good friends. We can just talk it over. Some of the agents have been around twenty-five years. I ask them what they think about it if its a close question."

The interviews with agents suggested that they exerted considerable influence, over new assistants in particular. "If there is a new U.S. attorney or assistant, we'll help him in drawing up indictments," commented one. Another reported that new assistants are "pathetic." "We tried the case for them. Whoever initiated the case would sit in court and husband him along."

In contrast, the pattern of prosecutor domination lacks informality and warmth. Interaction in this pattern is business-like, correct but curt. The prosecutor clearly controls the proceedings, restricting investigator opportunities to influence and rebuffing those attempts that are made. The pattern of overt conflict between assistant and agent undoubtedly occurs, though I only encountered the example described above where the U.S. attorney and the FBI's special agent in charge disliked one another. Usually, the perceived costs of such conflict, particularly from the agents' standpoint, are so high that agents permit it to develop only in the most exceptional circumstances.

Several factors determine the character of assistant–prosecutor interaction. The most important, the prosecutor's beliefs about the proper role of investigators and the significance he attaches to maintaining friendly relations with others, have already been identified. The assistant's evaluation of a specific investigator's integrity, reliability, and competence are also relevant. The better an investigator's reputation with an assistant the more influence he exerts. As noted above, some assistants place so much confidence in certain agents that they authorize cases presented by them almost as a matter of course. A few investigators possess such poor reputations that skeptical assistants refuse to prosecute until they have carefully scrutinized the case. Agents' aggressiveness also shapes encounters with assistants. Some press for prosecutions as a matter of course, appeal declinations, and offer advice on how to try cases. Others employ more passive tactics. The degree of sophistication and understanding of the legal process is another important factor. Agents who comprehend what securing a conviction entails appear more likely to concur with prosecutive decisions. The more an agent dislikes the prospect of losing cases, the more willing he is to defer to negative prosecutive decisions based on the difficulty of securing a conviction. The investigator's age relative to the assistant's also is relevant. When the agent is considerably older (a frequent occurrence), the encounter tends to be formal and the assistant deferential. Rapport builds more quickly when agent and assistant are approximately the same age.

Relations between assistants and individual agents can also depend on the overall quality of relations between the two organizations. "I got along with all of them except the Agriculture Department and the Wild Life Service," observed a former U.S. attorney. "We were not on friendly terms with them."

Finally, several attributes of the environmental context account for variation in interaction patterns. Region is one. Rapport appears to be higher between agents and assistants in both rural and southern districts. Tensions increase when an investigator's agency finds few violations in a district and must fight for prosecutions to justify its continued existence. In New England and parts of the West, for example, few violations fell within the jurisdiction of the old Alcohol and Tobacco Tax Division of the Treasury. In these districts, ATT agents seized upon any violation, investigated it thoroughly, and pressed vigorously for authorization. Bringing a minimum number of cases was more important than securing convictions.[21] An office's workload is another factor. Where it is heavy, some cases must be declined that would merit prosecution if sufficient staff were available. Such declinations often provoke conflict and appeals. The most important feature of the environmental context, however, is the size of the district. Larger offices handle more cases and consequently decline more. Serious cases arise more often, reducing the relative seriousness of offenses that smaller offices prosecute readily elsewhere. Small districts, especially in the South, enthusiastically prosecuted marijuana violations routinely declined in large urban districts. Large offices more often have a core of experienced assistants, reducing the need to rely upon agents for assistance and guidance. Furthermore, so many assistants and agents work on cases that individual pairs encounter one another too infrequently to build the rapport and close working relationships found in small offices. Procedures for authorizing cases are more formalized, contributing additional obstacles to the building of rapport. As a result, the more formal and business-like relations that typify the "prosecutor dominant" pattern emerge frequently in large offices.

### United States Attorney–Investigative Agency Interactions

Except in the smallest offices, the U.S. attorney does not routinely deal with investigators. Only when a "big" case develops or an adverse prosecutive decision is appealed does he interact with field investigators. The quality and content of interactions between his subordinates and investigative agents, however, does depend on his actions. He establishes procedures for making prosecutive decisions which determine whether or not agents can "shop" for their favorite assistant. If he asks assistants to specialize in a narrow range of cases, they will interact regularly with the same agents and will likely develop close relations with their agents. Office policies on what kinds of cases to authorize and what kinds to decline determine how much discretion assistants have in making prosecutive decisions. Pressures on assistants to secure convictions are transmitted and in part generated by the U.S. attorney himself. The most important contribution a U.S. attorney makes to the character of relations with investigative agencies in his district, however, emanates not from his interaction with field investigators, but from dealings with their administrative superiors in the various agencies. United States attorneys adopt two distinctive styles of behavior toward investigative agencies—the "manager" and the "innovator."

Most of the U.S. attorneys interviewed concentrated on managing their office's dealings with the agencies, reacting to problems as they arose, and smoothing over disagreements. "We have no problem with any of the agencies of a serious nature," observed one such U.S. attorney. "At times we will turn them down on a case and the head of the agency will come in a little angry, but it doesn't last long. We'll discuss and maybe we'll retreat and maybe we won't." "Managers" rarely take the initiative in dealings with the agencies. They primarily react to the problems that arise as the result of the agencies bringing cases to them. Some U.S. attorneys, however, aggressively seek to shape agencies' priorities and to open new lines of investigation. They not only pursue opportunities to develop significant cases that arise fortuitously, but actively seek to uncover and exploit such opportunities on their own initiative.

The field research revealed a number of factors that affect the success of an innovator's efforts to shape investigative agencies' activities. Larger offices often contain personnel with expertise in the subject matter of a complex investigation. They also have sufficient manpower to permit assignment of assistants to long-term projects. In addition, the "big" cases, best able to attract the cooperation of investigative agencies, arise primarily in large metropolitan areas served by large offices. The higher prestige and greater independence from the department and from judges enjoyed by U.S. attorneys in larger districts enhances their ability to elicit cooperation from the agencies. The administrative structure and policies of the agency with jurisdiction over a potential case also affect an innovator's success. The field offices of highly centralized agencies like the FBI cannot readily be induced to investigate a matter initiated by the U.S. attorney's office.[22] Investigations that require the cooperation of several such agencies often encounter severe obstacles stemming from interagency rivalry. When asked how he got the agencies to cooperate in joint investigations, one very aggressive U.S. attorney replied ruefully, "You have to have meetings till you are blue in the face." It takes tenacity to induce agencies to work on the big cases. The man just quoted reported spending about 75 percent of his time arranging for the investigation of such cases. Relations between agencies are so bad in some districts that cooperation between long-time rivals is virtually impossible, regardless of the efforts expended.

The political skill of an innovative U.S. attorney in devising and implementing strategies to secure investigative agency cooperation is a crucial determinant of success.[23] One strategy requiring considerable skill involves winning the confidence, friendship, and gratitude of the agency. A former U.S. attorney in one of the largest districts claimed great success with the FBI in this endeavor. "What you do when an investigative agent presents a case to a lawyer—a lawyer first of all has got to be a lawyer. He's got to say to the guy, 'Bullshit, that's no good. That's not proof. It's a lousy statement. Bring the guy in, let me talk to him.' At the same time he has to publicly support them. He has to establish a personal relationship with them. . . . He's got to give public credit to the investigative agency." To counteract the agency's emphasis on statistics, this man would "write to their boss and say this was a single prosecution and resulted in the conviction of five people. *But* here's who they were and this is what it meant to the community and here is the number of hours of your agents that we had to use and they did a phenomenal job. I'd send them the newspaper clippings, the credit that the agency got for doing it." He also facilitated the generation of statistics by getting the local police department to list the FBI as a joint investigator in stolen car cases. Finally, he developed a close personal relationship with the local special agent in charge of the FBI by being totally frank and by trying major cases himself.

The previous U.S. attorney in this district also sought to play the role of an innovator, but he enjoyed considerably less success. What he lacked in patience and sophistication in dealing with investigative agencies he made up for in aggressiveness and desire. His abrupt and abrasive personality probably precluded the development of close friendships. Rather than increasing the number of stolen car (Dyer Act) cases the FBI could claim, he reduced his office's prosecutions. Asked if this did not make the FBI unhappy, he replied, "A lot of things don't make the FBI happy. I'm concerned with prosecution, not with attention, public attention." By his own admission, aggressiveness, determination, and the resources at his command failed to win the FBI support. "I must say the Bureau—the Bureau. If it wasn't written out, spelled large, and underlined they wouldn't do it at all."

An aggressive style does not necessarily lead to frustration, even with the FBI. A U.S. attorney in an office with only about ten assistants explained how he was able to shape investigative policies.

The U.S. attorney is the ultimate decider of cases that are presented to the grand jury or filed on. And every federal agency coming into your office day in and day out wanting you to take this or that case, this or that position, they want you to file every case that they investigate. It's very important to them that they make a case. . . . And you let them know that you are going to do thus and so and tell them that there are cases that I will bring that you may or may not have worked on. If they understand that you are in charge of the office, that you will make the decision, that you will make them on a policy that you have announced yourself and they understand it, you get to this position.

But he also helped the agencies build statistics. When I asked what his policy was toward relatively minor but numerous violations like Dyer Acts, embezzlement of small amounts from banks, and minor thefts from interstate shipments, he replied: "I used those cases, I suppose, as satisfiers for the agencies that brought them. My policy was to allocate one of the older assistants to handle those cases. I wouldn't pay a damn bit of attention to them because anybody can handle them. . . . You know what their interest is. For example, you know what the FBI's interest is. Their interest is statistics. . . . So that's such a trivial thing—hell you give up on all that and bring all those cases."

## RELATIONS WITH CLIENTS
## IN CIVIL LITIGATION

Relations with federal agencies involved in civil litigation assume somewhat less significance than relations with investigative agencies, because U.S. attorneys' offices play a secondary role to the department in much civil litigation. Nevertheless, U.S. attorneys still have significant interactions with clients in civil litigation worth examining.

Because the department assumes control of civil litigation, federal agencies with civil cases depend less on U.S. attorneys. Consequently, client agencies enjoy enough freedom of action to engage in a number of practices that upset the U.S. attorney's office. They may seek to settle disputes with potential litigants before ever contacting the department. Even after court action begins, these agencies often negotiate with private attorneys and the department, by-passing the U.S. attorney. Such "end-runs" generate considerable resentment in U.S. attorneys' offices. Other sources of tension and conflict exist. United States attorneys feel that much of the civil litigation they handle results from the stubborness, stupidity, or narrow-mindedness of federal agencies. A U.S. attorney's vehement complaints about the Small Business Administration in his district provide a vivid illustration. "The SBA's procedures are very deplorable to say the least, particularly in the procedures they have for checking the security they have for their loans. And we inherit all of their errors." When an agency acquires land for a federal project, U.S. attorneys cannot settle cases litigating the purchase price without the approval of the acquiring agency. Because settlements must be paid from the agency's appropriation, it seeks to minimize payments. By refusing to offer reasonable settlements and disapproving the U.S. attorney's proposed compromises, an agency can unnecessarily force a case to trial. Agencies can also create unnecessary litigation by refusing to settle tort claims. But the role of agencies in these cases differs from land acquisition matters, because settlements are not drawn from the agency's budget. Therefore, the influence of U.S. attorneys on the outcome of these cases depends on their ability to negotiate a compromise with the opposing attorney and (if a large sum is involved) to convince the department to accept it. As described in preceeding chapters, field attorneys' superior information causes the department to accept their recommendations in most instances. Advantages accruing from superior information in other cases where client agency acquiesence in compromises is required explains much of the U.S. attorney's success in influencing the department attorneys in charge of the case.

## RELATIONS WITH PRIVATE ATTORNEYS

United States attorneys measure their success by how well they fare in court. Success depends in part on the outcome of their interaction with opposing counsel. Relatively few attorneys make up the local "federal bar." Most rank-and-file attorneys fear going to federal court and they accord the men who litigate there special prestige. Prestige also comes from the type of clients they often represent— corporations, financial institutions, and prominent private citizens— and from the status of the law firms to which they belong. Many are important members of what is loosely referred to as "the establishment," and share its dominant attitudes and interests. Some are well connected politically. Those who try jury cases are closely attuned to local attitudes as reflected in the decisions of jurors.

The federal bar has the best first-hand information about the overall performance of the U.S. attorney's office. The status of its members insures that this knowledge will be shared with influential individuals in a variety of spheres of activity in the community. Thus, the federal bar both transmits information about the office's performance to others and conveys local opinions and assessments of this performance to the U.S. attorney and his staff. Private attorneys, then, provide a crucial link between U.S. attorneys and the legal and political system in the district, as well as affect the success attained in litigation. Because the department controls all phases of civil litigation more tightly than in criminal cases, the description of U.S. attorneys' interactions with private attorneys will focus primarily on the criminal sphere.

In all but the smallest offices, only assistant U.S. attorneys routinely deal with private counsel. The U.S. attorney becomes involved only in the most important cases. The bulk of assistant–private attorney interactions occur in three circumstances. The first consists of discussions during the initial stages of a case. These discussions involve little or no negotiation. Instead, both sides seek information about the other's case and intentions. "It's a feeling type of thing." explained a criminal defense attorney when asked what he discussed with assistants in these encounters. "I go in there and say, 'Well Floyd, get your file. I'm trying to decide whether he has a defense.' ... He doesn't give anything away from the government."

Another defense attorney utilized a less direct approach during discussions.

If I wanted to try to work out something with those guys it would be a bad approach to call on them and tell them what you want. You have to just accidently run into them—this gets the best results. I make it a point to have my coffee break over there when they do so I can accidently run into them.... Sometimes, you can get some idea of what evidence they have. If you know they have something you can ask specifically for it and that's no problem. But if you don't, and perhaps even don't know what it is, you have to be very vague about the whole thing and fish around. You have to get them sitting down and talking about the case.

The second type of interaction involves explicit negotiations to reach a compromise settlement. The nature of such bargaining in criminal cases will be described at the end of this section. Finally, private and government attorneys interact before judges, both in the courtroom during trials or the hearing of motions and in chambers during pretrial conferences or other in-camera proceedings.

Interactions between assistants and private attorneys can be described on the same basis as relations with judges, investigative agents, and the department: the balance of influence; the general atmosphere (friendly—hostile); and the degree of conflict versus cooperation. Although the entire array of values is found, a dominant pattern emerges. The balance of influence is roughly equal. Neither party dominates the other. Since their cases cannot be processed without the active participation of both, a classic bargaining situation exists. Given equality in resources, the potential exists for acrimonious encounters and frequent trial after negotiations collapse. In fact, neither acrimony nor trials very often result. Assistants and private attorneys typically describe the atmosphere of their interaction as "pleasant" or "cordial," not acrimonious. Their adversary roles usually inject a degree of reserve and formality that precludes genuinely "warm" relations, like those between many assistants and investigative agents. But this reserve rarely degenerates into hostility.

Similarly, their interactions display a moderate degree of cooperation, certainly enough to permit negotiated settlements in most cases without a full trial. In fiscal year 1975, only 3.2 percent of civil cases went to trial.[24] That same year, only 11.1 percent of criminal cases disposed of involved a trial.[25] Furthermore, U.S. attorneys, as a rule, actively seek to cooperate with private counsel as a matter of policy. "The U.S. attorney should also maintain good relations with the bar," observed one U.S. attorney. "You should meet with the bar when court's in session, or on motion day, and chat with them. And you should try to help them in one way or another. This improves the feeling of the bar toward the U.S. attorney's office." United States attorneys find a number of ways to cooperate, including saving attorneys' time by improving the efficiency of scheduling techniques and calling if the start of proceedings will be delayed, helping attorneys inexperienced in federal procedures learn about federal discovery processes, interrogatories, and depositions, providing office space for private attorneys to use in the courthouse, giving them access to a telephone and the office's library, and sometimes even allowing them limited use of an office secretary. All but the largest offices visited provided such amenities and assistance.

The atmosphere of cordial formality, the even balance of influence, and the moderate cooperation that typically characterize U.S. attorney–private counsel relations flow naturally from the strategic environment within which they interact. They encounter one another as equals. Both are attorneys (and officers of the court) representing litigants. Both have the same opportunity to utilize formal legal procedures, including jury trials, in seeking favorable outcomes for their clients. Neither can call upon formal grants of authority to influence the other in the same way that judges or the department do to U.S. attorneys or U.S. attorneys do to investigative agents.

The fact that neither private nor government attorneys dominate the relationship does not mean, however, that they are totally independent. The actions of one inevitably affect the other's performance. In practice, they depend upon one another. Although they could eschew all attempts to influence each other or to maintain cordial relations and fight every case to the finish before a jury, strong incentives motivate each to try to influence the other to agree to a settlement. The behavior elicited by these incentives produces the dominant characteristics of the typical pattern of their interaction.

Research on state legal processes has firmly established the existence of powerful incentives to dispose of cases through negotiation rather than trial.[26] Attorneys practicing in the federal courts confront equally compelling reasons to settle cases. Private attorneys practicing in federal courts can no more afford to spend more time on a case then they will be compensated for than their counterparts in state criminal courts. Although federal defendants are somewhat better off financially than state defendants, relatively few can afford the fees justified by trial. Compensation schedules encourage indigents' appointed attorneys in particular to plead out their cases. In civil cases, attorneys for wealthy clients who can pay for the time spent encounter no financial incentive to settle. But those retained on a contingent fee basis find their assured cut of a negotiated settlement acquired without the effort of trial preferable to the uncertain outcome (and fee) of a verdict following trial.[27] Both sides respond to the pressure from judges to reach settlements that exists in many districts. United States attorneys face additional pressure to settle from the department, which likes high conviction rates and dockets that are current. Guilty pleas in criminal cases insure quick convictions with minimal effort and anxiety. United States attorneys under time-pressure are just as attracted by the advantages of efficient and anxiety-free settlements in civil cases as private attorneys.

United States attorneys recognize clearly the relationship between the ability to settle cases and the quality of relations with the private bar. Asked why relations with the bar were important, one replied, "If you had a closed-door policy, it would make for a bad relationship." His response to a "So what?" challenge was, "Well, you'd end up trying a lot of cases unnecessary to try." Because the opposing attorneys cannot coerce agreement on a negotiated settlement, they must rely upon persuasion. Their ability to persuade depends in large part upon their reputation. Attorneys known to be trustworthy (i.e., who will keep their word, who will not use information obtained during bargaining to pressure witnesses into changing testimony) and who possess highly respected trial ability and legal competence bargain effectively. Paradoxically, this fact creates an incentive to go to trial sometimes, if only to establish a reputation as someone who is willing to try a case and who can do so competently.

Both assistants and private attorneys rely upon their reputation to bargain successfully. But assistants have additional incentives to develop favorable reputations. "Basically they're young men," observed a former assistant. "They have their whole career ahead of them and want to start out well." Indeed, the overwhelming majority of assistants seek the position not for the inherent rewards of public service, but for the boost it can give their subsequent careers. It is an ideal position for an inexperienced and relatively unknown attorney. Assistants acquire extensive trial experience in a year that their contemporaries who go directly into private practice do not obtain for a number of years. They quickly and thoroughly become familiar with federal procedure. They learn the personality quirks and preferences of the judges and court personnel. They have numerous opportunities to demonstrate their legal prowess to the most distinguished and highly regarded members of the local bar. The visibility of their work permits them to make numerous contacts and some friendships with local attorneys.

Assistants recognize their reputation's significance for their prospects in private practice and they shape their behavior accordingly. They want to be known as competent, upstanding, knowledgeable attorneys. But they also want to be likeable, reasonable, and cooperative. A former assistant summarized succinctly the goals of most assistants when he reported he sought to cultivate a reputation as a "formidable advocate but not an S.O.B." The cooperation and cordiality that typify assistants' interactions with private attorneys reflect at least in part their eagerness to enhance their career prospects.

Incentives to demonstrate legal competence and to appear cooperative and reasonable may elicit contradictory behavior. This is an extremely sensitive area, and U.S. attorneys in particular approach it only obliquely. One U.S. attorney revealed concerns about his assistants' incentives during his explanation of why he did not resent the department's requirement that settlements in civil cases involving large sums be cleared with department attorneys. "If the [field] men are not of the highest capacity, they may be out to feather their own nest. This may not be necessarily dishonesty, but rather unconsciously dealing in too friendly a manner with defense attorneys. . . . [T]hey have an individual interest in what they will do in the future. You want to curry favor. In Washington, they're more detached."

Department attorneys show less reticence to discuss the topic. Indeed, one of their justifications for maintaining control and review over field decisions is their concern about attempts to curry favor with the private bar. Their concern extends to criminal cases as well. An assistant attorney general in charge of the Tax Division, discussing the "sensitive" nature of criminal tax prosecutions, observed that a U.S. attorney, "because he is a political appointment and therefore short term, doesn't necessarily have the vigor in some instances that one would like to see in a prosecuting officer." The validity of his concern was confirmed by his experience in prosecuting lawyers for tax fraud. "These people are usually well known in the community. On occasion I've had U.S. attorneys ask that lawyers from Washington handle these cases because they feel people will be overly sensitive to the local bar, particularly in small districts where the issue just becomes a family affair."

United States attorneys face some of the same incentives as assistants. They usually have already established a secure private practice, however, and they harbor a wider range of career ambitions. Those planning to return to private practice worry less about establishing a reputation and friendships than with maintaining and perhaps augmenting what they already have. Especially in smaller districts, interactions between the U.S. attorney and local private attorneys constitute only a small portion of an ongoing relationship of long standing. An older attorney in such a district refused to deal with assistants on any case, preferring to deal with his "good friend" the U.S. attorney. They had attended grade school, high school, college, and law school together.

The high proportion of U.S. attorneys who desire appointment to the federal bench[28] face a delicate task. They cannot afford to alienate the local bar, yet they must demonstrate legal ability and, above all, integrity and fairness. Although the specific strategies men with judicial ambitions pursue vary, all know the implications that their performance has for their prospects and shape their behavior in ways they hope will enhance their chances.

Interactions between individual pairs of assistants and private attorneys do not inevitably conform to the characteristics of the dominant pattern. The formality and reserve normally pervading the atmosphere sometimes give way to genuinely warm and friendly encounters. "You feel like you're going into the law office of some friends," observed one attorney. "They're very courteous and helpful." Personal friendships predating formal interactions apparently color the relationship. One attorney, observing that he was "good friends" with the last three U.S. attorneys, found everyone in the office "very very approachable." On the other hand, encounters are sometimes frosty. One private attorney described a U.S. attorney as "absolutely ruthless." "He wouldn't even talk to you."

The degree of cooperation and openess with respect to revealing the government's evidence in specific cases varies so much that there really is no "typical" pattern. Frequently, defense attorneys reported assistants willingly discussed cases in general terms and voluntarily revealed evidence obtainable by motion, but refused to show the actual file to opposing counsel. A U.S. attorney adhering to these guidelines described his office's practices thusly: "In criminal cases, all contact with the defendant and his counsel is at a minimum. We never talk to the defendant directly. But if the counsel has anything to discuss, we will hear him. . . . If the attorney requests, we will show them any written statement made by the defendant without them having to go to court to get it. If he made an oral admission, we will give him a summary of it. We never, however, open the file to him." A few defense attorneys indicated they received somewhat more information. One observed, "They're very cooperative in revealing their evidence. They let the defense counsel know what their evidence is. . . . They don't make you go through the motions." The attorney who claimed close friendship with three successive U.S. attorneys described an even more open policy. "Frank" discussions of what the U.S. attorney would prove and how he intended to prove it took place. Sometimes, the U.S. attorney even permitted him to look at the prosecutor's file. There were never any surprises at trial.

Several attorneys practicing in another district described a very different policy. "I've never been able to get them to tell me what their evidence is," observed one. "I find out what evidence they have when they surprise me with it on the stand." Another commented, "They hesitate to open their files on anything. You have to go into court and get a court order—that's required before they'll give me any documents."

The same variables that affect U.S. attorneys' interactions with judges, investigative agents, and the department help account for deviations from the typical pattern of interaction with private attorneys. Relations in large districts display more formality and coolness, those in the smallest districts are informal and warm. Offices that attract and hold competent assistants drive harder bargains. Where the U.S. attorney successfully imposes office policies on the extent to which evidence will be revealed, districtwide uniformities in this regard emerge. Heavy case backlogs impel both parties to seek compromises as the result of judicial pressure. The relative bargaining strength of opposing attorneys varies according to the proclivities of local juries. In regions where antigovernment sentiment is strong, convictions are more difficult to obtain and awards in civil suits against the government higher. In 1965 a number of districts still employed "blue-ribbon" juries, whose middle-class bias gave them a decidedly conviction-prone cast. This considerably strengthened an assistant's position in criminal cases.

Striking differences in private attorneys' characterizations of their relations with assistants in the same district suggest that personal characteristics and evaluations of opposing counsel operate irrespective of districtwide factors. For instance, one attorney complained that the U.S. attorney's office didn't "give you the time of day" in criminal cases. But another man in the same district found the office "open about revealing their case. . . . Here they tell you all about it. They brag." A lawyer in one of the largest districts reported "strained" relations, adding that "they are reluctant to talk to lawyers." In contrast, a colleague found "they're always willing to talk," and added that she sometimes was even shown the investigative report. She went on to suggest the origin of such differences. "There are those who deal with them day after day and they know you and get to trust you. They know you won't lie to them." A U.S. attorney confirmed the significance of opposing counsel's reputation in revealing evidence. "What you will tell him varies with the attorney. There are some that we will be quite free with information. There are others I wouldn't even tell the time of day."

A number of U.S. attorneys alter their behavior toward the opposing counsel in criminal cases, depending on whether he is retained or appointed to represent an indigent defendant, especially if (as often happens) the appointed attorney lacks experience in federal criminal cases. "If it's a court appointed attorney, we like to work with him," observed a U.S. attorney. "For instance, we'll tell him what we have—if we have a confession. I'm not that way if it's a hired attorney." The assistant's estimate of his opponent's intentions regarding trial also affect how much of the government's case he reveals. Asked how much he showed the defense, a former assistant recalled: "It depends on the particular attorney. There's no use giving him anything more than he'd be able to get anyway. Of course, there might be a man who has good sense and is thinking about pleading his client guilty. Then you might give him more information." This tactic seeks to reinforce inclinations to plea by demonstrating the strength of the government's evidence. By the same token, a defense attorney perceived as unlikely to plead his clients guilty gets little. "He might be a guy who would scrap with you all the way down the line," said an assistant. "I wouldn't tell him anything."

### Plea Bargaining in the Federal System

Vice-President Spiro Agnew's resignation and plea and the trading of testimony for reduced pleas by major figures in the Watergate scandal dramatically called plea bargaining in the federal courts to the public's attention. But plea bargaining in the federal system has attracted practically no scholarly attention.[29] The research conducted for this study did not especially emphasize plea bargaining, but I collected enough data to determine its distinctive features.

No study of U.S. attorneys' offices can ignore plea bargaining. As the second chapter argues, much of their significance rests on the number of defendants convicted and the charges upon which they are convicted. Plea bargaining produces the overwhelming proportion of federal criminal convictions. In 1975, for example, only 11 percent of criminal cases terminated went to trial; most of the rest were convictions resulting from a plea.[30]

Plea bargaining determines the character of assistants' interactions with private attorneys over criminal matters. Typically, they are either explicitly plea bargaining, engaged in preliminary maneuvering in anticipation of a possible plea, or confronting each other in trial because no bargain can be struck. Finally, the characteristic patterns of plea bargaining and the variations found in its particulars illustrate well the intimate connections between U.S. attorneys' offices and the legal, political, and social context in which they function.

Research on plea bargaining in state criminal justice systems has revealed several basic patterns, though no reliable estimates of the frequency of these patterns exist. In some jurisdictions, the plea bargains struck involve some agreement over the sentence to be imposed.

Such "sentence bargaining" sometimes involves only the prosecutor and defense counsel. They agree upon what sentence the prosecutor will recommend to the judge during sentencing, knowing that judges routinely follow such recommendations.[31] In other jurisdictions (Chicago provides one example), judges openly participate in the bargaining over the sentence.[32] The defendant normally knows before entering his plea just how much time, if any, he will have to serve. The other form of plea bargaining, by contrast, provides the defendant with no certain knowledge of what sentence the judge will impose. The bargaining conducted between defense counsel and prosecutor revolves around the number and level of charges to which the defendant will plead. The defendant offers a plea in return for a reduction in the number or seriousness of the counts charged, or both. These reductions limit the defendant's "exposure"—the maximum to which he could be sentenced.[33] Both forms of plea bargaining generally produce sentences substantially lower than the maximum that could have been imposed if the defendant had been convicted on the charges originally lodged. In fact, probation or "time served" often results from plea bargaining in the states.

Plea bargaining accounts for about the same proportion of criminal dispositions in the federal system as in most state jurisdictions. But much less variation in its content occurs. Sentence bargaining in any form is rare. In most districts I visited, respondents consistently reported absolutely no sentence bargaining took place. In a few, individual judges had the reputation of occasionally indicating what their sentence might be to a given plea. In only two districts did any sentence bargaining occur, but even in these, it was not the predominant mode of plea bargaining. Furthermore, few plea bargains in the federal courts involve reductions in the seriousness of the charges. Instead, the least significant component of state plea bargaining—reducing the number of counts—prevails. "Invariably they'll indicate that if we'll plead they'll dismiss the other counts," observed one defense attorney. "Usually, the U.S. attorney will put in as many [almost identical] counts as he can drum up." Typically, multiple charges against defendants carry roughly equivalent penalties. Thus, defendants charged with four counts of theft from an interstate shipment or five counts of forging and uttering stolen government checks will be allowed to plead to one. It is not uncommon, however, for defendants to enter a plea without obtaining any concessions whatsoever. Before the department was able to halt prosecution of joy-riding teenagers for taking a stolen car across state lines, such defendants charged with a single count often pled to that one count. I also found isolated instances of other variants of plea bargaining. Occasionally, assistants facilitate a defense attorney's efforts to "shop" for a light-sentencing judge in return for a plea. Opportunities for "shopping" are so restricted, however, that this does not comprise a significant element of bargaining. Assistants who have close relations with probation officers may offer to urge a lenient sentence. Some judges who forbid explicit recommendations do permit the government to make a statement at sentencing, and occasionally its content becomes a matter of negotiation.

Why do defendants accept the comparatively poor bargains available in federal court? They are unlikely to serve any more time if convicted of multiple counts of the same offense than if convicted upon only one, given the practice of most judges to impose concurrent rather than consecutive sentences. A few attorneys indicated they urged clients to accept them because they did not thoroughly trust some judges not to sentence consecutively. The desire of attorneys to plead out hopeless cases, especially when their client cannot afford to pay them for a full jury trial, is probably more important, however. Many defendants fail to realize that their lawyer has done little for them by getting four counts of a five-count indictment dismissed in return for a plea to the fifth. Furthermore, many defendants probably recognize their case is hopeless, making it pointless to go to trial. Finally, as in the state courts, the belief circulates that the judge may impose a harsher sentence upon those convicted after insisting on a trial.[34] "You better have a good case if you go to trial," cautioned a defense attorney, "because the sentence will be stiffer if you lose." Pleading guilty provides a small consolation for those who believe they may be avoiding the harsher penalty that a trial conviction would bring.

What accounts for the restricted nature of federal plea bargaining? To begin with, federal prosecutors handle far stronger cases than their counterparts in state courts. Careful screening of investigative agents' presentations eliminates weak cases that state prosecutors seek to get rid of by offering attractive bargains. Federal case volume remains low enough that screening mechanisms do not become overwhelmed, as happens in some state jurisdictions which seek to eliminate bad cases early. The quality of federal investigative personnel also contributes to the strength of the prosecution's case. By and large, investigations are thorough and the evidence good. The agents, particularly those from the FBI, display an impressive ability to elicit confessions that withstand court challenge. Most agents also make excellent witnesses. "Winning a criminal case in the federal courts is a very difficult proposition," complained a defense attorney. When asked why, he replied, "The jury thinks that a federal agent, especially an FBI man, is telling the truth beyond a doubt." As a result, federal prosecutors, by and large, deal from a position of considerable strength, a fact defense attorneys readily acknowledge and mildly resent. They recognize that most of their defendants are guilty and have few viable defenses.

Pressures from the strategic environment impose restrictions that may impede bargaining. State prosecutors have no superior supervisory organization analogous to the Department of Justice. As already noted, the department can review any case's handling, and dismissals of all charges require the explicit approval of a department attorney. Federal judges appear more willing to assume the responsibility of overseeing the work of the U.S. attorney's office than their state counterparts. Their disapproval of the more vigorous forms of plea bargaining makes it difficult to employ them. In addition, federal investigative agents handle fewer cases and more often become personally involved in the outcome of their cases than do local police. As a result, they possess both the incentive and information needed to monitor plea bargaining practices. It is not clear how successful agency attempts to shape bargains are. Robert Rabin's impressionistic study concludes that the extent of investigative agency participation in plea bargaining varies, but that agencies actively seeking to shape it are not very successful.[35] But prosecutor anticipations of agency reactions to overly lenient bargains undoubtedly contribute to existing stringent practices.

Several other factors restrict the concessions federal prosecutors can offer. The inability to affect sentences by making recommendations is the most significant. A defense attorney and former assistant summarized the situation well. "These judges here won't make deals. They won't even give you an indication of what the sentence will be. You have to plead blind." Although no statistics are available, it appears that the vast majority of federal judges heartily disapprove of sentence bargaining. The structure of the federal criminal code severely limits the alternatives available for "count" bargaining. There are relatively few misdemeanors. With the exception of narcotics and a few other crimes, not many "lesser included" felonies exist. In making prosecutive decisions, assistants authorize multiple counts on the same charge in part to create about the only "concessions" that can be offered to the defense during plea bargaining.

Finally, federal plea bargaining is restricted because the pressures to reduce the backlog are less compelling than those faced in more overcrowded metropolitan criminal courts. Defense attorney threats to go to trial do not normally intimidate assistants for another reason. "I couldn't care less about guilty pleas," observed a former assistant. "I like to go to trial. That's why I took the job—for the trial experience."

The striking similarity of the basic features of federal plea bargaining overwhelms in significance the differences found. Nevertheless, some variation occurs in the details of negotiations. The causes of variation, many of which have already been suggested, can be summarized briefly. In districts with conviction-prone juries, prosecutors can afford to be tougher. A prodefendant or proprosecution judge shapes negotiations in cases destined for their courtroom. Attorney perceptions of the opponent's competence are relevant. So are the specific details of the crime, the strength of the evidence, and the nature of the defendant. Indeed, nearly all of the variables identified in research on plea bargaining at the state level have some effect at the federal level.[36] The difference is that these variables exert their influence in a context which severely limits the range of variation.

## RELATIONS WITH OTHER PARTICIPANTS

### The Grand Jury

"The grand jury is pretty much a creature of the prosecutor—at least if the prosecutor handles it right," observed a U.S. attorney. "He's their legal advisor, and it's very difficult for them to disagree with him." This conclusion typifies the view of most respondents that I interviewed who dealt with grand juries. Although this domination grows naturally from the prosecutor's relationship to the grand jury, some U.S. attorneys reported that they took special care to cultivate a good relationship. "Grand jurors expect the United States attorney to attend. And if he didn't show up, it might indicate to them that they weren't very important. And they're very very important."

Most U.S. attorneys do not attach such great importance to grand juries, but they do acknowledge that they can be useful. Cases with weak evidence that are likely to go to trial can be tested out in the grand jury. "The grand jury is important because it's a dress rehearsal in two respects for the case. First, you can see the demeanor of witnesses before them. The other thing is you can see the reaction of the grand jury to the case. It's a pretty good indication of how the petit jury will react." A grand jury can supplement routine investigative techniques. "When people are brought before the grand jury, they are more likely to tell the truth," a federal prosecutor told me. "You can get information from a grand jury that an investigation can't get." It can also assist the U.S. attorney in dealing with other participants in the federal legal process. "To a large extent it is a tool in your hands.

You can frequently use a grand jury to get off the hook. The DJ might tell you to go ahead and prosecute. So you bring the indictment. You present it and get a No Bill. You say, 'See? I told you so. I can't control the grand jury.'" U.S. attorneys explained the subtle techniques employed in using the grand jury in this fashion. "I would never tell them not to indict. But I control the amount of evidence presented and how it's presented. And when setting up the case, of course, you emphasize all the weaknesses and none of the strengths of the case . . . no grand jury was ever in any doubt as to my position on any case."

Pressure from investigative agencies can also be deflected by the grand jury. If the agency demands prosecution, the U.S. attorney can agree to present the case to the grand jury knowing it will be turned down. Finally, some U.S. attorneys utilized evidence gathered from grand jury testimony to pressure into action investigative agencies initially reluctant to undertake an investigation.

When U.S. attorneys mobilize the grand jury to take the blame for a decision not to proceed with a case, they rarely fool either the department or the investigative agency involved, but there is little either can do about it. The department can dispatch one of its attorneys to present the case again, but limited manpower restricts its ability to do so, and there is no guarantee that the grand jurors will not recognize the case as one that "their" U.S. attorney previously indicated he wished dismissed and proceed to vote a second No True Bill.

### The Press

United States attorneys' offices rarely confront aggressive newspaper reporters. The men and women who cover the federal courts typically also cover other beats. They are relatively passive, relying upon information provided by the office. Often the office provides the only information available about a case until some public court proceeding occurs. Federal investigative agencies typically are stingier than local police in providing information. Department of Justice regulations specify the type of information that U.S. attorneys can provide. Though not always adhered to, these regulations effectively restrict what can be revealed. Essentially, U.S. attorneys can provide facts available in public records—the names and addresses of defendants, their ages and occupations, and the charges filed. The nature of the evidence, the details of the crime, the existence of statements or confessions, and assessments of the strength of the case or probable guilt of the accused may not be discussed.

Within the constraints established by these factors, U.S. attorneys display several noteworthy differences in their relations with the press.[37] Many attach little importance to the press. Their answers to my questions about press relations were perfunctory, suggested that they have not thought much about the topic, and described little contact with reporters beyond routine inquiries about important cases. By contrast, some U.S. attorneys regard the press as very important. Many of the dimensions of their concerns are illustrated by the following spontaneous observations of a former U.S. attorney.

[A U.S. attorney] owes it to the government, as a client, to maintain friendly relations with the press media. By that I mean not just the press, but radio and TV as well. Frequently, we had to do some pretty fast footwork with the press. If you don't have respect for your office among the people, then it's a bad situation. It's a matter of personal self-interest. One of the things about being U.S. attorney is, because you're before the people, you get known and you get respect. This is one of the reasons for taking the job. Also, you owe it to the government and the court, when a case has an interest, to see that the public gets everything it's entitled to. And in the most favorable light.

Most who stress the importance of publicity of their office's work mention its value in helping to deter crime. "If relations with the press are good," commented one, "you always get good press coverage in cases. This is good so far as the deterrence aspect is concerned." Building "good will" toward the office is also thought to be worthwhile, though the specific advantages that result are rarely mentioned. Publicity is also seen as a resource for attracting and rewarding assistants. "I try to get the assistants as much publicity as I can. If they're not going to make any money, the least I can try to do is to get them a little reputation." The boost in the U.S. attorney's own reputation and public recognition is also important, particularly to men who aspire to elective office.

Establishing good relations with reporters helps attain the goals just described, but it can also help avoid embarrassing or damaging publicity. The fear of criticism or looking bad powerfully motivates some. "It's human nature. You hate like hell to see your name in the newspaper in some bad connection. You keep thinking, 'How would it affect the kids? How would they take it?'" Easing the task of reporters and providing them with good information can reduce the chances of getting adverse publicity. One U.S. attorney, complimenting himself on his office's good relations with the working press, explained his success.

I talk to eight to ten of the media people every day, on a routine call. We make life easy for them instead of coming in and making them scramble. . . . (T)he average guy that comes in here is working on time limits and is inadequately prepared on the facts of the story he is supposed to get. He really doesn't know what to do to make his story a little different from the four guys who are standing right next to him. And if you give him some help on some of these things, you build a good relationship.

It can also make possible frank explanations of what is happening without fear of embarrassment. A U.S. attorney provided a specific example.

We have a case of a man, indicted for fraud, who's seventy-eight years old. You don't want to broadcast the fact that he's sick. Suppose he's faking. Then he'll get up and say that you're full of shit, and that he's ready to go to trial the next day. Then you'll have a lot of controversy over it and you'll have to explain to the press. But if you have good relations with the press, and explain the situation to them, then they don't put you in that position. What they would do, they would check with the fellow, however, to see if he was sick. They have checked.

United States attorneys pursue several different strategies in dealing with the press. Some, like an older U.S. attorney who accepted the post only after being pressured by the local bar, displayed little interest in cultivating such relations. "Actually, there isn't much contact with the press. Generally, they call us rather than we calling them. On civil cases, tax trials, the Department of Revenue will handle the case. They should handle it. Publicity has a deterrent effect, and they've worked with the case more and know just what they want to deter." His precedessor revealed a different story. "I took more of an interest in public relations. I thought it was important that the public think the government's legal work is in good hands. In order to do that, you have to get that information out to the press." Another difference found in policy is whether the U.S. attorney requires all press contact to be funnelled through him. Men who seek to restrict contact with the press and those who want to maximize their own exposure centralize press contacts. Others permit assistants to talk to the press on the cases they handle.

It would be extremely difficult to measure the impact publicity has on public attitudes toward the office in particular or federal law enforcement in general. Likewise, the deterrent value of publicity about convictions is almost impossible to assess. Even if we could determine the effect that a U.S. attorney's policies toward the press had on the amount and content of publicity, its impact on public opinion and crime rates would remain unknown. But we do know that some U.S. attorneys calculate the impact of newspaper publicity on proposed actions. It is also clear that the office has considerable potential for placing its occupant in the public eye. Those men with career ambitions who desire it and have the skill to obtain it often succeed well in establishing themselves as local celebrities. A Nixon appointee who was selected to run for statewide office directly from the U.S. attorney's office illustrates this point nicely. He deliberately sought to increase his visibility by speaking wherever he could in the community. He noted that while under his predecessor the press had to seek out members of the U.S. attorney's office, he had no hesitation in calling a press conference. The importance he attached to press relations is suggested by the time he spent on it. "I think we administered the office and had it set up right. I was in a position to spend three or four days doing nothing but dealing with the press on some of those big cases, which is important." At one point he was on national TV for several nights in a row discussing one case. His exposure undoubtedly increased his attractiveness as a potential candidate.

# CHAPTER 9

# U.S. Attorneys in the Political and Legal Systems

United States attorneys occupy a crucial position in the web of politics and policy making. In this final chapter, I will summarize the findings of the previous chapters by focusing on the links between U.S. attorneys and the political system generally. The chapter concludes with some impressionistic evaluations of U.S. attorneys' performance and various proposals for reform.

## THE STRATEGIC POSITION OF U.S. ATTORNEYS

Decision-makers in the legal process inevitably engage in making policy through the exercise of discretion in areas where professional "legal" criteria provide no clear guidelines. The elements of the strategic environment of U.S. attorneys described in the foregoing chapters, however, provide them with unusual opportunities to affect the course of public policy. As attorneys, they begin with a potent resource—the expertise that their legal training provides and the deference this recognized expertise creates in the minds of many people with whom U.S. attorneys interact. The recruitment process provides them with a number of additional resources. Men able to win the support that obtaining an appointment requires generally come to office with a thorough knowledge of the local community and personal contacts with many of its political and social leaders. They owe their appointment only in part to the department. The combination of independent bases of political support in the district, locally focused career ambitions, and the ability to leave office and establish quickly a successful private practice produce an outlook that generally precludes complete loyalty to the department.

The organizational structure of the department and the tasks it assigns to U.S. attorneys also contribute to the strategic environment. The department relies heavily on its large field staff to handle most federal litigation. The intricate tasks required in litigating cases insure that the individual actually handling a case must make a number of significant discretionary decisions. These decisions matter because they affect citizens' freedom, reputation, wealth, and legal rights. Furthermore, the various divisions and sections within the department divide responsibility for overseeing the operation of U.S. attorneys' offices, and coordination among the department's various components is difficult to achieve. The department's control suffers from its inability to transfer U.S. attorneys or assistants to another district or to headquarters, and from the difficulties entailed in removing a U.S. attorney.

The fact that U.S. attorneys serve as generalists who deal with a variety of specialists also constitutes a significant component of their strategic environment. The various divisions and sections within the department find that the U.S. attorney handles many other matters besides those in their field of expertise. Similarly, the specialized federal investigative and administrative agencies compete with each other for the limited resources of the U.S. attorney. Thus, U.S. attorneys perform the critical function of balancing demands from a variety of sources. The complexity of U.S. attorneys' strategic environment enhances their ability to balance these competing demands. With the exception of districts or branch offices which must deal with a single judge, U.S. attorneys do not depend excessively on any single actor. The department's divisions and sections, various investigative agencies, a variety of governmental agencies, bureaus and departments with civil litigation, judges, politicians, and the local bar, among others, all seek to influence the operation of a U.S. attorney's office.

These factors in the strategic environment combine to afford U.S. attorneys and their assistants substantial discretion. It would be difficult for anyone to exercise tight control over the performance of a task as complex as litigation. The complexity of the strategic environment and the lack of excessive dependence upon any of its components assures a measure of independence and provides them opportunities to maneuver. United States attorneys come to office with maturity, experience in both the practice of law and politics, and practical knowledge of what employment by government entails. Their independence is enhanced by the knowledge that they can, in most instances, leave their position to engage successfully in the private practice of law. Many are buoyed by the anticipation of further governmental service on the bench or some other position of importance, and (as the data reported in Appendix B show) a significant proportion find their hopes fulfilled.

## PATTERNS OF INTERACTION: A SUMMARY

Earlier chapters analyzed relationships between U.S. attorneys and a series of other significant positions they encounter. What generalizations can be made about U.S. attorneys' interactions with the entire range of significant others that their strategic environment produces? Put another way, how much autonomy do U.S. attorneys enjoy? For purposes of this discussion, autonomy refers to the ability to choose between significant alternatives without incurring severe sanctions. To the extent that significant "others" influence U.S. attorneys and constrain their choices, they lack autonomy.

Table 9.1 attempts to summarize the general pattern of autonomy and control by identifying four basic patterns of interaction and assessing the balance of the U.S. attorneys' autonomy and control in each with the major significant "others." The balance struck between complete autonomy and complete control is represented by a scale from one to five. A one indicates that the U.S. attorney dominates the relationship, influences far more than he is influenced. A five signifies domination by the other party. The total score in the right-hand column of Table 9.1 conveys my general assessment of the overall autonomy enjoyed by U.S. attorneys. If they uniformly dominated others and exercised complete autonomy, the score would be five. A score of twenty would signify complete lack of autonomy. Of course, these scores are not precise measures, but rather impressionistic evaluations. They range between eight and fourteen and a half. The obvious conclusion emerging from Table 9.1, and from the research in general, is that U.S. attorneys' offices fall somewhere between complete autonomy and complete control. Even the most autono-

Table 9.1. Schematic Representation of U.S. Attorneys' Patterns of Influence with Major Counterpositions

| Pattern | Counterposition | | | | |
|---|---|---|---|---|---|
| | Judges | Department of Justice | Investigative agents | Defense counsel | Total |
| Bounded autonomy | 3 | 2 | 1 | 2 | 8 |
| Normal | 3.5 | 3.5 | 2 | 3 | 12 |
| Judge-dominated | 5 | 3.5 | 3 | 3.5 | 14.5 |
| Department-dominated | 3 | 5 | 3 | 3.5 | 14.5 |

1 = U.S. attorney domination of mutual influence
5 = Counterposition domination of mutual influence

mous office is constrained by the intricate web woven by its status in a larger organization (the department), by its patterns of dependence on other key positions, and by the political and social values of its personnel. The picture of unbridled prosecutorial discretion conveyed by much of the prior research and writing on prosecutors is misleading.[1] On the other hand, even the least autonomous offices confront their personnel with a substantial and unavoidable degree of autonomy greater than that of most governmental decision-makers.

Table 9.1 also suggests significant variation exists in the relationships U.S. attorneys' offices establish with the major counterpositions, producing the four patterns indicated. Bounded-autonomy districts exhibit the most autonomy, judge- and department-dominated patterns the least. The relative influence exerted by each of the four counterpositions also differs. Judges are most important in judge-dominated districts, and the department in department-dominated districts. In both, investigative agents exert more influence over U.S. attorneys than in either of the remaining two patterns. In the normal pattern, the department and judges have equal influence. The influence of each counterposition is diminished in the bounded autonomy pattern, but judges remain relatively more important.

### The Importance of District Size

What accounts for the differences in the patterns of interaction summarized in Table 9.1? Although a number of factors (many of which will be discussed below) play a role, the size of the office is probably the most important. Larger offices tend to fall into the bounded-autonomy pattern; the smallest are more likely to be dominated by judges or the department. Size does not absolutely determine the pattern, of course. Small offices sometimes conform to the "normal" pattern; medium-sized offices become dominated by judges or the department, and even may approach bounded autonomy. Likewise, some large offices display the characteristics of the "normal" pattern.

Just what is it about larger offices that causes these differences? The previous chapters have presented in piecemeal fashion a number of the characteristics of offices associated with size. The following paragraphs summarize these characteristics.

The larger the office, the more differentiated its internal organization. United States attorneys in small offices supervise and consult with their assistants directly. Larger offices have several supervisory levels. The Southern District of New York, for example, has three tiers of supervisory personnel under the U.S. attorney. The first consists of the chief assistant, the administrative assistant, and the executive assistant; the second, the chiefs of the criminal and civil divisions; and the third the chiefs of the various sections within the criminal and civil divisions.

The larger the office, the more centralized decision-making is likely to be. For instance, in larger offices, one or two assistants review and make prosecutive decisions on all criminal cases. Smaller offices often rely upon haphazard and informal procedures. Sometimes, anyone in the office can authorize or decline prosecution on any case. As a result, investigative agents can more often "shop" for an assistant who will authorize prosecution, producing considerably less consistency on what is prosecuted.

The larger the office, the more time the U.S. attorney devotes to purely administrative duties and the less he devotes to actual litigation. In a two- or three-man office, the U.S. attorney, by necessity, must assume a significant portion of the caseload. United States attorneys in the largest offices as a rule appear in court only on rare occasions or not at all.

As a result, the larger the office, the less similarity there is between the activities of the U.S. attorney and his assistant. In small offices, U.S. attorneys do most of the things their assistants do—deal directly with investigative agents and defense attorneys on routine criminal cases, appear before the judges and juries, communicate with lower level department career attorneys. In large offices, the U.S. attorney rarely does any of these things.

The larger the office, the more flexibility the U.S. attorney has in managing its work. With just two or three men in an office, it is practically impossible to free a man to work on a time-consuming investigation, regardless of its potential. The never-ending struggle to keep up with the cases routinely referred to the office severely limits the ability to respond to unusual opportunities or initiate innovative policies.

The larger the office, the higher the prestige of the U.S. attorney. The mere fact that he presides over a large number of assistants enhances his status in the department. The importance of the cases that his office handles as a result of its location in a major metropolitan area reinforces the office's stature. The news media in large cities also provide wider exposure of the U.S. attorney's activities. As the number of judges increases, the uniqueness of the U.S. attorney rises, and the ability of the judges to coordinate their efforts to influence his office declines. The political support a U.S. attorney may enjoy from large city mayors counts more with the attorney general or the president than that of elected officials from cities served by small U.S.

attorneys' offices. The legal ability of assistants attracted from the larger pool of attorneys in metropolitan areas by the prospect of trying important cases provides the U.S. attorney with a powerful argument in disputes with the department over whether his office can handle important cases.

### Time, Location, and Personality

Although office size exerts the strongest influence over the patterns of interaction that U.S. attorneys develop with other significant positions, it shares its influence with several other variables. I have presented most of them earlier and will only summarize them briefly here. Offices display considerable variation over time. As the U.S. attorney and his assistants gain experience, they learn to exercise somewhat greater independence. The initial advantage the department enjoys at the outset of an administration begins to erode as the years pass. United States attorneys fortunate enough to have the personal support of a powerful senator can display a boldness and independence that less fortunate colleagues cannot. Location affects patterns in several ways. The potent political support some U.S. attorneys in metropolitan areas can win from local political officials has already been mentioned. Some districts enjoy a tradition of autonomy that assists new U.S. attorneys in preserving it through the sharing of information and the providing of support when disputes with others arise. Some variation associated with distinctive regions of the country also exists. Parts of the West, the rural Midwest, and most of the South display a distrust of Washington that tends to instill distrust of the department and to promote the formation of alliances among members of the local federal court community to thwart the department's efforts at control. Finally, two characteristics of U.S. attorneys' personalities and outlook shape interaction patterns. First, the aggressiveness and interpersonal skills possessed affect the ability to win autonomy. Some are aggressive, bold, and imaginative; others, timid, and cautious. The second characteristic is highly correlated with the first. Aggressive U.S. attorneys appear frequently to believe that they ought to play a major role in shaping the actions of their office. They feel that they ought to share decision-making with the department and resist domination by others. The attitudes of more timid men toward the U.S. attorney's role exhibit a corresponding modesty. They are likely to regard themselves as employees of the department and partners with investigative agencies and judges.

The multiple and complex causes of variation in patterns of interaction make estimates of the frequency of the various patterns difficult.

The distribution of U.S. attorneys' offices among the four patterns changes over the life of an administration, and thus depends in part on when a measurement is taken. Furthermore, individual districts can change substantially, regardless of an administration's age, when one or more of the major personalities involved (the U.S. attorney or a judge in a small district) changes. Undoubtedly, the "normal" pattern appears most frequently, but the field research suggests that all four patterns can be found.[2]

## U.S. ATTORNEYS IN THE POLICY PROCESS

The discretion, resources, and motivations U.S. attorneys' strategic environment provides create significant opportunities for them to shape the content of public policy. The discussion that follows describes the structure and content of these opportunities and the factors that determine when they are exploited.

### The Minimum Unavoidable Impact of U.S. Attorneys

Regardless of their personality, values or the size of their office, all U.S. attorneys inevitably encounter situations in which the decisions they must make affect policy. These decisions produce what I term their minimum unavoidable impact. The outlines of this impact have already been described in some detail in Chapter 2 and, consequently, will only be summarized briefly in the following paragraphs.

The process of enforcing federal criminal statutes provides a number of occasions requiring decisions that shape policy. Federal investigative agencies bring the cases they develop to the office for prosecutive decisions. Inevitably, the decisions made determine who will be prosecuted, on what specific charges, and with what result. The quality of justice that prosecuted defendants receive depends on how the U.S. attorney's office handles the case. When U.S. attorneys pass up opportunities to initiate investigations or establish no explicit policies on what to prosecute, the default decision to do nothing can have a profound effect. If a U.S. attorney adopts no policies on which marginal cases should be prosecuted, or if he makes no attempt to direct the energies of investigative agencies, then in effect he delegates such decisions to assistant U.S. attorneys and the investigative agencies themselves. Like it or not, the U.S. attorney determines whether there will be a conscious focus to federal law enforcement in his district. Thus, the effect on who gest indicted, tried, fined, acquitted, and imprisoned is both inevitable and profound.

Although less leeway exists in civil cases, every U.S. attorney chooses how to handle them. The quality of the government's courtroom presentation, and ultimately its success in civil cases, depends on the skill and diligence of his office. Whether cases are easily compromised in settlement (and for what amounts) depends largely on what the U.S. attorney's personnel do. In turn, this helps shape the policies of federal agencies that lead to the need for court action. Finally, he determines the vigor and harshness with which his staff pursues collection cases. Thus, as in the criminal area, the overall quality of justice depends upon the choices U.S. attorneys and assistants make.

United States attorneys also help shape the content of department policy, but the nature of their response to established policies and directives is even more significant. It is not merely a question of whether they will seek to implement policies faithfully and skillfully, although there are instances in which they do not. Even loyal and conscientious U.S. attorneys must make decisions in the ambiguous situations that inevitably arise in implementing policy. In so doing, they help determine the content of the policy. Finally, regardless of whether a U.S. attorney explicitly attempts to mold the images of federal law enforcement and the federal government generally through public speeches and publicity, the routine activities of his office necessarily affect them.

Taken together, the inevitable minimum impact the ninety-four U.S. attorneys' offices have is indeed formidable. The nature of the position guarantees that any incumbent, no matter how lethargic and unimaginative he is, will necessarily profoundly affect his district. He may not recognize his impact, nor may the choices he makes explicitly take into account what the impact will be. But for many of the significant decisions made in the federal legal process, U.S. attorneys have at least as much (and sometimes considerably more) to do with their outcomes as any other position.

## The Potential Impact of U.S. Attorneys

United States attorneys typically encounter opportunities to exert an influence on policy that extends considerably beyond their minimum unavoidable impact. They often possess an intimate knowledge of their district, a knowledge that permits them to pursue investigations and prosecutions far more effectively than strangers dispatched from Washington. Local prosecutors, of course, typically know their jurisdictions just as well. But U.S. attorneys enjoy more independence from local political forces than state prosecutors. Crucial support often comes from a U.S. senator, an individual with a statewide constituency. The U.S. attorney avoids entanglement with local political interests that state prosecutors who have successfully won nomination and election experience. He also enjoys greater career flexibility. He can more easily afford to undertake controversial and unpopular actions because he can return to his own law firm or because he anticipates an offer from a firm that depends upon clients with federal legal problems. Such firms enjoy a degree of insulation from local political forces. Furthermore, the federal judgeship many U.S. attorneys covet requires support from the department, the federal bench, the senators, and the "establishment" bar, a group that often admires an individual who displays the independence and integrity that bringing meaningful cases requires.

United States attorneys also possess the resources to exploit such opportunities successfully. First, they can call upon the support and resources of the Department of Justice. Local prosecutors enjoy no such support from another organization. Second, federal investigative agencies offer the U.S. attorney outstanding investigators whose Washington headquarters enjoy substantial immunity from local pressures that community police departments do not. United States attorneys' strategic advantages in dealing with federal investigative agencies help them to obtain their active cooperation in pursuing investigations. Third, U.S. attorneys enjoy substantially greater prestige than most local prosecutors. They preside over a jurisdiction which contains a number of local prosecutors. They are presidential appointees. If they choose, they can obtain considerable exposure in the mass media. Finally, they present significant cases to judges who are more insulated from local politics than their brethren on state courts.

### The Role of the Personal Characteristics of U.S. Attorneys

What determines whether a U.S. attorney exploits the potential for having a significant impact beyond what every individual who exercises the powers of the office enjoys? To some extent, circumstances play a part. Some U.S. attorneys encounter attractive opportunities through no efforts of their own. A U.S. attorney who instituted far reaching prosecutions of individuals promoting fraudulent creditor life insurance schemes found extensive investigative files when he took office. The investigative groundwork had already been completed. Sometimes U.S. attorneys confront a crisis in their office that forces them to alter fundamentally the organization of the office. In one district, the new U.S. attorney found the office in chaos. Few assistants from the previous administration remained, and the case backlog reached such proportions that drastic action had to be taken. Sometimes, big cases fall into a U.S. attorney's lap. Fruitful prosecution of political corruption requires that such corruption actually exists.

Most U.S. attorneys, however, encounter opportunities to take significant initiatives even if fortuitous circumstances do not arise to make them obvious. Yet many men lack the personal characteristics that enable them to exploit their office's potential. The two characteristics identified previously as shaping the pattern of interaction between a U.S. attorney and his environment—aggressiveness and interpersonal skills, and the conception of the position's prerogatives—also determine the impact he has. Men of intelligence, competence, and energy who recognize their office's potential and possess the motivation required to exploit it can transform a lethargic office into a dynamic one. Several such transformations were described to me by respondents who had observed offices under successive U.S. attorneys. In one instance, an official in the Civil Division of the department described the first U.S. attorney as "perhaps a well meaning man. But every time he was thrown the ball he fumbled it." His division avoided bringing cases in the district if possible. Under his successor, however, the division actively sought opportunities to bring cases there.

Often, energetic, dynamic U.S. attorneys make their own opportunities to have a significant impact. One U.S. attorney's efforts to attack water pollution in the local harbor illustrate what developing such opportunities entails. A report by two of his assistants, prepared at his request, revealed that the office played practically no role in the field at all. He determined that he would move against major polluters in the harbor under an 1899 statute forbidding the dumping of wastes in navigable waters. No one, including state and federal water quality control officers, even knew who the major polluters were. A series of meetings finally resulted in a joint program involving the Army Corps of Engineers and federal and state water quality control officers to locate and gather evidence against major polluters. A graduate student in sanitary engineering was hired to interpret the laboratory reports on effluent samples. At the time he was interviewed, a special grand jury had just been empanelled to hear the evidence that had been gathered.

The choices such innovative activists make on what to emphasize are doubly significant because they preclude their doing other things. An activist in a large district observed that he never really pursued criminal tax investigations against wealthy taxpayers. When asked why he did not try to get more investigation in this area he replied: "Because we had a volume of cases. We were working mostly to try to develop our organized crime cases." His successor confirmed this emphasis and by implication illustrated some of the opportunity costs paid by his predecessor. "I think there is a real temptation in a major city to just be popular and just go on organized crime. Without question, in my judgment, there was too much of that attitude when I took office. So I did go against, for instance, school segregation in [a local community] and we went against [a local union] for discrimination in employment and we went against the . . . real estate board for discrimination in housing and selling."

## U.S. ATTORNEYS IN THE POLITICAL PROCESS

### *"Pressures," Constituencies, and Representation*

In their study of federal district courts, Richardson and Vines observe that, "Although the representative functions of courts have rarely been recognized in legal theory, the linkage between political officials and the territory they service is not just a legislative function."[3] Legal theory also fails to recognize the representative functions of attorneys who appear in court on behalf of and give legal advice to governments. Public attorneys' discretionary powers inevitably permit them to shape public policy independently of the dictates of "law." Consequently, representation of popular values in making these policy decisions plays a legitimate role in a democratic society.

The representative functions performed by U.S. attorneys provide a fascinating, important, and difficult area of study. They perform this function while paying lip service to the widespread myth that they engage solely in professional legal activities. They belong to a national administration and carry out policies established by the president and his attorney general, who represent a national constituency. But they also represent their locality, and the interests and policy preferences of important segments of the local community sometimes conflict sharply with those of the national administration. Senators and representatives lack an explicit tie to the national constituency that the presidential appointment brings to U.S. attorneys.

The three chapters describing U.S. attorneys' relations with the Department of Justice examine in detail the mechanisms that link national policies to behavior in the field. Some of the links between elements in a U.S. attorney's local constituency and his behavior have also been examined (the press, the local bar, and federal judges). The following paragraphs, however, examine the relationship between a U.S. attorney and his district's preferences in more detail. Two broad mechanisms translate district preferences into policy. First, U.S. attorneys may act in accord with the values and interests of the constituency because they share those values and interests and automatically select a course of action compatible with the constituency's preference. Second, both direct and indirect pressures from the district affect their behavior.

The description of the appointment process and the characteristics of the men selected by it in Chapter 3 demonstrate that U.S. attorneys possess a thorough knowledge of their area and come from the dominant social and political stratum. They are well-connected, middle-aged, politically active members of the establishment. Their participation in the life of the community, a participation that continues after working hours and on week-ends and which will continue in the years after they leave the U.S. attorney's office, practically guarantees that if the dominant political stratum agrees on a policy issue, the U.S. attorney will share these views. Thus, most southern U.S. attorneys shared the distaste of whites in their districts for school desegregation and other policies designed to eliminate racial segregation. Usually, this first mechanism of representation does not provide guidance to a U.S. attorney on what to do in specific situations. The constituency typically possesses little information about or interest in the overwhelming majority of decisions made. Rather, it predisposes the U.S. attorney to view general questions in a way similar to his constituents. If most people in a district think marijuana constitutes a serious threat, marijuana prosecutions will be brought that U.S. attorneys in areas with a more lenient public attitude refuse to bring. If people regard "moonshiners" as eccentric characters engaging in a relatively harmless pastime, federal prosecutors will treat most infractions leniently.

The "pressures" directed toward U.S. attorneys and assistants from their districts almost always seek to influence decisions in a specific case. Their analysis and description present particular difficulties. The word "pressure" has acquired a negative connotation, and lingering beliefs about the sanctified and neutral nature of "law" regard "pressures" that interfere with its neutral administration as especially pernicious. Consequently, participants in the legal process find it difficult to recognize, analyze, and discuss how such pressures shape their behavior. The discussion of constituency pressures that follows makes no value judgments about them. It recognizes that a number of factors shape discretionary decisions made by U.S. attorneys, including communication of preferences from groups and individuals within the district. Some of these pressures clearly are not legitimate, but others are entirely appropriate in a democratic society.

The role pressures play in the representation process defies complete analysis. Whether a communication received about an impending decision assumes the status of "pressure" depends upon the recipient's reaction to the message. We can measure and analyze the content of overt communication, but we cannot ascertain whether it constitutes "pressure" in the sense that behavior is modified as a result. Nor can we examine the content of the decision itself, because decisions have multiple causes, making the assessment of the impact pressures play a matter of speculation. Even the self-assessments of those subjected to pressure provide imperfect evidence. People often fail to understand the sources of their own behavior. Furthermore, they more often report their successful attempts to resist pressure than the instances when they capitulate, especially if they think the capitulation may have been improper. The description and analysis of the pressures U.S. attorneys report, therefore, provides only an incomplete and imperfect picture of their nature and their impact.

When I explained to the men I interviewed that by pressures, I was referring to communications of all kinds that they received about matters in their office, including those that might shape their decisions, a number acknowledged their existence. "There are so many kinds of pressures," a U.S. attorney told me. "I mean, from the two-bit attorney who says, 'Just remember you will be on the outside some day and you will need a favor,' to somebody calling you up and just, you know, 'I don't want to interfere but I've heard this and it disturbs me. What is the picture on this?' You get calls from Washington, from a Congressman, and even a judge. There are a lot of pressures from people seeking to influence your decisions and a great deal of it is appropriate and proper."

Nearly everyone agrees that overt attempts to affect decisions by threats or bribes are improper. Harold Chase uncovered an example during his research on the appointment of federal judges. A U.S. attorney reported that the opposing counsel in a case he was trying promised to block the U.S. attorney's well-known ambition to obtain a judgeship. The opposing lawyer, who was being "roughed up" during the trial, formerly served as a member of the American Bar Association's judicial selection committee.[4] A department official related a similar incident in which a U.S. attorney received a phone call in his presence. The U.S. attorney reported that the call came from an important individual in his political party's state organization, who told him that if an indictment was returned against a major political figure, he would never realize his ambition to become a federal judge. Like most visible law enforcement officials, U.S. attorneys occasionally receive physical threats to themselves and their families. Southern U.S. attorneys in particular received harassing phone calls and veiled threats during desegregation crises. Men actively prosecuting organized crime cases also report such threats.

The question is not whether such blatant threats are ever made or bribes ever offered, but how often and with what success. No reliable way of measuring their frequency has been devised. Few discuss the topic readily, especially when the tactic has succeeded. If U.S. attorneys receive bribes and threats often, however, no evidence exists. Few U.S. attorneys have been prosecuted for official wrongdoing, though some have been fired for alleged improprieties.[5] United States attorneys with experience in state courts frequently contrasted the pressures encountered there with what they experienced at the federal level. "It was like a breath of fresh air when I came into the job, a breath of fresh air," observed one such man. "I sat on the city courts. There were all kinds of things that disturbed me going on." Furthermore, many U.S. attorneys volunteered that they had received no such pressure from those who would be expected to exert it. A southern U.S. attorney, pointing to the pictures of both his senators on his office wall, observed that he was friends with both, and particularly good friends with one. "In the years I've been here, I have never never received a call from the senators about a case. They've never asked me to rule any particular way, never presented opinions on how I should rule." Similarly, U.S. attorneys frequently recalled cases where one might expect intervention but none was forthcoming, such as a collection case against a U.S. congressman or prosecution of a state judge for income tax evasion. Finally, enough independent participants in the federal legal process exist who would detect either the transmission of such threats or acquiescence to them to make such activities risky—other members of the office staff, judges and their clerks, members of the federal bar, department attorneys reviewing the case, and investigative agents.

Most attempts to influence U.S. attorneys' decisions involve far less questionable practices than making threats or offering bribes. Frequently, private parties express an interest in cases involving a matter of principle which affects them. One U.S. attorney who began prosecuting small embezzlements from local banks found himself subject to subtle pressures from acquaintances in the banking industry, primarily in the form of disapproving remarks made in passing at the country club or in restaurants. Sometimes, groups seek to encourage the prosecution of certain types of cases. A spokesman for the Music

Publishers Protective Association in one district, for example, publicly praised the office's indictment of the publisher of a music "fake-book." Banks like fraud prosecutions in bad check cases to facilitate restitution. Oil companies like such prosecutions in stolen credit card cases. The pressures such interests exert are subtle. They offer public and private praise when a U.S. attorney undertakes favored prose-cutions, and repeatedly complain about violations and inquire about what is being done and why when he does not.

Often, however, individuals with a direct and personal stake in a case's outcome contact the U.S. attorney's office. They come "out of the blue" from friends and relatives of victims. They are, in the words of one U.S. attorney, "more nuisance calls than anything else," and "half of them are from people you know very casually. Then, all of a sudden, they think they know you very well." Of course, U.S. attor-neys know many people in the community, and their intervention cannot be so easily ignored. A U.S. attorney in a small southern dis-trict described the circumstances under which such contacts occurred. "For instance, suppose there was a cashier that worked for the bank for twenty-five years and was a thousand dollars short, and I asked the FBI to investigate. Well, he has a lot of contacts and friends over the years. And these people will call up and say, 'I don't know whether this person did what you're accusing him of or not. But he's been laboring under some difficulties lately. He's a fine person, and he did it under an emotional strain. Anything you can do for him why, I'd appreciate it very much.' This may be a grocer or some other promi-nent person."

Some contacts with U.S. attorneys about cases come from important politicians and even judges. For example, a U.S. attorney had a com-plicated case involving the failure of a furniture factory which had been financed by a Small Business Administration loan. "We got a call from the senator's assistant saying that he thought the contractor who did the building [for the furniture plant] had an equity in it and he ought to be paid." The southern U.S. attorney, who proudly pointed to the pictures of his two senators adorning his office wall, added the following comment almost as an afterthought to his vigorous assertion that he never received pressure: "Occasionally, I'll get a request from them on the facts in a case so that they can reply intelligently to requests for information I have." This theme was echoed by several other respondents. Observed one U.S. attorney: "I was a very close friend of the Democratic [state] chairman, and I never got any pres-sure from him. Sometimes he'd ask me what an indictment was about. He would call me up. But there was absolutely no threat and no question of anything improper on his part. He just wanted to know what was going on." Unlike bribes, threats, and pleas for leniency or harshness, such communications may not overtly request a particular outcome. Nevertheless, they can affect decisions. Most U.S. attorneys are astute enough to detect whether there is an underlying interest in the decision's outcome behind a request for information. They may not ultimately alter their decision, but the process they use to reach it may well involve calculations about what the reaction to the decision will be.

Because many U.S. attorneys know the local political community so well, they may feel pressure even if no one communicates with them at all. For instance, if a U.S. attorney is likely to be influenced by a senator's or a mayor's interest in a matter, he is usually also likely to be aware of this interest and will act in conformity with it without having to be asked. The modification of behavior in anticipation of community reaction is not confined, however, to avoiding offending political sponsors. Broader political considerations shape decisions because of intimate knowledge of the community. A Republican U.S. attorney in a large northern city provided an example of such pressures. "We had to indict a very prominent black militant here and there were some pressures that came to us not to indict him for a number of reasons. The indictment cost us some—I don't want to say support. I'm not in a position of needing or not needing support. But that's the kind of thing that you lose some friends maybe in the black community when you do." Later, when asked about the nature of preindictment pressures on this case, he revealed the role of anticipations of adverse reactions. "The preindictment stage wasn't, as I remember it, in the nature of phone calls or anything of that nature. The preindictment stage came somewhat—it was pressure based upon what we knew the community and newspaper reaction would be. It was pressure that grew out of knowing you were about to make a controversial decision."

In the foregoing example, recognition of such pressures did not alter the decision to prosecute, though it may have affected its timing. But I encountered other instances where U.S. attorneys modified their behavior in anticipation of adverse community reactions. An assistant in a large northern district had a matter pending which, if actively pursued, would have closed a hospital that served a large black neighborhood in the district. The office had refrained from initiating action for years. A veteran assistant in another district explained that they withheld news of the indictment of the local county supervisor's associates until after the supervisor's scheduled appearance on the same platform with Vice-President Agnew. For years, the department handled all civil rights cases in the South from Washington in the belief that local U.S. attorneys would either be unsympathetic or subjected to intense pressure. I uncovered ample evidence to indicate southern U.S. attorneys' sensitivity to the race issue. In fact, one refused to participate in the study until I convinced him that the research was not directed toward the handling of civil rights. A colleague in a neighboring district provided additional confirmation. "Regardless of whether they tell you this or not, every U.S. attorney in the South—and they might not tell you this—but they all have to weigh everything that may cause racial trouble. You don't want racial trouble. You want to have peace between the races."

The role of newspapers and newspaper coverage in cases plays an important part in anticipating community reactions. A U.S. attorney in a city with an alert, aggressive, and nationally known paper revealed his concern as follows: "A factor in my judgment on the case would be the possible publicity. It's not the *determining* factor, nor should it be. But all of us are human beings, and we hate like hell to be blasted in the newspapers. The newspapers are sometimes prompting us to push harder. They might just needle us a bit."

Not all pressures emanate from the larger political community. Some can stem directly from within the relatively small confines of the federal legal community. "I wouldn't overlook the fact that the judge was older than I was and that he had a lot of friends that were attorneys whom he'd known for a long time," commented a U.S. attorney in a two-judge district. "These people are friends of the judge's. They see him socially. . . . And when they were defending someone, I would realize that while they might be found guilty, the judge would exercise some clemency. That couldn't help but affect the whole case. I would be more inclined to arrange to have the fellow enter a plea."

Anticipation of what relations with opposing counsel and potential clients might be like after leaving office provides another source of such pressure on U.S. attorneys. The assertions of some department attorneys that U.S. attorneys frequently go easy on local attorneys who will affect their subsequent private practice are probably exaggerated. But their fears are not entirely groundless. "If you conduct yourself honorably and fairly, you meet a lot of people," observed a former U.S. attorney. "I represent now a group that was on the opposite side when I was a U.S. attorney. And I handled their case very fairly and managed to work out a settlement favorable to them and favorable to the government."

### The Impact of Pressures: An Assessment

"Pressures" broadly defined clearly have a significant impact on the behavior of U.S. attorneys. But it would be a mistake to assume that the federal legal process is riddled with the intrusion of illegitimate

political considerations. Several conclusions emerge from the impressionistic data gathered on the impact of such pressure. The vast
majority of cases involve routine matters that generate few if any
significant pressures. Cases that arouse the interest of politically significant individuals and interests occur infrequently. Even in circumstances where one would expect pressure to be exerted, it often is not.
A former U.S. attorney recalled his conversation with his political
sponsor (one of the most powerful politicians in the country) shortly
after he assumed office. "He chuckled, 'You know, when you got a job
like that, you got to get your orders from the boss.' And I said, uh oh,
now I'm going to learn. And he said, 'I got three orders for you. Be
true to the court, be true to the law, and most important, be true to
the [respondant's name] that I know.' And that was it. In all the time I
was in here, he never interfered, never said a word, anything like
that." That is evidently not an isolated phenomenon. Senators, local
politicians, even some defendants, believe it would be improper to try
to influence a U.S. attorney's decisions directly. Certainly, attempts to
influence decisions occur far less frequently than in most state court
systems.

No one is totally immune to pressures, and U.S. attorneys are no
exception. Politically appointed men who harbor ambitions that require the support of others for realization cannot ignore how others
will react to their decisions. As long-term residents of their community, they cannot isolate themselves completely from their acquaintances. At a minimum, this gives the prominent and well-connected
an opportunity to be heard that others do not enjoy, as the comments
of a former U.S. attorney suggest. "My approach there is when you
meet with friends, your friends in a sense get more time to be heard.
Access. You are courteous to your friends and you listen." Furthermore, they belong to the Department of Justice, which itself receives pressure which can be effectively transmitted to the field.

When U.S. attorneys encounter direct and overt pressures, however, the results are not predictable. Different sources of pressure
may request conflicting outcomes. A prosecution unpopular in the
district may be welcomed by the department and the investigative
agency. Restraints on the U.S. attorney's discretion limit opportunities
to succumb to pressure. Some U.S. attorneys refuse to be affected.
"It's just not in my makeup," said a U.S. attorney who described how
he reacted when defense attorneys would tell him what fine Democrats their clients were. "Oh, maybe if you had some petty politician in
the job, maybe it would have some influence. But not for me." The
application of pressure can also backfire. A southern U.S. attorney
related what happened when a prominent businessman and civic

leader had committed a technical violation: "He had a lot of friends, and a lot of people called me. If I hadn't had all those calls, I probably wouldn't have filed the case. . . . If I hadn't prosecuted it, then I think they would have all felt that talking to me had done some good." Even the prior reputation of some U.S. attorneys may deter attempts to influence them that otherwise might be forthcoming. An individual in a community known for the prevalence of political intervention at the local level attributed the lack of pressure to just such a reputation. "When I first started to do that public work, I went through all that bullshit. 'You know who I am' bullshit. And I'd tell them, you know, forget it, get out of here. So it was over with."

Finally, some U.S. attorneys are stubborn and principled, and they proceed with cases that they know will generate tremendous pressures and ruin their subsequent careers. The most striking example I encountered involved a U.S. attorney in the South whose office became heavily involved in civil rights litigation. "I had a job to do. It wasn't a tough decision. I got my assistants together and told them if they had any moral misgivings to get out right now. We've got to stand together on this. You've got to take the pressure and now is the time to get out. And they all stuck by me." The formidable pressure included heavy attacks in the newspapers and the state legislature. The federal judgeship coveted by the U.S. attorney never materialized, and in his first year back in private practice he reported he earned only $3,000.

Of course, sometimes pressures affect decisions. Undoubtedly, some men become U.S. attorneys who would be classified as "petty politicians." The clearest example was provided by a man who served as U.S. attorney in the Truman administration. Referring to the office of U.S. attorney, he observed, "What you have is a political set-up. You get favors done because you've been getting favors done through politics since the beginning of the country." He went on to describe in general terms how defendants in federal cases could bring extraneous matters to the federal attorney's old law firm and pay a fat fee. His Republican successor clearly implied his predecessor allowed political considerations to affect decisions. "For any normal man, a Democrat or Republican, politics is only a means of getting the appointment. It doesn't play a role in the administration of the office. But apparently it did under him, because the Democrats seemed to be surprised when I came in that they were treated courteously, surprised that they received fair treatment." It is not likely that there are many such clear-cut examples. Rather, many men are probably "petty" at some times and not at others.

Assessing the impact that pressure generated by a U.S. attorney's own anticipated reactions in the absence of overt communication from others presents insurmountable problems. Undoubtedly, politically astute men who owe their appointment and allegiance to an influential individual shape their decisions on their own initiative with no communication whatsoever. Sometimes such decisions even attain some visibility.[6] But low-visibility discretionary decisions (are an office's energies directed toward organized crime or corruption among the mayor's close associates?) affected by such considerations normally cannot be detected. Hence reliable estimates of their frequency cannot be made.

Partisan considerations and pressures emerge most often in cases involving prominent individuals and matters that affect the political fortunes of officials and political parties. As indicated, routine cases stimulate little overt direct pressure and require no modification of behavior in anticipation of adverse reactions. But cases involving the prominent give everyone pause, and it makes little difference if the decision-maker is a U.S. attorney or career bureaucrat in Washington. A U.S. attorney who prosecuted prominent local union officials described the prosecution as one that was "very very risky." As a lifelong Democrat, he knew the case would generate considerable pressure. If he lost the case, some would accuse him of deliberately throwing it and criticize him for not bringing in someone else with more trial experience. Thus, even when prosecution is undertaken in such cases, it is only done after careful calculation of the costs and consultation with others. Prosecutors scrutinize the strength of the evidence with special care, since a vigorous defense can be predicted and public examination and questioning of motives is likely. Such calculations also increase the time it takes to make a decision. Although prominent members of the president's party do not enjoy immunity from prosecution, these factors do often discourage prosecution in some cases and delay it in others. Many U.S. attorneys exhibit an understandable reluctance to undertake the prosecution of cases with political overtones, especially when the individuals belong to their own party. But officials of the department may be no less reluctant. Furthermore, some U.S. attorneys display courageous enthusiasm for prosecuting prominent law violators, regardless of party. Their knowledge of the local community, its jurors, and the judges enhances their ability to pursue such prosecutions effectively.

## PERFORMANCE AND REFORM: AN ASSESSMENT

Most attempts to evaluate the work of public policy makers (legislators, bureaucrats, judges) encounter serious problems. Systematic assessments require operationalizing what "good" performance consists of and well-designed and executed field research. The evaluation of the performance of U.S. attorneys presents problems equal to those arising when assessing other decision-makers. This research, moreover, was designed to provide information about the impact of U.S. attorneys on policy and the dynamics of their interaction with other positions in the federal legal process, not to evaluate their performance. Consequently, I cannot provide definitive or authoritative assessments of U.S. attorneys. My research, nevertheless, provided opportunities to form some judgments. Since others will evaluate U.S. attorneys regardless of the quality of the information upon which their judgment rests, and since proposals for reform based on alleged shortcomings will continue to be made, I shall conclude this book with a few thoughts on the topic.

The criteria for evaluating several aspects of U.S. attorneys' and assistants' performance generate little controversy. These include: their personal integrity and ability to resist rendering decisions on the basis of illegal payments, personal friendships, or narrow partisan considerations; their ability to administer their offices and handle their work efficiently; and their legal competence in representing the government's interests. But other criteria of performance produce less consensus. For instance, some believe U.S. attorneys can be evaluated by how faithfully they carry out the department's policies and directives to produce uniformity throughout the country in legal policy. However, others reasonably argue that the local variation in federal legal policy introduced by the actions of semiautonomous U.S. attorneys representing local values produces the flexibility that our federal political structure requires. Similarly, some value vigorous prosecution to control crime and protect the interests of society; others stress the importance of insuring that the federal criminal process adheres strictly to the requirements of due process. Finally, some argue that U.S. attorneys should play an active role in shaping the priorities of federal law enforcement, even to the point of initiating significant prosecutions. Others, however, feel that U.S. attorneys ought to play a more passive role, relying upon federal investigative agencies and the Department of Justice to establish priorities.

If U.S. attorneys frequently take bribes, succumb to partisan pressures, or conduct personal vendettas, my research did not uncover it. No major scandals involving U.S. attorneys have attracted the attention of the news media in the past decade. Some officials in the Department of Justice, particularly in the Johnson administration, alleged that U.S. attorneys too often let personal and partisan political considerations shape their behavior, deferring to the wishes of senators and friends and improperly accommodating opposing counsel in anticipation of future employment. However, I doubt that these officials discovered many provable, flagrant instances of such behavior. Given their desire to change the appointment process, they probably would have utilized such evidence in a strategy to win approval for their desired reforms. While the frequency of such occurrences cannot be measured accurately, useful comparisons can be made with state courts. Without exception, respondents familiar with both state courts and the federal district court reported the standards of conduct of federal prosecutors surpassed what they knew occurred at the state level.

United States attorneys' administrative capabilities vary widely. The selection process rarely operates to select men who display administrative ability. Consequently, some districts experience administrative difficulties, from the management of the office's work to the selection of assistants.

The most serious problems arise in the quality of legal representation provided. Criticisms from department personnel lack credibility. They have a vested interest in reserving the handling of important and interesting cases for their own staff attorneys. Furthermore, they acquire information about the handling of a biased sample of cases tried by field personnel. They naturally remember those cases that ended in disaster and required their intervention at a later stage. Judges and private attorneys, however, possess better information. A few districts, especially those in large metropolitan areas, received high ratings from the bench and the private bar. In most districts I visited, however, both judges and the private bar felt that the government suffered from poor representation too often. The problem lay not so much in the innate incompetence of assistants, but rather in their inexperience. The quality of representation suffers especially during the severe manpower shortages that often occur when the incumbent administration faces defeat and the new personnel either have not been appointed or lack any experience.

The chapters describing relations with the Department of Justice demonstrate that U.S. attorneys sometimes fail to implement Washington's wishes. Particularly after an administration begins to age, the field offices' responsiveness to departmental directives falls short of that enjoyed by most federal headquarters agencies. However, the department succeeds in prevailing on those matters of policy that it considers most important. The balance between central control and local autonomy faithfully reflects the diversity of American society and the federal nature of its governmental structure. This blending of national policy with local and regional values does not run counter to the fundamental principles of the American political system.

Evaluating the balance struck between effective law enforcement and the principles embodied in the notion of due process presents an especially challenging task. We remain ignorant of the relationship between law enforcement in general and crime, and we lack reliable measures of crime. Hence, we do not really know whether federal law enforcement is effective or not. How much respect for the notion of due process exists? Again, comparisons with the state courts provide about the only reliable guide. In general, federal prosecutors (and investigative agents) appear to be more dispassionate, restrained, and respectful of defendants' rights than their counterparts on the state level.

Finally, to what extent do U.S. attorneys realize their potential to shape the direction of federal law enforcement and to affect the policies of agencies requiring representation in civil litigation? For a variety of reasons, including relatively small staffs, domination by judges or the department, and the lack of personal initiative and interpersonal skills, many U.S. attorneys fail to lead their offices much beyond the routine processing of the litigation that comes to them as a matter of course. Only a minority, perhaps a small minority, seize the opportunities available to them to take significant initiatives. However, whether this is a strength or weakness depends on whether or not one believes in a forceful, activist stance on the part of government.

Most of the proposals for reform come from officials of the Department of Justice and seek to enhance their ability to control the field offices. They argue that if the attorney general could hire and fire U.S. attorneys, and that if assistants belonged to a career service permitting their transfer to any district or to Washington, problems of incompetence and susceptibility to pressures generated by political contacts and career ambitions would diminish or disappear. Proponents of such reforms, however, rarely examine the possible disadvantages of these measures. Clearly, they would increase the control departmental officials wield over the field office, but no guarantees that this power will not be used improperly can be built into reform proposals. As U.S. attorneys like to point out, the department's top personnel also receive their jobs through political appointment. A highly centralized department conceivably could be used more effectively to implement a uniform policy of violating defendants' rights or prosecuting cases against political enemies. The fact that Republican U.S. attorneys indicted former Attorney General John Mitchell, Vice-President Spiro Agnew, and the Republican chairman in New Jersey illustrates that the current decentralization of the department insulates its branch offices from potential political pressures as well as reduces the capacity for implementing uniform policy. The basic weakness underlying such reforms lies in the fact that no scheme for choosing either U.S. attorneys or department officials can change the fact that many of the decisions made have political ramifications, both for who gets what generally in society and for the political fortunes of party officials.

Nor will placing U.S. attorneys and assistants on a career civil service basis guarantee increased competence and nonpartisanship. Even civil service systems can be subverted by a determined administration, as some reports of the Nixon administration's abuses of civil service procedures suggest. The prospect of a legal career in the government's service, complete with frequent moves from one jurisdiction to another, will not consistently attract attorneys of great courage, vigor, and intelligence. Few members of the legal profession travel from jurisdiction to jurisdiction. And while many of the career attorneys I interviewed displayed remarkable dedication, intelligence, and (as best I could judge) competence, I doubt if the entire contingent of some 1,600 or so attorneys staffing the field offices would uniformly exhibit these characteristics if put on a career basis. It is difficult to attract outstanding attorneys and hold them in a career service while simultaneously weeding out the mediocre.

An attorney general determined to recruit outstanding U.S. attorneys can largely succeed in most districts. Department officials can easily blame "the senators" for poor appointments. But the department appears to be the single most important participant in the appointment process. Though it must defer to the choices of powerful senators in a few districts, it can succeed in attracting good attorneys if it chooses to emphasize intelligence and legal competence over political credentials. The department could encourage the assistance of others, particularly the organized bar, in eliminating men with good political credentials but questionable legal skills or reputations. Delegating the choice of a U.S. attorney to bar associations through a merit selection plan presents problems of its own, for it permits bar association politics to enter into the selection process. But the department could ask the bar to evaluate the candidates who emerge from its negotiations with senators. This would preserve the presidential appointment feature of the current selection process, a feature that accounts for much of the ability of U.S. attorneys to resist domination by the department and gives them the resources to become innovative and effective policy makers.

The government's representation suffers during the interregnum between administrations. Establishing a small corps of career assistants, limited to 20 percent or less of the authorized assistants in each district, would do much to alleviate this problem. A rigorous selection procedure for choosing career assistants could reduce the likelihood that the position would be used as a retirement post for men who cannot succeed in private practice. If these posts could go to the handful of men of integrity and competence who enthusiastically seek the U.S. attorney's office as a lifeswork, such individuals would provide a strong basis for insuring continuity and adequate representation when the political appointees left the office at the end of an administration.

By far the single most serious problem I discovered rests in the inexperience of assistant U.S. attorneys. The work provides enough valuable experience, excitement, and prestige to attract people of ability initially, but the pay is not high enough to keep them much past the time when they feel they have gained the experience that caused them to seek the job. Although some department officials lament the fact that the U.S. attorney's office serves as a "training ground" for young attorneys, in fact this might be one of the useful functions it performs, particularly in light of recent criticisms leveled at the quality of the trial bar. Eliminating assistant U.S. attorneyships would reduce the opportunities for young attorneys to obtain extensive federal trial experience.

Ironically, the most effective reform for improving U.S. attorneys' offices also appears to be one of the easiest to implement. It takes about two years for an assistant to gain the experience necessary to begin to realize his potential as a litigator. The department could improve the quality of representation by taking steps to increase the time assistants stay in office to four or five years. Requiring aspirants for the job to sign a pledge to stay at least four years might help somewhat, but structuring financial incentives to encourage their staying probably would be more effective. Salaries for first-year assistants should be kept at about their current levels in relation to salaries for comparable positions in private practice, with modest increases in the second year. In the third and fourth years, however, substantial monthly increases should be awarded. A lump sum termination payment that increases in size with every month served past three years for a maximum of five years also could be added to an incentive plan. The improvement in the quality of representation that longer tenure would bring would be well worth the additional cost.

Finally, several things can be done to promote the likelihood that U.S. attorneys, relying upon their knowledge of their districts, will become vigorous, innovative shapers of policy. First, they need to learn early in their tenure about the potentials of their office and their ability to exercise some independence from Washington. Second, those involved in the appointment process may seek out aggressive individuals if they better understand the office's potential. Third, the department can continue the recent practice of assigning investigative personnel directly to the U.S. attorney's office. Lastly, the department can continue to assign additional manpower to the field rather than headquarters, providing U.S. attorneys with the manpower and flexibility required to act vigorously. These steps will enhance the probability that U.S. attorneys will continue to play a crucial role in the shaping of public policy in the federal legal system.

# APPENDIX A

# Methodology

This appendix summarizes the history and methodology of the research upon which this study is based. I conducted the initial data-gathering in 1965 as part of my disseration work. A second wave of interviews were obtained in 1970 and 1971.

I embarked upon the topic initially at the suggestion of Herbert Kaufman, then in the political science department at Yale University. He believed instructive comparisons could be made between the organization of the Justice Department, with its semiautonomous field offices, and the Forest Service. I soon discovered that practically nothing had been written about U.S. attorneys. The elementary information about them required before their relations with headquarters could be compared with Forest Rangers simply did not exist. However, my preliminary inquiries indicated that U.S. attorneys had a significant impact on federal legal policy and that they offered an attractive opportunity to observe the politics of headquarters–field relationships. This led me to shift the focus of the research to a broad, exploratory study that would provide the background needed for subsequent research on specific aspects of U.S. attorneys' behavior and impact. The proposed study formed the basis for my successful application for a Dissertation Fellowship from the Woodrow Wilson Foundation, permitting me to proceed with the research design.

In developing a research design, I immediately encountered what Robert Dahl has aptly termed the "dilemma of rigor vs. relevance." His comments are instructive: "Attempts to meet high standards of logical rigor or empirical verification have produced some intriguing experiments and a good deal of effort to clarify concepts and logical relationships but not rounded and well verified explanations of complex political systems in the world. Conversely, attempts to arrive at a better understanding of the more concrete phenomena of political life and institutions often sacrifice a good deal of rigor and logic of verification so as to provide more useful and reliable guides to the real world."[1] The lack of hard information on U.S. attorneys, coupled with a preliminary indication that the position was an important and

213

interesting one, caused me to emphasize providing a useful and reliable guide to the real world.

The absence of significant published research forced me to move directly to preliminary field research in the U.S. attorney's office in Connecticut. The U.S. attorney there provided access to the office's operations. I read case files, talked to assistant U.S. attorneys and secretaries, and observed assistants' interactions with investigative agents. In addition, I began interviewing investigative agents, judges and their clerks, and former members of the U.S. attorney's office. I ultimately conducted interviews with nearly a dozen individuals with different perspectives and knowledge of the office's operation. These interviews, coupled with direct observations, provided the opportunity to develop, pretest, and revise my interview guides.

The pretest experience resulted in a number of important changes and strategic choices. First, I soon learned that strict reliance on role theory as a guide to the questions asked worked poorly. The time spent inquiring about mutual perceptions of what counterpositions ought to do could be better spent asking respondents directly about what they did, why they did it, and what impact it had. In addition to obtaining a general picture of each respondent's formal duties, the final interview schedule sought to determine what calculations influenced their behavior.

Second, the pretest interviews revealed the pitfalls of rigidly adhering to an interview schedule that asked all respondents the same questions in the same order. Not all respondents were knowledgeable in all areas. For instance, some assistants handle no criminal cases; of those who do, some have extensive contact with a number of investigative agencies, while others deal with only one. The amount of contact with the Department of Justice varies similarly. Thus, it would have been pointless to ask each assistant about relations with all investigative agencies and the Department of Justice. However, I asked the same questions to all respondents who knew something about an area of inquiry. It proved useful in building rapport and generating a smooth development of the interview to alter the sequence in which topics were covered, depending upon the assignment and principal activities of the respondent. The interview guides (see the two examples reproduced below) provided both a check-list of topics to cover as well as a check-list of questions to ask within each topic. These techniques, developed during the pretest stage, permitted thorough coverage of relevant topics with respondents while enhancing rapport, even though not all respondents could answer questions about all the topics covered in the interview guide.

Third, I found taping the interviews directly undesirable. I broached topics that most respondents considered sensitive, and it seemed best to minimize inhibiting factors. Pretest interviews suggested that tape recording hindered the rapid development of rapport. Consequently, I took notes during the interviews and read them into a tape recorder as soon as practicable. When this proved impossible, I sought to expand my notes from the interview immediately. With practice, it became possible to reconstruct the interviews with a high degree of precision. A typist transcribed the taped reports of the interviews onto note cards. In a few instances, I typed the interviews directly onto note cards from the shorthand notes.

Although role theory proved a poor guide to constructing interview guides, it did suggest who to interview. The pretest district demonstrated the value of interviewing incumbents of the "focal position" (U.S. attorneys and assistants) and the major "counterpositions" (judges, private attorneys, investigative agents, Department of Justice personnel, and probation officers). Occasionally, other participants, such as court clerks and newspaper reporters, provided useful background information. This meant that six interview guides had to be developed and pretested before interviewing in the field could begin. In addition, separate questions had to be devised for Department of Justice personnel. Two of the guides, one for U.S. attorneys and former U.S. attorneys, the other for investigative agents, are reproduced at the end of this appendix.

Some districts had to be eliminated from consideration for the field research due to their physical location (Guam, the Canal Zone, Puerto Rico, the Virgin Islands, Alaska, and Hawaii). The District of Columbia office prosecutes crimes that state district attorneys handle elsewhere and is fundamentally different from the other districts, and it too was eliminated. Limitations of time and travel money made it impracticable to draw a random sample of the eighty-six remaining districts in the continental United States, but a purposive sampling technique designed to maximize variation along the dimensions of size of office (measured by the number of assistants), caseload, region, population size, racial composition, per capita income, urbanization, and party strength produced a sample that permitted the research to be conducted and still provided a good representation of all eighty-six districts. Thirteen of the districts were visited in the summer of 1965; the fourteenth, the Southern District of New York, was studied in the fall of that year.

The characteristics of these fourteen districts can readily be matched to those of the eighty-six districts in the continental United States on three important dimensions: office size, caseload per assistant, and region. The results of this comparison are presented in

Table A.1. Despite the small size of the sample, it appears to conform to the universe of eighty-six districts rather closely. Considerable variation among the fourteen districts on the other dimensions (population, party competition, and so forth) was obtained.[2]

The field research consumed thirteen weeks of the summer of 1965. One week was allotted for each district, with weekends used for travel to the next district. My wife, a first-year student at Yale Law School with an undergraduate honors degree in political science from Oberlin College, conducted the interviews with federal judges and private attorneys.

Prior to beginning the field interviews, I had written the U.S. attorney in each of the districts selected, enclosing a letter from the Department of Justice authorizing cooperation. All cooperated, granting interviews and permitting free access to their assistants.

Interviews with judges, private attorneys, postal inspectors, probation officers, and occasionally newspaper reporters and agents from other investigative agencies were arranged after arriving in the district. As many former U.S. attorneys and judges as possible were interviewed in each district. In smaller districts, there often was only

Table A.1.  Comparison of 14 Districts Studied in 1965 with 86 Districts in the Continental U.S.[a]

|  | *Sample of 14* *(%)* | *86 Districts* *(%)* |
|---|---|---|
| Office size:[b] |  |  |
| 4.0 or fewer AUSAs | 43 | 45 |
| 4.1 to 8.0 AUSAs | 43 | 40 |
| 8.1 or more AUSAs | 14 | 15 |
| Caseload per AUSA:[c] |  |  |
| less than 100/AUSA | 21 | 13 |
| 100.1 to 150/AUSA | 29 | 35 |
| 150.1 to 200/AUSA | 21 | 20 |
| 200.1 or more/AUSA | 29 | 32 |
| Region of office's location: |  |  |
| South (Confederacy) | 29 | 30 |
| Border | 14 | 14 |
| East | 14 | 16 |
| Mid-West | 29 | 23 |
| West | 14 | 16 |

[a]The District of Columbia office has been excluded. See text.

[b]These figures are calculated from data in The United States Department of Justice, *Annual Report of the Attorney General of the United States for the Fiscal Year ended June 30, 1963* (U.S. Government Printing Office, Washington, D.C.), Table IX, col. 1, "Average Number of Assistant U.S. Attorneys," pp. 95–96.

[c]*Annual Report of the Attorney General,* pp. 95–96.

one probation officer and one available postal inspector. Since there was time to interview only one individual in each of these positions, no set sampling procedure was used in larger districts. However, I sought interviews with rank-and-file probation officers and postal inspectors rather than their supervisors. A number of techniques for choosing the private attorneys interviewed had to be adopted. Often suggestions were received from members of the U.S. attorney's office, judges or their clerks, or the clerk of the court. In several districts, it was possible to examine the docket book to locate those men who most frequently opposed the government. The interviews with members of the U.S. attorney's office and federal judges in the Southern District of New York were conducted in the fall. I interviewed in Washington, D.C. both prior to and following the summer field research. The total number of individuals in each position, including the pretest, who were interviewed appears in Table A.2.

The fundamental reconceptualization of the 1965 data that preceded the writing of this book suggested that I needed to conduct additional research in two crucial areas: the impact of U.S. attorneys' offices on who gets what, and the relationship between U.S. attorneys and administrative personnel in the department. Consequently, more narrowly focused interviews concentrating on these matters were conducted in late 1970 and early 1971. This stage of the project was funded by a Ford Foundation Faculty Fellowship.

I spoke with sixteen current and former members of the Department of Justice: two deputy attorneys general or attorneys general, five assistant attorneys general, a chief assistant to an assistant attorney general, three men in the Executive Office for U.S. Attorneys, and five career or former career attorneys. Of the twelve men with a clear party identification among this group, six served in Lyndon Johnson's administration and six in Richard Nixon's. I interviewed

Table A.2. Number of Individuals Interviewed in Each Position in 1965

| | | |
|---|---|---|
| U.S. attorneys | 14 | |
| Former U.S. attorneys | 20 | |
| AUSAs and former AUSAs | 58 | |
| U.S. district judges | 17 | |
| Private attorneys | 37 | |
| Probation officers | 12 | |
| Justice Department officials | 13 | |
| Postal inspectors | 11 | |
| Other investigative agents | 4 | (1 FBI, 1 ex-narcotics, |
| Miscellaneous | 6 | 2 Alcohol–tobacco tax) |
| Total respondents interviewed | 192 | |

nineteen men who had served in U.S. attorneys' offices. Six were incumbent Republican U.S. attorneys and six were Democrats who served under Johnson. Four of the Democrats had been interviewed in 1965. I conducted these interviews in four districts included in the 1965 sample plus a new district. Seven assistant U.S. attorneys agreed to be interviewed, five of them in the Southern District of New York.

Exploratory research such as this cannot utilize systematic techniques of data analysis that studies of voting behavior, public opinion, or class mobility do. In this respect, this work resembles a number of recent studies exploring the operation of the legal process.[3] The analysis of such data presents the researcher with a number of troublesome challenges. However, it is not true that analysis of quantitative empirical data is a "science," while qualitative data is merely an "art." Anyone who has worked extensively with quantitative data knows that its analysis is also in large part an art. In fact, in many respects, substantial similarities emerge in the process of analyzing both kinds of data. The primary difference lies in the precision with which hypotheses can be tested. Exploratory studies such as this generate such hypotheses and provide what Dahl refers to as "useful and reliable guides," but they do not test such hypotheses rigorously.

Although the intensive, lengthy, and complex procedures used to analyze the data gathered for this study cannot be described easily, something of the flavor of the analysis can be conveyed by relating briefly the techniques used to analyze the 192 interviews obtained in 1965. The interviews filled over 3,500 five-by-seven-inch note cards. I read each of these cards a number of times. All interviews from a given district read at one sitting helped uncover patterns of interaction within the district. It also permitted comparisons with patterns in other districts. Another technique utilized was to read all interviews with respondents occupying the same position regardless of district. After determining an outline of the points to be analyzed, a color coded scheme of gummed tabs was used to index the individual note cards. Thus, all cards with a black tab contained information about U.S. attorney relations with private attorneys. Finally, summaries of the principal points contained in each interview with a U.S. attorney or assistant on a number of topics were entered in a notebook. This permitted a quick method of reviewing what each U.S. attorney and assistant had said about the degree of autonomy he had from the department.

# Interview Guide for U.S. Attorneys

Ø & EX-Ø*

*Introduction*

1. One of the areas I'm quite interested in concerns the differences from district to district in just how the Ø handles his job. Perhaps we could start by discussing the activities and areas that you personally handle (handled) as U.S. attorney.

> Probe: How do (did) you spend your time?
> supervision
> handling own cases
> hearing I.A.† reports
> handling relations with press, defense attorneys, Department of Justice

2. What do you consider the primary functions and obligations of a Ø in executing his office to be?

> (*If nec.*) Well, what sorts of things should he try to see are done in his district, and in what sorts of ways?
> Anything else?

3. A somewhat similar question is: In what ways can a Ø affect the patterns and practices in the federal legal process, from investigation through sentencing?

> (*If nec.*) Well, how can the Ø's actions and policies influence the way in which the federal legal machinery operates in his district?
> Anything else?

> (*If not mentioned*): How about influencing the areas in which investigative resources are concentrated?

---

*Ø = U.S. attorney
†Investigative Agents

Are there any other ways in which the Ø can have an impact on his district? I'm thinking of all sorts of areas, not necessarily just the field of federal law enforcement.

> e.g., local police practices; areas of investigation

4. Perhaps we could turn now to the quality and nature of your working relationships with some of the individuals you frequently come (came) into contact with as Ø.
Suppose we start with the investigative agents. Could you tell me a little about the nature of your relationship with them?

5. Which agencies do (did) you have the most satisfactory relationship with?
Why is (was) that?

6. With which agencies do (did) you have the least satisfactory relationship?
Why is (was) that?
Could you elaborate a little (give an example or two)?

7. Do you think the investigative agents are prosecution-minded? Does this vary between agencies? Between agents from the same agency? Both? Examples?

8. Does (did) the attitude and enthusiasm of an agent vary according to how good a case he is presenting, or are the presentations straightforward; *or* does it depend on the agency involved? How?

9. When you are (were) dealing with an investigative agent, who is (was) in charge of what areas? This is, what are (were) his responsibilities and what are (were) yours?

How do (did) you depend on him?
What does (did) he depend on you for?

10. Could you tell me a little about the nature of the working relationship that develops (developed) with agents whom you see (saw) often?

Are (were) you on a first name basis with many of them?
Do (did) you ask some of them for their frank, down-the-line assessment of a case?
(*If yes*) How much confidence do you have in their opinions?

11. Do (did) you find that conflict and rivalry among the investigative agencies affects (affected) the way you conduct (conducted) your office?

12. I know that an investigative agency will occasionally appeal a negative prosecutive opinion either to their superiors or to the Justice Department. What has been (was) your experience in this area?

(*If yes*) What sorts of cases? What was the outcome? Could you give an example?

13. Let's turn to the judges in this district. How would you characterize your relationship with them overall?
In what ways do (did) your relationship with them vary from one judge to another?

14. How important is it for a ∅ to have a good working relationship with the judges in his district?

15. What can a ∅ do to maintain good relations with the judges? What sorts of things should he avoid doing to maintain good relations?

16. How can a judge assist or harm the ∅'s efforts to represent the government?
How can the judge make the ∅'s work easier? Harder?

17. How often do (did) you see the various judges outside of the courtroom?
On what occasions? What sorts of things did you discuss? [*quote page if necessary*]

18. Do (did) you find that the attitudes and preferences of the judges, both spoken and unspoken, affect (affected) the way you conduct (conducted) the government's business in this district? How?

19. I've found that in some districts it is often possible to know which judge will hear which case. Is (was) that true in this district?

(*If yes*) Do (did) you prefer to have certain cases heard by certain judges, or perhaps prefer to have certain judges *not* hear some types of cases?
(*If yes*) Could you give me an example or two?

20a. Are (were) any of the judges in this district former ∅?

(*If yes*) How do you think their experience as ∅ affects (affected) their (his) behavior and style on the bench?

20b. I've been told that I would find that there are some judges who are considered to be generally unfriendly to the government, at least in some types of cases, while others may be "friendly." What's the situation in this district? Who, what areas?

21. Another area of interest concerns the relations between the Ø and the Department of Justice. Could you tell me a little about your relationship with the department, particularly regarding its supervision or control over your work?
How well you know (knew) people in department? Any on first-name basis?

22. Over-all, do (did) you consider yourself primarily a semiautonomous decision-maker, utilizing the advice and resources of the Department of Justice as a sort of legal consultant?
*or*
Do (did) you think of yourself more as a member of the Department of Justice, working under the direction of the attorney general, executing departmental policies in the field . . . a sort of junior partner in the federal law firm?

23. Are (were) there any areas in which the department currently makes (made) or strongly influences (influenced) decisions where you feel (felt) they should be delegated to the Ø's in the field?
What are they? Why should they be delegated?

24. Are (were) there any areas within the discretion of the Ø that you feel (felt) might be better handled in one central place, that is, the department?
What are they? Why should the department handle them?

25. What has been (was) your experience in the matter of the way in which your recommendations have been (were) handled by the department?

   (*Ask about*):  recommended compromises in civil suits—torts & condemnations
                 dismissals or reduction in charge in criminal cases
                 tax suits
   (*If nec.*)  When the attorney in the department handling a case disagrees (disagreed) with your recommendation, do (did) you usually go along with his decision, or do (did) you take it up with his superior (depty. atty. gen.).
                 What is (was) usually the outcome?

26. When you do make (did make) a recommendation to the department on something like a settlement in a large civil case or a dismissal in a criminal case, what are (were) some of the most important factors "going for you" so to speak, that is, what are (were) some of the more important reasons why your recommendation might be accepted?

27. Have you evolved any policy regarding when an assistant should call the department for advice?

(*If nec.*) Do you like to have them check with you first?

28. What are the areas in which you find departmental assistance in the form of a lawyer coming out from Washington to try a case most welcome?
Least welcome?

29. It's practically axiomatic that whenever you have a central agency that has some control over the actions of units in the field, there are always some areas that cause more difficulties than others. In your experience, what are (were) these areas of greatest difficulty (you may have mentioned some)?

30. Now I'd like to turn for a few minutes to your relationship with the AUSAs.* Could you outline for me what sort of supervision and review you exercise(d) over their work?

Is (was) this supervision more prior consultation or *review* of decisions?
How closely do (did) you review suggestions for compromises, or requests to dismiss or reduce charges in criminal cases?
Do (did) you usually take these matters up with the department when some question arises (arose) or do (did) the AUSA's handle their own recommendations?
(*If app.*) What sorts of matters do (did) you discuss with the chief asst(s)?

31. Which cases do (did) you handle personally (or keep close watch on)? Why?

32. Could you tell me a little about your relations with the press? Anyone cover the Ø regularly?

33. I'd like to turn from the area of your relationships with some of the people you come (came) into contact with to a more general question. In almost every position there are always what one might call "external factors" that aren't directly connected with the office but nevertheless play an important role in shaping the conduct of the individual. I guess this might be the underlying truth to the old saying that a case may turn on what the judge had for breakfast. I'm interested in your views as to what some of these external factors are for Ø.

[*probe only briefly private practice; att. of judges, no-fire Ø*]

*AUSA = assistant U.S. attorney.

34. One area in which I've found quite a big difference between districts is in the appointment of AUSAs, particularly the extent to which the choice of an ASST is influenced by political parties. Could you describe the general process to me in this district?

∅'s choice? With or without clearance—with whom? ∅'s choice from people sent to him? Who sends them? Who is the most important sender? ∅ presented with one choice—must accept or reject?

35. I wonder if you would mind telling me something about your own appointment? I know people are sometimes reluctant to talk about this, not only because it involves politics but also because in order to get the position you have to seek it yourself to some extent, and it is sometimes difficult to speak about this. But political scientists know appointments do involve politics (and we approve, I might add). What we have been lacking is a true picture of how the process works. I'm not interested in all of the details of one appointment, but rather the general patterns that emerge. If you don't want to go into too much detail on this, I'll understand, though I can assure you I will keep everything strictly confidential.

Who else trying; what factions took part; role of senator(s); what *activities or associations in past helped* get appointment; how appointment affected pol. situation in the district?

36. What were your reasons for wanting to become a ∅, what is attractive about the position?

37a. [*Ex ∅'s only*] How do you think your stint as ∅ helped your subsequent career?

37b. [*Current ∅'s only*] Almost without exception, the position of ∅ is a temporary one. How do you think your stint as ∅ will help you in your future endeavors? (Probe as rapport allows.)

38. Do you think that a ∅ should resign if his term extends over into a change of administration? Why?

39a. What do you think of the proposal to make the position of ∅ a civil service position? Why?
What effect would such a change have on the office and how it is executed?

39b. What differences have you noticed between the way you execute(d) the office of U.S. attorney and the way others who have held the position have handled their job?

40. When you are (were) in doubt as to how to handle a particular

problem that comes (came) up in the course of your work, where do (did) you turn for help?

Where else? Any other sources?

(*If says DJ.:*) Are there any areas in which you think it is better not to consult the department?

Do you (did you) ever contact former ∅'s or AUSA's for advice?

41. Suppose you were faced with a difficult decision as to which of several courses of action to take and you couldn't make up your mind which to choose. Generally speaking, do you think it would be best to:

1. Rely on your personal judgment.
2. Rely on the suggestions of the Justice Department (who in particular there?).
3. Choose the course of action you feel will be regarded as correct by most of the people who regularly follow your work as ∅—your AUSA's, the bar, judges, the press.
4. some other source.

42. We have already discussed the process of appointment, but I wonder if there are any other ways in which the position of ∅ impinges on the local political scene?

What difference can it make politically who the ∅ is?

E.g., success of party at polls; career of ∅ and other politicians; making or influencing policies or practices in a number of areas.

# Interview Guide for
# Investigative Agents

1. To begin with, could you tell me a little about the quality and nature of your working relationships with the AUSAs in this district?

2. Do you have much personal contact with the Ø here?
(*If yes*) What sorts of things do you see him about? Nature of relationship?
(*If no*) What about former Øs? Why did you see him (them) more often?

3. I'm interested in the ways in which your relationship with the AUSAs varies from one man to the next. Does it make a difference what the individual AUSA is like, or are personality differences relatively unimportant?

Could you elaborate? (Give a few examples?)
In what ways, if any, does the character of your contact with the AUSAs change when there is a change of Øs?

4. How important to you is a good working relationship with the AUSA's (& Ø) in your job? Why?

Could you tell me some of the sort of things that help establish and maintain a good working relationship? (What can you do to get a good relationship?)
What are the most frequent occurences that make a good relationship more difficult to establish and maintain?

5. How about the other side of the coin. How important is it to the AUSAs to have a good working relationship with the investigative agents?

Why? (or Could you give me an example of what you mean?)
What are some of the things occasionally done by AUSAs that are not conducive to the best relationship with investigative agents?

6. What are the chief difficulties of government attorneys in their dealings with investigative agents—what is most troublesome?

How well do you think AUSAs recognize the problems you face? How do you know this?

7. I know that investigative agencies occasionally appeal negative prosecutive opinions. Could you tell me a little about this in your experience?

What sorts of cases are usually involved, could you give me an example?
Are any other matters ever taken up with superiors besides prosecutive opinions?

8. How often do you get to know the AUSAs on a first name basis?

Do you feel free to call them at home, or does this vary from man to man?
Do any of the AUSAs ever ask you your assessment of a case?

9. Do you find that the AUSAs differ in the types of cases that they prefer to take—that is, do some like some kinds of cases more than others? Could you give me an example or two?

(*If yes*)  Do you generally try to bring these cases to their attention? How is this done?
(*If no*)  Go to question 10.

10. From my interviewing, I've discovered that one of the differences between AUSAs is that some like to be more certain of getting a conviction than others. Some like to be sure that if they bring a case into court, they are going to win. Others are content with a case that gives them a "good shot" at getting a conviction. They don't mind losing a case so much. Have you found this to be true in your experience?

What would you do if you had a case that you felt some of the AUSAs would prosecute, but others would not because they weren't sure enough of winning it?
Has this ever happened?
If an AUSA unexpectedly turned down what you thought was a good case, would you take it to another assistant whom you thought would take it?

11. Do you find agents differ in their willingness to prosecute certain *types* of cases—leaving aside the question of how tight a case is, do

some tend to decline on certain types of offenses where others will authorize?

What kinds of cases are like this? [*If not covered by "yes" to Q.9*]
Do you try to bring these cases to the attention of those who like to take them?

12. What role do the AUSAs play in the actual investigation of a case?

Have you ever received a request from the Ø or a AUSA to undertake or initiate an investigation?

13. Do you think the AUSAs are prosecution-minded or not, or does it vary with the individual? (*If it varies*) How?

14. In what ways have you noticed that the behavior of the Ø and his assistants is influenced by the judges in this district . . . you know, the personal likes and dislikes of the judges regarding procedure, type of cases brought, things like that?

15. Do the attitudes and practices of the judges affect the sort of cases you bring to the attention of the Ø's office or the way you handle a case for investigation?

16. From your vantage point, how much of a role have you found the Department of Justice playing in directing the work of the Ø and his assistants?
Could you cite an example or two?

*If not already covered:*
17. How can an investigative agent help a new Ø or new AUSA in his work?

18. What sorts of official instructions did you receive concerning your relationship with government counsel?

19. Do you find there are many differences in the relationship of different investigative agencies with the Ø and AUSAs?

20. How is the decision made as to whether a case will be brought into the state courts or the federal courts when dual jurisdiction exists?

21. How do AUSAs reach decisions on whether to prosecute or not—what factors are important?
Post Office—obscenity cases—how handled; differences between AUSAs; are a lot of good cases not prosecuted?

# APPENDIX B

# The Subsequent Careers of U.S. Attorneys

What happens to U.S. attorneys after they leave office? Several of the findings reported in the text of this volume suggest many may go on to hold other important positions. As Chapter 3 shows, U.S. attorneys come to office with substantial prior experience in government, and naturally some would want to continue a public career after leaving office. Their ability to secure the appointment testifies to their proven capacity to attract the support of politically important individuals and groups. In addition, U.S. attorneys themselves admit to harboring ambitions for higher office. Indeed, some seek the post because they believe it will prove to be a valuable steppingstone to another position. Finally, once in office, they acquire the visibility and experience required to compete for other posts.

The research on U.S. attorneys' characteristics and careers prior to appointment reported in Chapter 3 provides some information about their activities subsequent to leaving office. As the discussion there implies, the results of this research must be interpreted cautiously due to the many problems encountered in getting reliable data. Several sources had to be consulted to create a list of the men who served as U.S. attorneys between 1961 and 1973. Some who served only a few weeks or months as court appointees or acting U.S. attorneys appear in the *U.S. Government Organization Manual* or *The Department of Justice Register*. I eliminated men who never received a presidential appointment and served only a very brief time; but those with court appointments who served for at least a year were included. Since the date of appointment and date of departure is not always available, a few of the men on the roster probably served only a few weeks or months. Many men who serve as U.S. attorneys never attain the visibility or status required to receive an invitation to submit a biography to *Who's Who In America* or the other biographical directories consulted. However, I found some information on 163 of the 261 (62 percent) people on the roster.[1] Few of the remaining 38 percent probably attained a governmental position considered important (a federal judgeship, governorship, seat in Congress) by 1975, the last year for which biographies published in 1976 have information. Because those included furnish the data about themselves, the information lacks the comprehensiveness and comparability that a detailed and systematic analysis of careers requires. However, the data do provide reasonably accurate estimates of the minimum proportion of U.S. attorneys who go on to hold important positions.

According to the available biographical information, 75 men on the basic roster of those holding the office between 1961 and 1973 still served in 1975. If we eliminate them, 186 men remain who could have attained a significant post after leaving office. This figure overestimates the actual number somewhat, since some of the 186 died before they had an opportunity to hold another post and others left office past the age when they could expect to move to another position.

The analysis of those among the 186 for whom data exists (a total of 101) reveals that an impressive number go on to hold an important policy-making position. Thirty-two of the 186 (17 percent) became "successful alumni"—a governor, state appellate judge, state attorney general, member of the U.S. House or Senate, assistant attorney general in the Department of Justice, or federal appellate or district judge. A majority of the successful alumni (twenty-three of the thirty-two) became federal district or appeals judges. Thus, about one of every eight U.S. attorneys appointed between 1961 and 1973 and no longer serving in 1975 became a federal judge. Close to another 10 percent of the 186 alumni listed a less important position in government, and more extensive information on those whose biographies could not be located would raise this figure. For instance, one man not located in the biographies served in a leadership role in the Democratic caucus in the Pennsylvania Senate.

The biographical data show, then, that 27 percent of recent alumni held a governmental position in 1975, and the true figure is higher. Many of these alumni still have many years left in their active careers, and the absolute number who move to higher positions undoubtedly will increase. However, fewer of the seventy-five men still serving in 1975 will become district judges unless the Republicans capture the presidency in 1980.

The basic features of the office of U.S. attorney that make its incumbents strong candidates for other important governmental posts have remained unchanged for many years. Consequently, U.S. attorneys should have enjoyed comparable success in the past. An analysis of the subsequent careers of men who served between 1896 and 1960 in a randomly selected group of thirty districts confirms this supposition.[2] I compiled a roster of 352 men who served in these districts by systematically examining the *U.S. Governmental Organization Manual* and the *Department of Justice Register* for this time period. I located biographical data on 272 of the 352 (77 percent). Seventy-two men became successful alumni, about 20 percent of the total roster of 352. They included a member of the cabinet, two solicitors general, six U.S. Court of Appeals judges, two senators, three governors, four members of the House of Representatives, six justices of state supreme courts, eight U.S. assistant attorneys general, one state attorney general, six lower state court judges, and thirty-two federal district judges. The predominance of federal judgeships in the careers of successful alumni thus rests on a firm historical record. A spot check of the careers of a sample of 187 district judges, drawn from the rosters of those sitting in 1916, 1936, and 1959, offers a different perspective on the importance of U.S. attorneys in staffing the judiciary. Fifteen percent of the 187 served as U.S. attorney, and another 7 percent had been assistant U.S. attorneys. Thus, over one in five of these judges worked in a U.S. attorney's office.

The historical sample provides a good perspective on the general patterns in the subsequent careers of U.S. attorneys. Five patterns emerged: the "successful alumni" (20 percent of the roster); the "careerists," men who served at least ten years and held no major position after leaving (about 6 percent of the roster); the "retirees," men who held the position up to or very close to the normal retirement age (11 percent of the roster); the "private practitioners," men who left office before their late fifties and indicated that they became partners in law firms or directors of business concerns (about 10 percent of the roster); and the "residuals," men for whom no information was located or who left before retirement age but listed no important governmental post or partnership in a law firm (about 53 percent of the sample). The more recent alumni display a similar pattern. Thirty-two are successful alumni, five "retirees," seventeen "private practitioners," and eighteen held a less important government job. Almost all of the rest for whom biographical data exist engaged in the private practice of law. The "residual" category accounts for about 61 percent of the recent alumni.

# NOTES

## PREFACE

1. Several worthwhile articles dealing directly with the office exist: John C. Heinberg, "Centralization in Federal Prosecutions," *Missouri Law Review* 15 (June 1950): 244–58; John Kaplan, "Prosecutorial Discretion—A Comment," *Northwestern University Law Review* 60 (May–June 1965): 174–93; Whitney North Seymour, Jr., "Why Prosecutors Act Like Prosecutors," *Record of the Association of the Bar of the City of New York* 11 (June 1956): 302–13; Robert L. Rabin, "Agency Criminal Referrals in the Federal System: An Empirical Study of Prosecutorial Discretion," *Stanford Law Review* 24 (1971): 1036–91. As their titles indicate, the last three deal only with prosecutive decisions. Relations between U.S. attorneys' offices and the organized crime strike forces are described by Richard S. Frank, "Federal Strike Forces Dominate Government's War on Organized Crime," in John F. Bibby and Robert J. Huckshorn, eds., *Current Politics: The Way Things Work In Washington* (Minneapolis: Winston Press, 1973), pp. 258–70. A description of the formal structure of the office and its duties in the mid-1920s can be found in Albert Langeluttig, *The Department of Justice of the United States* (Baltimore: The Johns Hopkins Press, 1927). Other publications discuss U.S. attorneys, but not in any detail. Homer Cummings and Carl McFarland, *Federal Justice* (New York: Macmillan, 1937) has interesting information on the history of the office. L. B. Schwartz, "Federal Criminal Jurisdiction and Prosecutors' Discretion," *Law and Contemporary Problems* 13 (Winter 1948): 64–87, discusses the problems raised by the dual jurisdiction of states and the federal government for many types of crimes. Robert A. Jackson, "The Federal Prosecutor," *Journal of the American Institute of Criminal Law and Criminology* 31 (1941): 3–6, is a reprint of a speech of Attorney General Jackson, emphasizing the importance of prosecutors in general and U.S. attorneys in particular. Several journalistic descriptions of U.S. attorneys' activities in office have recently appeared. One is by a former U.S. attorney, Whitney North Seymour, *United States Attorney* (New York: William Morrow, 1975). The other is by Paul Hoffman, *Tiger in the Court* (Chicago: Playboy Press, 1973).

2. The author has attempted to summarize this research elsewhere. See James Eisenstein, *Politics and the Legal Process* (New York: Harper-Row, 1973). One indication of the rapid growth in this area is the appearance of a number of interdisciplinary journals in recent years, including *Law and Society Review, The Journal of Legal Studies,* and *The Journal of Criminal Justice.*

3. The methodology employed in this research is described in Appendix A.

## CHAPTER 1

1. Leonard D. White, *Introduction to the Study of Public Administration,* 4th ed. (New York: Macmillan, 1955), p. 100.

2. The department's authorized budget for fiscal year 1976 was $2,132,415,000. Only $265,583,000 (12.5 percent) went for legal activities and general administration. Of the total authorized manpower of 51,878, only 9,560 (19.4 percent) worked in general administration or legal activities. *U.S. House of Representatives, Subcommittee of the*

*Committee on Appropriations: Hearings on the Departments of State and Justice, the Judiciary, and Related Agencies Appropriations for 1977.* U.S. House of Representatives, 94th Congress, 2nd Session (1976), calculated from tables appearing on pp. 4-5.

3. These include the Office of Policy and Planning, the Office of Public Information, the Office of Legislative Affairs, the Office of Management and Finance, the Pardon Attorney, the Board of Immigration Appeals, the Board of Parole, and special units created from time to time, such as the Watergate Special Prosecution Force. *House Appropriations Hearings, 1977,* p. 6.

4. For descriptions of the responsibilities and activities of the various divisions, see Luther A. Huston, *The Department of Justice* (New York: Praeger, 1967), ch. IV-XI.

5. 5 U.S.C. § 310 permits specially appointed counsel to "conduct any kind of legal proceeding, civil or criminal, including grand jury proceedings and proceedings before committing magistrates, which U.S. attorneys may be by law authorized to conduct, whether or not he or they be residents of the district in which such proceeding is brought."

6. 28 U.S.C. § 507 (a).

7. In *United States* v. *San Jacinto Tin Co.,* 125 U.S. 273, 278-79 (1888), the Court declared that the attorney general "has the authority, and it is made his duty, to supervise and conduct all suits brought by or against the United States . . . and his district attorneys who do bring them in the various courts are placed under his immediate direction and control." President Franklin Roosevelt affirmed the attorney general's supervisory power in Executive Order No. 6166, which transferred control of federal litigation formerly lodged in other agencies to the Department of Justice. See Carl Brent Swisher, "Federal Organization of Legal Functions," 33 *American Political Science Review* (1939): 980.

8. See, for example, Huston, *The Department of Justice.* Huston devotes about three pages to U.S. attorneys in the entire book.

9. In fiscal year 1976, 1618 of the department's 3325 (48.7 percent) attorneys worked in the field. *1977 House Appropriations Hearings,* p. 20.

10. For a discussion of the concept of malapportionment in federal courts, see Richard J. Richardson and Kenneth N. Vines, *The Politics of the Federal Courts* (Boston: Little-Brown, 1970), ch. 3, especially pp. 43-48.

11. United States Department of Justice, *Annual Report of the Attorney General: 1968* (Washington, D.C.: U.S. Government Printing Office, 1969), table V, pp. 93-94.

12. *Annual Report of the Attorney General: 1968,* pp. 93-94. They were the Southern District of New York (67), the Eastern District of New York (32), the District of Columbia (46), the Central District of California (43), and the Northern District of Illinois (32).

13. *Annual Report of the Attorney General: 1975,* p. 4.

14. According to department calculations, "each new judge generally moves cases through the pipeline at a rate to require the services of two new Assistant U.S. Attorneys." *House Hearings, 1977,* p. 283.

15. *Annual Report of the Attorney General: 1975,* calculated from information on pp. 26-27.

16. Ibid.

17. Ibid.

18. Ibid.

19. Ibid., pp. 24-25.

20. A former U.S. attorney in the Southern District of New York, Whitney North Seymour, reported spending approximately 20 percent of his time on press relations. His recollections of his tenure provide an excellent description of the work environment and duties of a U.S. attorney in a large district. See *United States Attorney* (New York: William Morrow, 1975), pp. 48-59. Chapter 11 deals exclusively with his press relations.

21. Whitney North Seymour described his job as "administrator, trouble-shooter, enforcement planner, interviewer, litigator, statesman, paper pusher, back slapper, advisor, writer, researcher, negotiator, interviewee, and a dozen other things as well." *United States Attorney,* p. 48.

22. The department consistently emphasizes the workload and its constant growth, in part to justify its requests for additional manpower. See, for example, *Annual Report of the Attorney General: 1975*, p. 4, or *House Appropriations Hearings, 1977*, pp. 396–97.

23. Homer Cummings and Carl McFarland, *Federal Justice* (New York: Macmillan, 1937), especially chapters VII and VIII; John C. Heinberg, "Centralization in Federal Prosecutions," 15 *Missouri Law Review* (June 1950): 244– 58; L. B. Schwartz, "Federal Criminal Jurisdiction and Prosecutors' Discretion," 13 *Law and Contemporary Problems* (Winter, 1948): 64–87; Carl Brent Swisher, "Federal Organization of Legal Functions," 33 *American Political Science Review* (December 1939): 973–1000; Seymour, *United States Attorney*, pp. 45–46; Albert Langeluttig, *The Department of Justice of the United States* (Baltimore: Johns Hopkins Press, 1927).

24. The Judiciary Act of 1789 provided for the appointment "in each district a meet person learned in the law to act as attorney for the United States in each district . . . to prosecute . . . all delinquents for crimes and offenses, cognizable under the authority of the United States, and all civil actions in which the United States shall be concerned." I Stat. 92–93.

25. Schwartz, "Federal Criminal Jurisdiction," pp. 64–65.

26. Cummings and McFarland, *Federal Justice*, pp. 121–22.

27. Schwartz, "Federal Criminal Jurisdiction," pp. 64–65.

28. *Annual Report of the Attorney General: 1975*, pp. 17, 20.

29. *Annual Report of the Attorney General: 1963*, p. 98. *Annual Report of the Attorney General, 1975*, p. 27.

30. For discussions of the attorney general's lack of authority and control over U.S. attorneys before the Civil War, see Langeluttig, *The Department of Justice*, ch. 1; Seymour, *United States Attorney*, p. 21; Cummings and McFarland, *Federal Justice*, ch. VIII; and Heinberg, "Centralization in Federal Prosecutions," p. 246.

31. Cummings and McFarland, *Federal Justice*, p. 78.

32. Ibid.

33. Ibid., p. 159.

34. Heinberg, "Centralization in Federal Prosecutions," p. 246.

35. The department's creation is described in the following sources: Cummings and McFarland, *Federal Justice*, ch. VIII and ch. XI; Huston, *The Department of Justice*, pp. 12–15, 35–38; and Langeluttig, *The Department of Justice*, pp. 9–13.

36. Cummings and McFarland, *Federal Justice*, pp. 218–19. Referring to the post Civil War period, they observe: "The scattered district attorneys, whom the Judiciary Act of 1789 had made responsible for both criminal and civil litigation in the district and circuit courts, remained all but completely independent." The attorney general had little time for supervision of U.S. attorneys, and some felt it improper for him to attempt it.

37. Swisher, "Federal Organization of Legal Functions," presents an excellent summary of this struggle through the 1930s.

38. Heinberg, "Centralization in Federal Prosecutions," p. 247.

39. Swisher, "Federal Organization of Legal Functions," p. 980.

40. Ibid., p. 998.

41. White, *Introduction to the Study of Public Administration*, p. 102.

42. Ibid., p. 105.

43. James Fesler, *Area and Administration* (University, Alabama: University of Alabama Press, 1949), p. 64.

44. Ibid., pp. 58–59.

45. I am using "resources" in the sense that Robert A. Dahl has used the concept— things possessed that allow influence to be exerted. See "The Concept of Power," 2 *Behavioral Science* (July 1957): 201–15.

46. In fiscal year 1968, for instance, about 20,000 of the 70,000 (29 percent) civil actions begun in federal district courts involved the federal government. Sheldon Goldman and Thomas Jahnige, *The Federal Courts as a Political System* (New York: Harper & Row, 1971), p. 101.

47. Fesler, *Area and Administration*, p. 64.

CHAPTER 2

1. United States Department of Justice, *Annual Report of the Attorney General: 1975* (Washington, D.C.: U.S. Government Printing Office, 1976), pp. 4–16.

2. Ibid., p. 19.

3. This is not a new area of activity for U.S. attorneys. In his book *Federal Protection of Civil Rights: Quest for a Sword* (Ithaca, New York: Russell Sage, 1948), Robert Carr describes specific instances in which U.S. attorneys convinced individuals to modify conduct which infringed on the liberties of citizens in their districts. He also indicates (p. 129) that the Civil Rights Section urged them in a 1943 circular to seek voluntary cooperation before instituting suit.

4. In fiscal 1975, U.S. attorneys' offices received 174,173 criminal matters, but filed only 46,951 criminal cases. *Annual Report of the Attorney General: 1975*, p. 27.

5. U.S. House of Representatives, Subcommittee of the Committee on Appropriations: *Hearings on the Departments of State and Justice, the Judiciary, and Related Agencies Appropriations for 1961*, 86th Congress, 2nd Session (1960), p. 25.

6. See, for example, James W. Davis, Jr., and Kenneth M. Dolbeare, *Little Groups of Neighbors: The Selective Service System* (Chicago: Markham, 1968), which describes the impact of local draft boards in the implementation of the Selective Service Act.

7. Whitney North Seymour, in his book *United States Attorney* (New York: William Morrow, 1975), p. 51, mentions dealing with investigative agencies as one problem facing a U.S. attorney in a large district, and observes that these agencies "are notorious prima donnas when it comes to their prerogatives."

8. For a fascinating account of the Agnew prosecution, see Richard M. Cohen and Jules Witcover, *A Heartbeat Away: The Investigation and Resignation of Vice President Spiro T. Agnew* (New York: Viking, 1974).

9. The importance of discretionary choices in these cases declined markedly after the Nixon administration sought to discontinue prosecution of routine violations involving joy-riding teen-agers. A number of other types of cases in which differences emerged between districts exist, including failure of aliens to register their addresses each January, widows who continue to collect Social Security checks of deceased husbands, and failure to list all previous arrests on post office temporary employment forms. Seymour, *United States Attorney*, pp. 58–59, also notes differences in emphasis among districts.

10. Seymour, *United States Attorney*, ch. 9, paints an entirely different picture of the Nixon administration's policy on civil rights, charging the civil rights division with a "slowdown." Limited information on the role of U.S. attorneys in the early portion of the struggle to achieve desegregation can be found in Jack Peltason's study of federal judges in the South. See *Fifty-Eight Lonely Men* (New York: Harcourt, Brace, and World, 1961). Individual U.S. attorneys can effect department policy and procedure in other ways. One is to serve as a testing laboratory for new policies or procedures. Another is as a source of new ideas. One respondent, for example, claimed that he instituted a record-keeping system in his district that was adopted by the department and adapted into the machine listing system. Another claimed to have initiated a variation of the Brooklyn Plan—the deferring of prosecution of youthful offenders as long as they stay out of further trouble. A third is as a source of information on violations in areas of particular concern to the department. This was particularly true with respect to civil rights and civil liberties in the mid-1940s. See Carr, *Federal Protection*, pp. 124–26.

11. Admiralty cases and civil tax refund cases (with a few exceptions), for instance, are handled by department attorneys. Civil cases involving unusually large sums of money or particularly important issues are frequently taken over by Washington.

12. Seymour, *United States Attorney*, describes this effort in chapter 10.

13. *Annual Report of the Attorney General: 1975*, pp. 15–16.

14. Ibid., p. 25.

15. *Berger* v. *U.S.*, 295 U.S. 78, 88 (1935).

16. The field research confirmed differences among districts in how such questions are answered. In one district, the U.S. attorney said that many defendants in untaxed

liquor cases plead guilty even though the evidence was obtained illegally. He explained that the defendants were guilty of possession and that their attorneys never raised questions about the legality of the evidence. Federal prosecutors in other districts would not bring such cases as a matter of principle even if they anticipated a guilty plea. If they did, defense attorneys would successfully raise the illegal evidence defense. The proportion of criminal cases plea bargained and civil cases compromised in various districts described in the first chapter provide more rigorous confirmation of interdistrict differences.

17. *Annual Report of the Attorney General: 1975,* p. 4.

18. One U.S. attorney who prosecuted local police officers expressed concern about the negative impact such cases can have on the public. "I want the public to react to an indictment of ten policemen that there are forces in government who are working on the bad apples and sorting them out. And I don't want them to forget that five or ten police officers out of a police force of 4,800 isn't all that bad. . . . You elaborate and tell them that the investigation has also showed it is a fine department that you can be proud of."

19. Carr, in *Federal Protection,* pp. 152–63 indicates that in the mid-1940s, these cases were very often handled by U.S. attorneys with the assistance of the civil rights section. He presents several specific examples where local law enforcement officers were prosecuted and the U.S. attorney reported a beneficial deterrent impact on the local community. Here too, attempts to get voluntary compliance were made: "The Agency (Civil Rights Section of the Department) believes that a tactful word from a United States attorney often persuades local police officers, who are perhaps unaware of the existence of federal criminal statutes which they may be violating, to alter their conduct" (p. 163).

20. From accounts in the *New York Times,* something very much like this happened in the Southern District of New York in 1965. A local minister had gathered evidence of a bookie ring operating in his community, and after discovering that furnishing the information to local authorities "produced no results," he turned it over to the U.S. attorney. A prosecution resulted. "Citizens Root Out Seven Bookie Suspects," *New York Times,* October 26, 1965.

21. Of course, U.S. attorneys also provide the Department of Justice with information and recommendations on how to enforce statutes, on the success of new policies, and on major problem areas that require new policies. Presumably, the attorney general's U.S. Attorneys' Advisory Committee will institutionalize such feedback.

22. "69 in Coast Jail for 1964 Sit-Ins," *New York Times,* July 24, 1965.

23. "Church Stands on its Bid to Dr. King," *New York Times,* April 25, 1965.

24. These cases are described in detail in Paul Hoffman, *Tiger in the Court* (Chicago: Playboy Press, 1973).

25. For an interesting account of the development of this investigation, see "White House-Backed Form of Immunity a Key Weapon in the Agnew Inquiry," *New York Times,* Sept. 1, 1973. See also Cohen and Witcover, *A Heartbeat Away.*

26. The decision on whether to seek an indictment against Vice-President Agnew on charges involving kickbacks is a perfect example. According to newspaper accounts, the assistant attorney general for the Criminal Division went to Baltimore to review the case and the ultimate decision was to be reviewed by the attorney general. "Action in Baltimore on Agnew Awaiting Richardson Ruling," *New York Times,* August 18, 1973. For a full discussion of the department's role, see Cohen and Witcover, *A Heartbeat Away.*

27. An excellent interpretive article describing the appointment of Herbert Stern as U.S. attorney in New Jersey expressed the prevailing view of incentives in politically sensitive areas quite well. As the reporter delicately stated, "both parties attempt whenever possible to name established party figures to the sensitive post of United States attorney, on the theory that they will vigorously prosecute crime and corruption while keeping in mind the party that put them in office. . . . However, Justice Department officials are understood to feel that any party loyalty will not count with Mr. Stern. 'It will be like having a loaded gun in there—you'll never be certain it won't be pointed at you,' a top Republican remarked." "Nixon Seen Ready to Appoint Stern," by Ronald Sullivan, *New York Times,* September 10, 1971.

28. "Rolvaag Faces Party Fight in Bid for Reelection in Minnesota," *New York Times*, February 27, 1966. The U.S. attorney had been nominated for a judgeship subsequent to the prosecutions.

29. Sometimes maintenance of such friendships leads to trouble. A respondent told how he introduced an old family friend who was a lobbyist to his senators. The lobbyist subsequently was exposed for offering a bribe to another member of the Senate. The respondent had to resign as a result of his part in the episode.

30. Ramsey Clark, *Crime in America* (New York: Simon and Schuster, 1970). Clark asks (pp. 191-92), "Who is likely to learn first of evidence of crime with political implications—a Senator or the Attorney General? Who is likely to be influential in a case, or a grand jury investigation?"

31. Other examples where political intelligence is furnished were encountered. An assistant called the local mayor while I was in his office to observe that he could expect some unhappiness among his liberal supporters, because the chief of police publically stated he intended to continue to release information to the press on cases before trial.

32. Seymour, *United States Attorney,* pp. 61-62.

33. Ibid., p. 226.

34. Ibid., pp. 226-27.


CHAPTER 3

1. Title 28, Section 501 reads: "The President shall appoint by and with the advice and consent of the Senate, a United States attorney for each Judicial District."

2. The provisions relating to the tenure of U.S. attorneys are found in Section 504 of Title 28 of the U.S. Code. It reads:

"(a) The United States attorney for each judicial district shall be appointed for a term of four years.... Upon the expiration of his term, a United States attorney shall continue to perform the duties of his office until his successor is appointed and qualifies.

(b) Each United States attorney shall be subject to removal by the President. Each assistant United States attorney and each attorney appointed under section 503 of this title shall be subject to removal by the Attorney General.

(c) Each of such officials, before taking office, shall take an oath to execute faithfully his duties."

One other section is relevant to this chapter. Section 506 reads: "The district court for a district in which the office of United States attorney is vacant, may appoint a United States attorney to serve until the vacancy is filled."

3. Several studies examine the appointment process to positions in the federal legal system, including Joel Grossman, *Lawyers and Judges: The ABA and the Politics of Judicial Selection* (New York: John Wiley & Sons, 1965); Sheldon Goldman, "Politics, Judges, and the Administration of Justice: The Background, Recruitment, and Decisional Tendencies of the Judges on the U.S. Courts of Appeals—1961-64," (Ph.D. dissertation, Harvard University, 1965); and Harold Chase, *Federal Judges: The Appointing Process* (Minneapolis: University of Minnesota Press, 1972). They contain useful discussions of interaction among the Department of Justice, the president, the Senate, and others in the appointment process, but do not deal directly with the appointment of U.S. attorneys.

4. In *Congress and the Presidency* (Englewood Cliffs, N.J.: Prentice-Hall, 1964), Nelson Polsby aptly termed senatorial courtesy as "a co-operative device to ensure clearance" of appointments to federal posts in a state with the senator(s) of the president's party from that state. They can block an appointment by declaring to the Senate that the nominee is "personally obnoxious" to them. The most extensive study of senatorial courtesy is Joseph P. Harris, *The Advice and Consent of the Senate* (Berkeley and Los Angeles: University of California Press, 1953), particularly Chapters XIII and XIV. Discussions of courtesy can also be found in George B. Galloway, *The Legislative Process in Congress* (New York: Crowell, 1953), and most standard texts on American government. See e.g., Ogg and Ray's *Introduction to American Government,* 11th ed. (New York: Appleton-Century, 1956), p. 323.

5. Harris, *The Advice and Consent of the Senate*, p. 382. Most descriptions of senatorial courtesy generally support Harris' contention. See, for example, E. Allen Helms, "The President and Party Politics," *Journal of Politics* 11 (1949): 42–64. Helms asserts that where courtesy operates, the senator actually makes the nomination. Standard American government texts usually take a similar view.

6. C. Perry Paterson, "The President as Chief Administrator," *Journal of Politics* 11 (1949): 228, asserts that the president is largely free to nominate whom he wants, and that he usually wins the Senate's approval.

7. Others have also suggested neither the president nor senators dominate such nominations. See, for example, V. O. Key, *Politics, Parties, and Pressure Groups,* 4th ed. (New York: Thomas Y. Crowell, 1953), p. 366, and Roland Young, *The American Congress* (New York: Harper, 1958), pp. 208–12. Charles E. Merriam and Harold F. Gosnell, in *The American Party System* (New York: Macmillan, 1940), p. 191, observe that "the exact relation between the President and Senators and Congressmen in the selection of these officials has never been determined, and must depend to a great extent on the relative strength and weakness of the officials concerned." See also Chase, *Federal Judges*, p. 47.

8. Although I did not emphasize the appointment process in the field research, I asked a number of respondents about it. Several Department of Justice officials intimately involved in the appointment process gave especially helpful accounts. The discussion that follows applies to initial appointments, not reappointments. Reappointment is practically automatic, although according to department sources interviewed, the Johnson administration denied reappointment to a mediocre U.S. attorney with ties to a local union under investigation.

9. Harris, *The Advice and Consent of the Senate*, p. 224, states that a senator of the minority party may enter a personal objection to a nominee if he is in fact personally obnoxious to the senator. The Senate has sustained such objections, but it occurs only rarely. However, minority party senators cannot inject themselves into the selection of the nominee.

10. The Eisenhower administration found forty-five of eighty-five appointments (53 percent) to districts in the states involved at least one Republican senator. For the Nixon administration, the figure was fifty-four out of eighty-seven (62 percent).

11. The number of initial appointments in districts located in states with two senators from the president's party in recent years are: 1953, twenty-four; 1961, forty-five; 1969, nineteen; and 1977, thirty-five.

12. Harris, *The Advice and Consent of the Senate,* p. 227. He notes the Senate takes into account both the grounds for the objection and the standing of the senator. When a nominee is confirmed over an objection, it is usually because the objector is not highly regarded by his fellows. Huey Long of Louisiana and Senator Bilbo of Mississippi both failed to exercise courtesy successfully in the 1930s.

13. The following table summarizes the relationship.

| U.S. attorney appointed "mid-term" | Did U.S. Attorney Ever Serve as an Assistant? | | |
|---|---|---|---|
| | *Yes* | *No* | |
| Yes | 13 (36.1%) | 23 (63.9%) | 36 (100%) |
| No | 21 (17.9%) | 96 (82.1%) | 117 (100%) |
| Chi square significance level = .04 Cramer's V = .19 | 34 | 119 | 153 |

14. After praising the quality of one district, an official referred to a neighboring district by observing, "The judges are lousy, the assistants are lousy, and the U.S. attorneys are lousy." He said he would oppose a mediocre nominee in the first, but probably would acquiesce to one in the second.

15. The description of negotiations prior to the submission of a nominee's name to the Senate is primarily based on an extensive interview with a former department official involved in the selection of a number of U.S. attorneys.

16. Another aspirant for the post interviewed corroborated this description. By the time he got around to contacting the senators, he found them to be "evasive." They finally told him that "the pie had been divided" and that his faction did not get the U.S. attorneyship.

17. Southern senators were described as being more likely to be in this category, perhaps a reflection of their greater stature in the Senate, their more "political" orientation, and their interest in the attitudes of U.S. attorneys toward civil rights.

18. Harris, *The Advice and Consent of the Senate,* p. 222, describes something similar. "As a general rule, when the President turns down the recommendation of a Senator . . . he anticipates the opposition of the Senator and therefore is particularly careful to choose a person of outstanding qualifications."

19. Of course, the senator may be able to use this same strategy to get his man in office, provided his recommendation carries more weight with the chief judge than the attorney general's. Given the importance of senators in the selection of judges, such situations probably occur, though none were described to me during the field research.

20. Senator Edward Kennedy convinced the Johnson administration to nominate an old family friend and political supporter to the federal bench. Vigorous opposition to what many (including some sitting judges in Massachusetts) considered an unqualified appointee embarrassed Kennedy into requesting that the nomination be withdrawn. An account of the episode can be found in the *New York Times* from the end of September 1965 to early November, especially September 28, October 17, 19, 20, 21, 22, and November 6.

21. When this occurs, the department may try to cut its losses by exercising considerable control over the selection of assistant U.S. attorneys and scrutinizing the office's operations and handling of litigation more closely than normal.

22. This does not mean that "out" senators never engage in any activity on behalf of a candidate. In one case, after a congressman convinced a man to seek the post, one of the "out" senators, in the words of the appointee, "took the lead in the Judiciary Committee." In another instance, a U.S. attorney (more from etiquette than necessity) requested and received the support of the "out" senators for an already assured *re*appointment. In neither case did the senator play a crucial role.

23. A U.S. attorney described what someone in his district did after receiving a court appointment. "It turned out to be a Frankenstein monster. He got the bit into his mouth and turned out to be very difficult to replace. He'd gone about garnering support for the permanent appointment."

24. Chase, *Federal Judges,* pp. 29–35.

25. For a comprehensive study of the American Bar Association's role in the selection of federal judges, see Grossman, *Lawyers and Judges.*

26. The man who eventually got the appointment independently confirmed these events. His initial reluctance to accept the post was partially overcome by his opinion of the prospective appointee as "the sort of fellow you knew wouldn't do a good job."

27. The appointment is described in Paul Hoffman, *Tiger in the Court* (Chicago: Playboy Press, 1973), ch. 8.

28. For a description of the survey, see Appendix B.

29. A few men reported very aggressive activities in pursuit of the nomination. "I had good information that the incumbent was grossly unhappy . . ." reported one such man. "So I began working to lay the foundation. I went to all of the city Committeemen and talked to other people." By the time the incumbent resigned, "I had the inside track."

30. In some districts, a number of former U.S. attorneys have moved to higher posts. Of the seventeen men who served in the Northern District of Illinois between 1896 and 1976, five became federal district judges, one a U.S. Court of Appeals judge, and three governors.

31. I would like to express my appreciation to three work study students who assisted me in this research—Robert Gilboy, Nancy Rehak, and especially Jack Stein.

32. A major portion of the work for this study was performed ably by an undergraduate student, Jack Stein. We received usable replies from 144 of the 241 individu-

als left in the roster after eliminating those whose questionnaires were returned marked "deceased". As of this writing, only incomplete results from this study were available.

33. In a news story discussing possibilities for appointment to new judgeships, the *San Francisco Examiner and Chronicle,* March 27, 1965, claimed that the U.S. attorney, Cecil Poole, was the first Negro in the post in history. Though this in itself is not strong evidence, none of the sources on U.S. attorneys mentioned any Negro appointments. The first Negro federal judges were not appointed until FDR's second term. See Samuel Lubell, *The Future of American Politics,* rev. ed. (Garden City, New York: Doubleday, 1955), p. 83.

34. John R. Schmidhauser, "The Justices of the Supreme Court: A Collective Portrait," *Midwest Journal of Political Science,* 3 (1959): 30.

35. The relationship between the administration appointing a U.S. attorney and his religion is summarized in the following table.

|  | Democratic appointee | Republican appointee |  |
|---|---|---|---|
| Roman Catholic | 14 (33.3) | 5 (16.7) | 19 |
| Jewish | 7 (16.7) | 1 (3.3) | 8 |
| Protestant | 21 (50.0) | 24 (80.0) | 45 |
|  | 42 (100.0) | 30 (100.0) | 72 |

Chi square level of significance = .03
Cramer's V = .32

36. Four of the sixteen men serving in the Pacific and Mountain states born out of state came from another state in this region. In the rest of the country, eighteen of the thirty men born out of state came from another state in the same region.

37. Over a quarter of the men from these regions attended a prestigious undergraduate institution, compared to just 4 percent from the rest of the country. The comparable figures for attendance at one of the prestigious law schools are 25 percent and 8 percent.

## CHAPTER 4

1. Robert L. Peabody, *Organizational Authority* (New York: Atherton, 1964), p. 118.

2. James Fesler, *Area and Administration* (University of Alabama Press, 1949), p. 62.

3. Leonard D. White, *Introduction to the Study of Public Administration,* 4th ed. (New York: Macmillan, 1955), p. 113.

4. Robert A. Jackson, "The Federal Prosecutor," *Journal of the American Institute of Criminal Law and Criminology,* 31 (1941): 3.

5. In a book published shortly after leaving office,,President Johnson's last attorney general, Ramsey Clark, expressed these concerns as follows: "How independent will some chief prosecutors be when they have associated all their adult life with a Senator, when he secured their appointment, when he approved the selection of their assistants, when the close association between the Senator and the United States Attorney will continue after administrations change and ostensible superiors in the Department of Justice have retired to private life?" *Crime in America* (New York: Simon and Schuster, 1970), p. 191.

6. An assistant attorney general in the criminal division during a Democratic administration gave this rough breakdown: a handful are superb, a larger group very competent, a small handful real "clinkers," and the rest in between (mediocre). Others were less harsh, but still found some U.S. attorneys lacked basic ability. One department attorney felt most were professional, responsible, competent, and dedicated. "But not all. Some are petty people."

7. Fesler, *Area and Administration,* p. 65.

8. For example, trying a police officer for violating the rights of a minority group member can have an important deterrent effect. A few income tax evasion cases judiciously spaced out over the year can decrease the incidence of such crimes, regardless of the outcomes of the cases.

9. Other reasons for handling cases are offered. Some in the department feel an office might "trade-off" and settle several entirely unrelated cases in a package deal with a law firm. Recommended compromise settlements must be scrutinized carefully because the assistant might not drive a hard bargain with a law firm he hopes to join after leaving office. Finally, the department just does not feel it can trust several of its U.S. attorneys in some types of cases (e.g., organized crime).

10. The Criminal Division, for example, merely exercises general supervision over the handling of cases—reading investigative reports, approving requests for dismissals, and (on nonroutine cases) making specific recommendations on procedures. In contrast, the admiralty section handles most cases itself, relying on U.S. attorneys' offices primarily as functionaries who handle preliminary matters (such as the filing of papers) under explicit and detailed instructions from headquarters.

11. Many other less independent respondents expressed the same view. The answer of one, when asked what happened when he disagreed with the department over whether a case should be prosecuted, is typical. "Ultimately, the decision rests with them. The Department of Justice is really the attorney general, and he could decide . . . . If the attorney general says prosecute, then you have two alternatives: either prosecute or resign. Anything else is insubordination."

12. He was referring to 28 U.S.C. § 507 (a), which sets forth the duties of U.S. attorneys without mentioning the department. Though this position was rarely encountered, the fact that it existed at all is rather extraordinary.

13. Analysis of interviews with both incumbent and former U.S. attorneys revealed the existence of three basic positions on the question of headquarters control versus field autonomy. This was confirmed by a questionnaire distributed to U.S. attorneys attending the 1965 annual conference in Washington. The questionnaire asked them for answers to the following question: "Views of current and ex-U.S. attorneys on what the proper relationship between the Department and U.S. attorneys should be have ranged between two 'polar' views. At one pole is the belief that while some general direction is necessary, the U.S. attorney, as a presidential appointee confirmed by the Senate, should be largely autonomous from the Department. Opposed to this is the view that the U.S. attorney is primarily an officer of the Department of Justice, an arm of the Department executing its policy in the field (and hence should not be autonomous). Both views have been expressed to me. Briefly, how do you feel on this matter?" Excluding U.S. attorneys from the territories, replies from 38 of the 88 U.S. attorneys were received. Ten said their view was somewhere in between the two poles, 14 gave responses placing them toward or at the autonomous pole, and 14 indicated they regarded themselves as officers of the department. Since the response sample may not be representative, caution must be exercised in estimating the distribution among all U.S. attorneys. However, it seems safe to assume that at a minimum, a significant minority (on the order of 15 to 20 percent) of U.S. attorneys adhered to each of these positions. Officials in the Nixon administration who had read the results of this questionnaire indicated that it appeared to characterize the distribution of views among Republican U.S. attorneys as well.

14. Two answers to the U.S. Attorneys Conference questionnaire item on relations with the department (see note 13 above) coded as "field officer" responses follow: "I feel that uniformity in policy, as regards the problems which beset us, must be mandatory. For this reason, the U.S. attorney must assume a subordinate role." "Necessity of the Department of Justice following a substantially uniform policy in all districts makes it advisable that a U.S. attorney be in name and fact an arm of the Department."

15. The three additional examples of the "autonomous" outlook below are drawn from the U.S. Attorneys Conference questionnaire item referred to in note 13.

"I think that if an administration has faith enough in an attorney to have him appointed he should make most of the policy-making decisions. He is on the ground and knows the situation best."

"The Department of Justice exercises to (sic) much control over the U.S. attorney. There needs to be a national policy for the attorneys to follow, however, I feel that the U.S. attorney should run the affairs of his district."

"Something should remain autonomous in this tremendously centralized government."

16. It is difficult to assess the accuracy of this statement based on available data. This respondent went on to suggest that part of assistants' resentment stemmed from perceived discrimination, especially with respect to salaries. At one time, salary discrimination was fairly substantial. A survey conducted by the department found that assistants were paid about 15 percent less than other federal attorneys with comparable experience (Clark, *Crime in America*, p. 190). Since the gap between salaries in the field and in Washington has narrowed, a major cause of differences in the attitudes of assistants and U.S. attorneys has been eliminated.

17. Sometimes, this resentment is exacerbated by the contrast with a U.S. attorney's previous experience. Said one U.S. attorney: "I'd been a Circuit Judge for four counties, 75,000–80,000 people in there. It *galled* me to come over here and have to write Washington and have some young fellow make a decision for me. . . . They wouldn't give me any authority, even for the smallest decision. I had to submit them to Washington."

18. For example, the Tax Division ordered an assistant to prosecute a nurse for failing to report all of her income as a deterrent to other nurses. After explaining what a sympathetic character the defendant was, the U.S. attorney observed tartly, "This was a loser. The jury wasn't going to send this person to prison. If I brought that, the judge would chew me out every day for it." Just after the airplane bomb hoax statute was enacted, the department required U.S. attorneys to obtain permission to decline prosecution. The department's policy of bringing charges against passengers who made wisecracks about the bomb in their lunch bag struck many U.S. attorneys as ridiculous.

19. The compliment is often returned. Department attorneys were referred to as "luminaries" in one district. The individual quoted in the text observed, "I never had an attorney from the department that I thought would be competent to be one of my assistants."

20. Whitney North Seymour, a former U.S. attorney, expresses in his book views voiced by a number of individuals I interviewed. "A good U.S. attorney's office, however, is usually much better equipped to handle a complex criminal prosecution than the young trial assistants from the Department of Justice, who travel around the country primarily because they are looking for courtroom experience." *United States Attorney* (New York: William Morrow, 1975), p. 48.

21. Seymour, *United States Attorney*, p. 51, describes the department in similar terms. "The Department itself can be extremely slow in answering mail, and frequently reacts in a bureaucratic, negative way to simple requests."

22. See the *New York Times*, October 23, 1964. The judge agreed to stay execution of the sentence for five days to allow an appeal to the Circuit Court. The Circuit Court threw out the contempt citation, sparing the U.S. attorney from jail. See *United States* v. *Cox*, 242 F. 2d 167 (5th Cir. 1965), *cert. denied*, 85 S.Ct. 1767 (1965).

23. This individual also succeeded in avoiding a jail term. The judge agreed to see the files himself before turning them over to defense counsel. After seeing them, he reversed his earlier ruling granting the motion.

24. Fesler, *Area and Administration*, pp. 65–66.

25. The crime issue has been a salient one for some time. In 1972, for example, newspaper articles appeared reporting on a suppressed study of the conviction rate in federal criminal cases prepared for a Senate subcommittee. The study showed a five-year drop in the conviction rate, a decline in the proportion of guilty pleas, and an increase in dismissals before trial. The story not only made the front page of the *New York Times* but also was carried by the major wire services. See "Convictions Drop in Federal Cases," *New York Times*, April 1, 1972; "Convictions Down in U.S. Courts," *Ann Arbor News*, April 10, 1972 (UPI).

26. For a description of Rooney and his subcommittee, see John W. Kingdon, "A

House Appropriations Subcommittee: Influences on Budgetary Decisions," *Southwestern Social Science Quarterly* 47 (1966): 68–78.

27. Kingdon, "A House Appropriations Subcommittee," p. 72, describes the subcommittee's behavior as follows: "Subcommittee questioning in the hearings on the requested increase places a premium on furnishing numerical measures of the agency's workload—number of pending cases, prisoners in institutions, and so forth—and on providing detailed breakdowns of the request into more manageable units."

28. There is some evidence that the department's concern over minor budgetary items goes back even further. After examining communications between U.S. attorneys and the department extending back to the 1920s, John Heinberg, writing in 1950, concluded, "There is far more evidence of constant control by the Department over small expenditures by the attorneys than of Departmental intervention in the processing of individual cases." "Centralization in Federal Prosecutions," *University of Missouri Law Review* 15 (June 1950): 248.

## CHAPTER 5

1. For a penetrating analysis of this and other factors shaping outcomes in such situations, see Thomas G. Schelling, *The Strategy of Conflict* (Cambridge, Mass.: Harvard University Press, 1960).

2. One independent district with an outstanding reputation for competence regarded the recruitment of outstanding assistants an essential component of its success. In fact, this was a major justification for vigorously resisting Washington's efforts to take control of important cases. Key administrative personnel in this district believed they got good assistants because of the prospect of trying fascinating and difficult cases. Because they got good assistants, they were able to handle them successfully.

3. Herbert A. Simon, Donald W. Smithburg, and Victor A. Thompson, *Public Administration* (New York: Knopf, 1956), p. 218.

4. James G. March and Herbert A. Simon, *Organizations* (New York: John Wiley & Sons, 1958), p. 165.

5. The lack of cooperation in the use of the reporting system was evident in the comments of department officials trying to explain modifications of the system to U.S. attorneys at the 1965 Conference. Private conversations with some attending the conference indicated a willingness to cooperate, but others intimated that they would continue to subvert the system.

6. A disloyal assistant can give the department information on activities within the office, sabotage local policy by conforming to central directives when conflicts exist, and place the U.S. attorney in a very embarrassing position by adopting the headquarter's view in open confrontations. Though such patent disloyalty is unlikely, even ambivalent neutrality can be harmful.

7. Another form of resistance is to rewrite drafts of complaints sent by the department for assistants to file. Asked if he did not get flak from the department for this practice, one assistant indicated that he did, but that it didn't stop him from continuing the practice.

8. There are times when grand juries can be used as a technique for frustrating an investigative agency's goals. Les Whitten, an investigative reporter for Jack Anderson, was arrested by the FBI for illegal possession of documents stolen from the Bureau of Indian Affairs while he was assisting in their return to the agency. The grand jury refused to indict, and one newspaper report stated: "Lawyers close to the case suggested that indictments could have been obtained if there had been more vigorous prosecution by the Government. But, they said, the United States Attorney's office here was reluctant to press the charges because of a dislike within the Department of Justice for the acting director of the Federal Bureau of Investigation, Patrick Gray, III, because Mr. Gray did not alert the Justice Department to plans for the arrests." See "Reporter Freed in Indian-Data Case," *New York Times*, February 16, 1973.

9. A department official suggested that there may be occasions when the opposite

tactic is employed. An assistant who wants to prosecute a case that the department orders him to dismiss can convince the judge to refuse the request for the dismissal.

10. A judge described a similar technique. If the U.S. attorney cannot get department approval of a compromise when the government is plaintiff, and if he agrees not to appeal the case, the judge tells him to put on one witness. Judgment is then rendered for less than the government is asking but near the compromise figure agreed upon by local counsel and rejected in Washington.

11. An assistant attorney general or section chief can also improve the reasonableness and acceptability of his staff's supervision of U.S. attorneys by dividing responsibilities on a geographical basis so attorneys come to know the assistants and judges well in a few districts and by requiring career attorneys to try an occasional case to keep in touch with trial problems.

12. The various divisions differ in the frequency with which they resort to outright conflict and seek to establish reputations for firmness rather than helpfulness and expertise. When conflicts do arise, however, all of the divisions want to prevail.

13. In what one official admitted was an organized campaign, the deputy attorney general sounded the major theme of the importance and value of reducing the case load. Subsequent speakers then introduced plans for the expanded reporting system, emphasizing the following points: it will reduce case loads; it will mean more paper work temporarily, but less in the long run; there will be more time then to do true "lawyers' work"; it isn't being used to "check-up" or "embarrass" anyone; it will help identify problem areas within the office. An attempt to give the impression that plans were tentative and that suggestions and reactions of U.S. attorneys were wanted was also made. While some seemed unconvinced, a good number—perhaps a majority—appeared willing to cooperate. Several felt it would be a very helpful administrative aid.

14. For a brief description of the Advocacy Institute, see United States Department of Justice, *Annual Report of the Attorney General, 1975* (Washington, D.C.: U.S. Government Printing Office, 1976), p. 3.

15. Although the impact of such conferences is difficult to assess, officials in the Executive Office for U.S. attorneys believed that they resulted in greater uniformity in policy. A former department official, however, expressed reservations. He noted the conference would make section chiefs more aware of the problems facing assistants in the field and would allow assistants from different districts to compare notes regarding their problems with the department and the techniques they used for dealing with them.

16. The Tax Division has a regional office in Fort Worth, Texas, which handles tax cases in a number of neighboring districts.

17. A related strategy, as yet little used, is to encourage headquarters attorneys to become assistants in their home districts. Such individuals retain ties to the department and generally accept central direction. This was tried briefly with mixed results during the Johnson administration. See The American Bar Association, *Preventing Improper Influence on Federal Law Enforcement Agencies: A Report of The American Bar Association Special Committee to Study Federal Law Enforcement Agencies* (1976), pp. 44–45.

18. Another reason for such loyalty and enthusiasm for Kennedy is that, as members of the department acknowledged, he was willing to back up U.S. attorneys against lower department officials on occasion.

19. An official in the deputy's office described these efforts: "The deputy attorney general has taken a very active and personal interest in U.S. attorneys. He has met personally with each one. This has developed good rapport. He wants to see them when they are in town."

20. For example, it instructs U.S. attorneys to decline prosecution of Mann Act violations that involve no commercial aspects.

21. For example, the *Manual* warns U.S. attorneys to avoid involvement in jurisdictional disputes between investigative agencies and advises that success in important illegal liquor prosecutions may be jeopardized if judges become antagonized because they bring too many petty liquor tax cases. Though many of these suggestions appear obvious, newly appointed assistants often find them extremely useful.

22. "When I first came in," he explained, "they were ready to dismember the office. They felt, 'Now is the time to move in on them.'" An assistant described how the department, as it was to do again nine years later, tried to take over cases previously handled by the office. "Right away they tried to steal some appeals." The U.S. attorney's reponse also anticipated later events. "The U.S. attorney had to go to bat right away. They were not really interested in those appeals. They were testing his political strength with the attorney general."

23. For a brief summary of early recommendations for changes in the appointment process, see The American Bar Association, *Preventing Improper Influence.*

24. Ibid., pp. 13–14, 42–48.

25. "President Opens Narcotics Drive," *New York Times,* January 29, 1972. The article noted, "The legal staff in the field would have powers in the narcotics law enforcement area equivalent to those of United States attorneys." Attorney General Mitchell announced a similar centralization the year before. "Mitchell Sets Up Special Network to Combat Radicals," *Ann Arbor News,* June 6, 1971.

26. One fairly good article on the strike forces has appeared. See Richard S. Frank, "Federal Strike Forces Dominate Government's War on Organized Crime," in John F. Bibby and Robert J. Huckshorn, eds., *Current Politics: The Way Things Work in Washington* (Minneapolis: Winston, 1973), pp. 258–70. Shortly before he resigned over the firing of special prosecutor Archibald Cox, Attorney General Elliot Richardson, a former U.S. attorney himself, met with a group of U.S. attorneys urging the abolition of the strike forces. He set up a sixteen-member committee composed of U.S. attorneys to advise him on the strike forces. "U.S. Considers Abolition of Crime Strike Forces," *New York Times,* September 23, 1973. The task force's efforts may have begun to pay-off from U.S. attorneys' standpoint, because just before the Ford administration left office, the assistant attorney general in charge of the Criminal Division (a former U.S. attorney) proposed abolishing the strike forces and turning their functions over to the local U.S. attorneys.

27. Thus, a gung-ho assistant who insisted on prosecuting when the department's Criminal Division felt it was ill-advised was finally sent a telegram reading: "You are hereby ordered not to prosecute this case." Even if such a prosecution proceeds, the department may have a remedy. The department can ask the appellate court to reverse the conviction on the grounds that the prosecutor did not follow department policy. See *Petite* v. *United States,* 361 U.S. 529 (involving federal prosecution of an offense for which the defendant had served time after conviction in a state court) and *Redmond* v. *United States,* 384 U.S. 264 (prosecution of husband and wife for mailing nude pictures of themselves to each other).

28. See, for example, "U.S. Attorney Ousted over Tax Leak," *Washington Post,* September 23, 1972. Here, the U.S. attorney was fired for leaking information from the tax returns of a prominent member of the opposition party. The article also reports on several firings for other reasons, however. "[A] federal prosecutor in Nevada was asked to resign for allegedly 'embarrassing' the Justice Department in his public statements, and another in Los Angeles was required to step down after he refused to sign an indictment against Daniel Ellsberg for disclosure of the top secret Pentagon papers."

29. An unusually well-publicized firing of an assistant occurred in New York in early 1971. The assistant, handling a pollution suit against General Motors, was quoted in a newspaper article as criticizing the department's softening attitude in the suit. The assistant claimed his firing by the U.S. attorney was under pressure from the department. "U.S. Denies Any Softness in Its G.M. Pollution Suit," *New York Times,* January 13, 1971.

30. This evidently was the case with respect to the Democratic U.S. attorney in the Southern District of New York. See "Morgenthau Gets Mayor's Support," *New York Times,* August 3, 1969; "Morgenthau Ouster Sought, With Post to Go to Seymour," ibid., August 15, 1969; "Nixon Moves to Replace Morgenthau, Naming Seymour as Prosecutor Here," ibid., December 18, 1969; and "Morgenthau Resigns Post, Citing Nixon 'Ultimatum'," ibid., December 23, 1969.

31. Robert K. Carr noted this some time ago: "The extent to which U.S. attorneys

rely on the facilities of the department—particularly the criminal division, the FBI, and the office of the solicitor general, is not generally realized." *Federal Protection of Civil Rights: Quest for a Sword* (Ithaca, New York: Cornell University Press, 1947), p. 143.

32. Other types of cases are also gladly surrendered to the department. A Democratic U.S. attorney interested in a political career was understandably relieved when the department undertook the prosecution of a powerful local union leader. A former state party chairman escaped a rather sensitive situation when it handled the prosecution of officials of the other party for election fraud.

33. At the 1965 Annual Conference, U.S. attorneys were invited to refer requests for information from the press that had to be denied to Washington. The message, in effect, was "We'll be happy to be SOBs with the local press for you."

34. The department can permit field attorneys to try a few specialized cases themselves, allow them to observe their preparation and trial, and can hold training seminars with lectures, mock trials, and so forth.

35. The relatively rapid turnover of U.S. attorneys also can lessen the desire to resist the department. I interviewed in one district where the Democratic U.S. attorney had engaged in prolonged and heated conflict with the department's organized crime strike force personnel dispatched to his district. But his Republican successor, while acknowledging the existence of prior difficulties, explained he had no quarrel with them: "You've got to remember it was easier for us to accept the task force. They were here when we arrived. They were part of the status quo."

36. The criteria include monitoring cases handled by newly appointed personnel, monitoring cases handled by men with poor reputations, and monitoring all cases in a particularly sensitive, important, or newly enacted area of law.

37. An illustration of circumstances like those referred to here appeared in the press in mid-1971. According to one report ("Kleindienst Postscript," *New Republic*, June 17, 1972, pp. 7–8), the U.S. attorney for the Southern District of California blocked a grand jury subpoena of Frank Thornton and interfered in an IRS investigation of his advertising agency. Thornton was reported to have been instrumental in the U.S. attorney's appointment. He was also President Nixon's 1968 campaign chairman in San Diego, and his advertising agency was controlled by C. Arnholt Smith, a long-time friend of the president's. A career department official would think twice before urging the firing of a man with these connections. Regardless of the actual difficulties involved in firing U.S. attorneys, department career officials *believe* they are substantial, and they modify their behavior accordingly.

38. John C. Heinberg described the basic problems encountered in firing U.S. attorneys in 1950. He observed that considerations leading to their initial appointment, especially appointees' standing in state and local politics, inhibit removal. "Centralization in Federal Prosecutions," *Missouri Law Review* 15 (1950): 245.

39. Several strategies not mentioned above appear to be of value only in enhancing one's ability to persuade as opposed to prevailing in open conflict. One U.S. attorney made several trips to Washington, both before and after assuming office, for the express purpose of building personal relationships with the assistant attorneys general. A career man in the frauds section explained why he got along with men in a district notoriously at loggerheads with the department. "We tried to be helpful and not take over the cases. We came to be trusted and got to the point where we could talk to them. As a consequence, we had some influence over them."

40. Another reason for equalizing pay was to try to slow the rapid turnover of assistants which continually confronted the department with problems created by the large proportion of inexperienced assistants. According to a former assistant attorney general, the average stay increased about a year after the pay was equalized.

CHAPTER 6

1. The exploratory nature of the field research precluded studying a random sample of districts that would permit reliable estimates of the frequencies of the patterns of

interaction depicted in Table 6.1. However, as appendix A indicates, I made an effort to pick districts displaying a variety of characteristics found throughout the country. The distribution of patterns among the districts studied probably corresponds roughly to the nationwide distribution. Of the thirteen districts studied which could be classified, eight were normal, one semiautonomous, one in conflict, and the remaining three "controlled" or ideal field offices.

2. As suggested in the previous chapter, there are exceptions. Some men form very close personal and working relationships with their counterparts. One department official indicated that he had such high respect for several assistants that he regarded them "as one of my staff," even dispatching them to neighboring districts in lieu of sending his own men out to try difficult cases.

3. Respondents in the department expressed their reluctance to issue orders directly. One man waits for an invitation to send a department attorney to try a case; if none is forthcoming on a difficult case, he will "invite" a request. If this fails, he usually lets the matter drop rather than ordering his own man out.

4. See the *New York Times,* June 5, 1966. The lead paragraph reads: "Sam (Momo) Giancana was reported to have played golf this week while the Justice Department and the United States Attorney here disagreed publicly about his future, the Department's wisdom, and the attorney's skill." The article hinted the department wanted the U.S. attorney to resign; he publicly stated he would not. An interesting sidelight was the public backing of the U.S. attorney and criticism of the department by the chief judge of the district court in a press conference.

5. In his book on his experiences as U.S. attorney in the Southern District of New York during the Nixon administration, Whitney North Seymour reprints his farewell speech to his staff on what it means to be an assistant in the district. His remarks, he notes, reflected his strong convictions about the traditions and goals of the office. His last point to his assistants was, "Above all, be independent." See *United States Attorney* (New York: William Morrow, 1975), pp. 15–17.

6. For a number of years, a banquet attended by current and former members of the office has been held. The Southern District is the only district where this is done.

7. When the U.S. attorney who served during the Kennedy and Johnson years left office, his Republican successor retained the chief assistant U.S. attorney and chose two of his predecessor's assistants to head the civil and criminal divisions. For a description of the transition, see Seymour, *United States Attorney,* p. 212.

8. See, for example, his account of his disagreement with Assistant Attorney General L. Patrick Gray over how to handle the occupation of the Statue of Liberty by some Vietnam war veterans. Seymour, *United States Attorney,* pp. 42–44.

9. Robert Peabody, *Organizational Authority* (New York: Atherton, 1964), p. 137.

10. Ibid.

11. An official in the Executive Office for U.S. Attorneys talked of the "aura of excitement and newness" throughout the department at the start of the Kennedy administration. His counterpart in the Nixon administration claimed to detect close cooperation and rapport between U.S. attorneys and the new deputy attorney general.

12. The comments of a knowledgeable and experienced career official in the Civil Division are particularly noteworthy in this regard. He observed that the department can give orders and "a certain number of them will be obeyed, especially before U.S. attorneys learn what it is all about."

13. A Democratic holdover provided one example. "With civil rights, for instance, there were differences between Ramsey's administration and Mitchell's administration. You could get more cooperation from Ramsey's in school [desegregation] matters than you could from Mitchell." Seymour, *United States Attorney,* ch. 9, confirms this assessment. He characterizes the policy of John Mitchell's department, especially the Civil Rights Division, as a "slowdown" in civil rights.

14. For general accounts of the department under John Mitchell and his Democratic predecessors, see Richard Harris, *Justice: The Crisis of Law, Order, and Freedom in America* (New York: Avon, 1970); and Greg Rathjen, *Law and Reorder: A Comparative Assessment of the Johnson and Nixon Administrations of Criminal Justice* (forthcoming).

15. The history of the organized crime strike force in their district demonstrates the

sharp swings in the nature of relations with the department that sometimes result after the U.S. attorney changes. This respondent's Republican successor reported close cooperation with the strike force. Evidently, there was little communication between the two men and almost no mechanism for maintaining traditions, for the successor told me, "But this office has worked better with the strike force traditionally than any other office in the United States as far as I can tell." In truth, relations were among the most strained.

16. Recall that in Chapter 1, small offices were defined as having seven or less assistants, medium offices eight to fourteen, and large offices more than fifteen. I have discussed the relationship between office size and relations with the department previously in *Politics and the Legal Process* (New York: Harper–Row, 1973), pp. 166–70.

17. This advantage is offset somewhat by the fact that U.S. attorneys from small districts (especially Democrats in the South) frequently have the support of powerful U.S. senators. The support of a Senator Ervin would more than offset the inability of the mayor of Asheville to provide strong backing.

18. Three studies of headquarters–field relations can be used as a basis of comparison: Herbert Kaufman, *The Forest Ranger* (Baltimore: Johns Hopkins Press, 1960); James W. Davis, Jr., and Kenneth M. Dolbeare, *Little Groups of Neighbors: The Selective Service System* (Chicago: Markham, 1968); and Bernard H. Baum, *Decentralization of Authority* (Englewood Cliffs, N.J.: Prentice–Hall, 1961). For a rare example of a study that explicitly seeks to compare administrative agencies (though not on the question of centralization–decentralization) see Herbert Kaufman's stimulating little book, *Administrative Feedback* (Washington, D.C.: Brookings, 1973).

19. Baum, *Decentralization and Authority*, p. 21.

20. This is essentially the view of Herbert A. Simon, George Kozmetsky, Harold Guetzkow, and Gordon Tyndall, *Centralization vs. Decentralization in Organizing the Controller's Department* (New York: Controllership Foundation, 1954), p. 4. "An administrative organization is centralized to the extent that decisions are made at relatively high levels in the organization; decentralized to the extent that discretion and authority to make important decisions are delegated by top management to lower levels of executive authority."

21. Davis and Dolbeare, *Little Groups of Neighbors*, note (pp. 46–47), that Selective Service headquarters did not "in any meaningful sense supervise, control, or review the actions of state headquarters and their local boards. Uniform action is not a goal and national headquarters has not developed performance standards or systematically collected the data required to measure and evaluate either system performance as a whole or the performance of various units."

22. For a description of the centralization of administrative structures in the federal judiciary, see Carl Barr, "The Growth of Federal Judicial Administrative Structures: Implications for Judicial Behavior," paper delivered at the 1970 Annual Meeting of the Midwest Political Science Association. For an empirical examination of increasing central control in the Seventh Circuit, see Beverly Blair Cook, "Federal District Judges in the Seventh Circuit: Trial Judge Roles in the Courtroom and in the Court Structure," paper delivered at the 1970 meeting of the American Political Science Association. For an exhaustive examination of the entire topic of federal judicial administration, see Peter Graham Fish, *The Politics of Federal Judicial Administration* (Princeton, New Jersey: Princeton University Press, 1973).

23. Included in these figures are the Tax Division, the Criminal Division, the Civil Division, the Lands Division, the Civil Rights Division, the Office of Drug Abuse Law Enforcement, and the Office of National Narcotics Intelligence. Figures were obtained from *U.S. House of Representatives, Subcommittee of the Comittee on Appropriations: Hearings on the Departments of State and Justice, the Judiciary, and Related Agencies Appropriations* for 1969 through 1974.

24. These calculations are based on figures found in *U.S. House of Representatives, Hearings, 1976*, p. 19, and *U.S. House of Representatives, Hearings, 1977*, p. 18.

25. Seymour, *United States Attorney*, argues in Chapter 3 ("A Less-Than-Hallowed Place") that the department suffered from political influence and possible corruption at the same time U.S. attorneys performed in a nonpartisan and upstanding fashion.

CHAPTER 7

1. Assistants are keenly aware of the strategic advantage enjoyed by the defense and the necessity of compensating for it. A former assistant expressed this attitude in print. "The prosecutor must be prepared to fight against rulings from the bench which may be harmful to the government's case. There is no appeal for the government from these rulings, and therefore if the government seeks to have them changed, it must do so by prompt and thorough legal research and argument during the trial itself." Whitney North Seymour, Jr., "Why Prosecutors Act Like Prosecutors," *Record of the Association of the Bar of the City of New York,* 11 (June 1956): 331.

2. The University of Chicago Jury Project found that in personal injury cases at least, the extent of agreement between judge and jury is not affected by whether the judge gives written instructions to the jury, summarizes the evidence, or comments on the weight of the evidence. See Dale W. Broeder, "The University of Chicago Jury Project," *Nebraska Law Review* 38 (1959): 744–60.

3. Judges possess several other procedural powers. If a key witness is late, a cooperative judge can juggle the day's docket to give the government a chance to locate him. Judges also empanel, dismiss, and extend the life of grand juries. If a new one must be empanelled every few weeks, investigations in progress would have to be begun from scratch. If allowed to run too long, the grand jurors become bored and restive.

4. "U.S. Court Blocks Disbarment of 6," *New York Times,* March 13, 1974.

5. Some judges remind attorneys on occasion of their power. A senior judge known for his acumen and no-nonsense approach called the clerk, the U.S. attorney, and the defense attorney together after word of a grand jury indictment appeared in the press and curtly remarked, "One of you gentlemen leaked the news to the press and one of you gentlemen is going to end up in prison."

6. Peter Graham Fish, *The Politics of Federal Judicial Administration* (Princeton, New Jersey: Princeton University Press, 1973), p. 55.

7. Ibid., p. 73.

8. Ibid., p. 349. Fish notes, "Court congestion and the utilization of various procedures to alleviate it often dominate the general sessions (of circuit conferences)."

9. Quoted by Fish, *The Politics of Federal Judicial Administration,* p. 377.

10. For instance, Chief Justice Burger's report on the federal courts' backlog was printed in *The Third Branch,* a newsletter sent to all federal judges. The yearly per judge output, according to the chief justice, has increased from 239.1 in 1968 to 309.8 in 1972–73. "This increase is due to the adoption of modern techniques, as well as to judges working harder than ever before." *The Third Branch,* 5 (September 1973): 2.

11. In her study of district judges in the Seventh Circuit, Beverly Blair Cook reaches a similar conclusion. "The message from Judicial Conference resolutions and from AOC [Administrative Office of the U.S. Courts] statistical reports come through clearly to the trial judge: dispose of pending cases and handle the incoming cases expeditiously." "Federal District Judges in the Seventh Circuit: Trial Judge Roles in the Courtroom and in the Court System," paper delivered at the Sixty-sixth Annual Meeting of the American Political Science Association, 1970, p. 10.

12. Several defense attorneys stated that they sometimes went to trial on nearly hopeless cases on the chance that an inexperienced assistant would botch the presentation of the case. The poorer the reputation of the office, the more attorneys will be tempted to go to trial. The importance of settlements in keeping docket backlogs down is suggested by Cook, who reports that in the Seventh Circuit, almost three times as many cases are settled by pretrial bargaining and compromise as go to full trial. "Federal District Judges in the Seventh Circuit," p. 11.

13. United States attorneys reduce the work load of judges in other ways. In a few districts, they are called upon to write drafts of opinions when the judge has decided to rule for the government. They can also prepare papers and orders that formally are the responsibility of the judge.

14. Cook provides a rare glimpse into some of the mechanisms for sensitizing district judges to reversals. At the executive session of the Seventh Circuit Judicial Conference,

attended by all the judges in the circuit, the circuit chief judge discusses cases appealed from the districts, with special attention paid to reversals. Here, the errors made by district judges are exposed to all of their brethern. "Federal District Judges in the Seventh Circuit," p. 16. Of course, not all judges fear reversal, as the following remark attributed to Judge Sirica when an attorney questioned the propriety of Sirica's cross-examination of Hugh Sloan during the original Watergate burglary trial in early 1973 reveals. "I exercise my judgment as a Federal judge and as the Chief Judge of this court . . . and as long as I'm a Federal judge, I'll continue to do it. . . . I could care less what happens to this case on appeal." "Jury Is Told Nixon Aides Knew of Watergate," *New York Times*, January 27, 1973.

15. A fascinating study of the socialization of new federal district judges by Robert Carp and Russell Wheeler provides empirical confirmation of the existence of anxiety. "In addition to their initial legal and administrative problems, most new federal trial judges experienced psychological discomfort as well." Robert Carp and Russell Wheeler, "Sink or Swim: The Socialization of a Federal District Judge," *Journal of Public Law* 21 (1972): 372.

16. Comparisons of West German prosecutors with American prosecutors reflect the conventional wisdom that in the United States, few if any effective restraints exist on the decision to prosecute. See, especially, John H. Langbein, "Controlling Prosecutorial Discretion in Germany," *University of Chicago Law Review* 41 (1974): 439–67; Joachim Herrmann, "The German Prosecutor," in Kenneth Culp Davis, ed., *Discretionary Justice in Europe and America* (Urbana, Illinois: University of Illinois Press, 1976), ch. 2; and Professor Davis's comments on Professor Herrmann's chapter in the same volume, pp. 60–74.

17. For a description of research that found similar reports on judicial influence on the decision to prosecute, see Robert L. Rabin, "Agency Criminal Referrals in the Federal System: An Empirical Study of Prosecutorial Discretion," *Stanford Law Review* 24 (April–June 1972): 1036–91.

18. On rare occasions, such efforts attain public visibility. The distinguished Judge Charles Wyzanski, Jr., of Boston publicly requested assistants in his district to file sworn statements that they had never smoked marijuana in an effort to turn prosecutorial attention from simple marijuana cases to more serious crimes. However, he shortly thereafter retracted his request and admitted he had "grievously erred." The episode, originally reported by the Associated Press, is described in Walter F. Murphy and C. Herman Pritchett, eds., *Courts, Judges, and Politics*, 2nd ed. (New York: Random House, 1974), p. 204.

19. Cases frequently mentioned as falling into this category include: Dyer Act cases (interstate transport of stolen autos) not involving organized theft rings; moonshine cases involving small quantities ("pint liquor cases"); failure to list all previous arrests on applications for temporary post office employment; mail fraud or forgery cases involving small dollar amounts; migratory bird cases; violations of acreage allotments (e.g., planting two acres too many of peanuts); and Mann Act violations involving consenting adults and lacking a commercial aspect. For a similar list of such cases, see Rabin, "Agency Criminal Referrals," pp. 1052–53.

20. Rather subtle and complex variations of such influence were found. A U.S. attorney refrained from prosecuting minor offenders of a statute, fearing the judges would become habituated to giving light sentences and cease imposing stiff sentences on major offenders.

21. If a judge is too enthusiastic about hearing certain types of cases, it may discourage a conscientious prosecutor from bringing all such cases. "You have to protect yourself—govern yourself on the basis of what you know about the judge," observed a southern U.S. attorney. "For instance, this judge was very vigorous on the subject of white slavery cases. I wouldn't let a case get to him unless it was a very serious violation, because he'd give a sentence of five years on anything."

22. Often, the local office will assign someone to sit with a department attorney during trial. Since the U.S. attorney may be chastized by a judge for the misbehavior of a department attorney, the practice of sending someone to "baby-sit" with department

lawyers is partly self-defense. Some judges encourage the presence of a local attorney: "I want the U.S. attorney to be in Court to guarantee [department lawyers'] responsiveness to the orders of the Court."

23. When asked if he had perceived differences in the types of cases prosecuted by U.S. attorneys over the years, one judge widely known for his domineering nature expressed surprise. "I thought that was pretty much controlled from above." Such gross misperceptions are not held by former U.S. attorneys now on the bench.

24. Impeachment has been so rarely used, and only then for flagrant misconduct, that it is not a significant factor. Peltason reports that only four federal judges have ever been removed by this process; another eight resigned before impeachment procedures could be completed. See Jack W. Peltason, *Federal Courts in the Political Process* (New York: Random House, 1955), p. 36. For a summary of the federal judges who have been the subject of congressional inquiry, see the appendix to Joseph Borkin's *The Corrupt Judge* (New York: Clarkson N. Potter, 1962). The Court of Appeals is the most significant institution capable of constraining district judges' behavior. In addition to the power to reverse decisions, the judicial councils of each circuit have acquired the power to strip district judges of their right to hear cases. See *Chandler* v. *Judicial Council of the Tenth Circuit* (398 U.S. 74). For a thorough discussion of the role of Circuit Judicial Councils, see Fish, *The Politics of Federal Judicial Administration*, ch. 11.

25. It is necessary to distinguish between the responsiveness of individual members of the office who appear in a specific courtroom in specific cases and the responsiveness of the office as a whole with respect to general policy. The overwhelming dominance of judges over attorneys who litigate before them compels nearly every assistant U.S. attorney to be responsive to trial judges. Although not all assistants are equally likely to make such accommodations, it is a rare individual indeed who is willing deliberately to engage in behavior known to anger the judge. There is considerably greater variation in the extent to which U.S. attorneys modify office policies in response to judges.

26. In another small district which exhibits many of the attributes of a partnership, the judge invites the U.S. attorney and the probation officer into his chambers to get their opinions of the appropriate sentence for convicted defendants. United States attorneys sometimes influence sentences by influencing a probation officer's recommendation to the judge.

27. A sampling of observations made by other respondents in this district follows. Regarding the interest of judges in the office, an ex-U.S. attorney said, "They have a lot of interest, particularly the Chief Judge." Another observed: "They all have different opinions about what should go on in the U.S. attorney's office . . . . If you lose a case or two, they'll bring you down to the office and tell you what was wrong." An experienced assistant, when asked if judges took much interest in the office, explained, "They certainly do! Fifty percent of their work comes out of this law firm. They like to see the office run efficiently." And the incumbent U.S. attorney commented, "They feel we should win a large percentage of the cases. When you start to lose some cases, they're interested in why." Another assistant confirmed discussion on matters of administration. "The U.S. attorney and I talk to them every day about what's pending, what problems there are. It's all very informal . . . . We don't discuss cases unless they ask about it."

28. As mentioned in note one of Chapter 6, the districts studied do not constitute a random sample of districts permitting reliable estimates of these patterns' frequencies. Any such estimate, of course, would describe the distribution only at a given time. As noted later in the text, patterns of interaction with judges change over time.

29. It is difficult to predict attitudes toward judicial attempts to exert influence, much less actual behavior. The apparent susceptibility of this individual to judicial influence was belied by his contention that he would resist a suggestion from a judge that one of his assistants never be sent into his courtroom again. "I'm afraid I would be constrained to say I am going to be the sole judge of who is going to represent the government and whether it meets with the court's displeasure or not—I don't want to lose a case but on the other hand, there is a principle involved that has to be vindicated."

30. In his book on the appointment of federal judges, Harold W. Chase concludes

that incumbent federal judges do seek to influence who is appointed. Their opinions on prospective nominees are solicited by the department and the American Bar Association Standing Committee on the Federal Judiciary. But they also frequently take the initiative in urging the appointment of favored candidates. See Chase's *Federal Judges: The Appointing Process* (Minneapolis: University of Minnesota Press, 1972), p. 34. Joel Grossman, in *Lawyers and Judges: The ABA and the Politics of Judicial Selection* (New York: Wiley, 1965), p. 40, relates that a number of judges from the Southern District of California went to Washington to oppose the nomination of Ernest A. Tolin for a judgeship because he was inexperienced and had an "unclean reputation" as U.S. attorney. Tolin, however, was confirmed.

31. For instance, few if any federal judges let unruly or unethical conduct by attorneys persist. Nearly all feel trials must be conducted to assure a "just" outcome and will take steps to insure that they are. Few can resist evaluating the importance of the cases brought, particularly with the heavy emphasis placed on the condition of their dockets. For a discussion of internalized restraints most judges accept, see Herbert Jacob, *Justice in America*, 2nd ed. (Boston: Little, Brown, 1972), pp. 207–13.

32. "The 'Chicago 8' Judge," *New York Times*, October 9, 1969. The judge's own comments made when he sentenced defense lawyer William Kunstler to four years in prison for contempt of court support this assessment. "If crime is, in fact, on the increase today, it is due in large part to the fact that waiting in the wings are lawyers who are willing to go beyond professional responsibilities, professional obligations, professional duty in their defense." "Kunstler Given 4-Year Sentence for Contempt by U.S. Judge in Chicago," *New York Times*, February 16, 1970.

33. In a study of lower Ohio judges, Larry Baas verifies a relationship between judges' perceptions of what their functions ought to be and their behavior. The average case disposition rate for two "adjudicators" was less than for two "administrators." Larry Baas, "Judicial Role Perceptions: Problems of Representativeness, the Identification of Types, and the Study of Role Behavior," paper delivered at the Midwest Political Science Association Convention, April 27–29, 1972, pp. 16–17.

34. In one district, the story is told of a judge who was strongly pro-government in tort claims cases except when the Post Office was involved. It seems that he was nearly run down by a Post Office truck while leaving the courthouse one afternoon.

35. Of course, personality traits of judges also affect relations with U.S. attorneys. Few litigating attorneys deny personality's importance in shaping a judge's courtroom behavior. For a brief and fascinating portrait of a federal judge with a strong personality and outspoken views, see David Shaw, "United States Judge Lets Chips Fall Where They May," in Murphy and Pritchett, *Courts, Judges, and Politics*, pp. 197–203.

36. Cook, "Federal District Judges in the Seventh Circuit," p. 4.

37. In the Seventh Circuit, for instance, eight of the twenty-six judges sit as "solitary" judges, even though only one of the seven districts in the circuit has but one judge. Cook, "Federal District Judges in the Seventh Circuit," p. 4.

38. Ibid., p. 8.

39. Ibid., pp. 7, 12.

## CHAPTER 8

1. Relations with less significant components of U.S. attorneys' strategic environment that will not be described here include U.S. marshals, probation officers, court personnel, and their office clerical staff.

2. These include the Federal Bureau of Investigation, the Internal Revenue Service, the Postal Inspection Service, the Immigration and Naturalization Service, the Alcohol, Tobacco and Firearms Division of the IRS (formerly the Alcohol and Tobacco Tax Division), the Securities and Exchange Commission, the Department of the Interior (Wildlife Service), the Bureau of Customs, the Department of Agriculture, and the Secret Service.

3. Although little published research on U.S. attorneys and assistants exists, two

excellent articles deal with relations between assistants and investigative agents. One is an impressionistic account of a former assistant describing how prosecutive decisions were made. His comments are confined to his own experience in the Northern District of California, one of the larger offices. See John Kaplan, "The Prosecutorial Discretion—A Comment," *Northwestern University Law Review* 60 (1965): 174–93. The other also focuses upon the decision to prosecute. The methodology employed is quite similar to that used in the research described here. Open-ended interviews were conducted with supervisory personnel in the Department of Justice and with members of the U.S. attorney's office and investigative agency personnel in nine districts. The interviews concentrated upon the decision to prosecute. However, the research excluded cases under the jurisdiction of the FBI. The FBI furnishes the largest number of referrals, and relations between its agents and assistants constituted a major focus of the interviews conducted during my field research. In most respects, the conclusions reached in this second study are strikingly similar to those reported here. Together, they provide a fairly complete description of the basic elements of assistant–agent interaction. See Robert L. Rabin, "Agency Criminal Referrals in the Federal System: An Empirical Study of Prosecutorial Discretion," *Stanford Law Review* 24 (1971): 1036–91.

4. For a brief description of the "post-referral investigatory" aspects of assistant–agency interaction, see Rabin, "Agency Criminal Referrals," pp. 1067–68. A U.S. attorney provided an example of the close relations that can develop when he told me, "It was a five-week trial. I didn't have any assistant. The FBI agent who handled the case was really my assistant. He sat at the counsel table with me and helped me prepare the case."

5. In most districts, the Alcohol and Tobacco Tax unit could make arrests involving illegal alcohol without prior authorization. The department's Tax Division authorizes criminal income tax cases. Also, prosecutive decisions are centralized when a new criminal statute is being "broken in." Of course, agents can make arrests in all instances when they catch prospective defendants "red-handed."

6. The state of Michigan provides a notable exception. For a brief description of how the decision to prosecute is made in Detroit, see James Eisenstein and Herbert Jacob, *Felony Justice: An Organizational Analysis of Criminal Courts* (Boston: Little, Brown, 1977), pp. 127–29.

7. I do not have good evidence about the precise content of incentive structures established by federal investigative agencies. My research led to the impression that both the number of arrests and the number of convictions were important. Rabin, however, suggests "While the U.S. attorney may regard its conviction rate as of central importance, the agency may regard the number of violations referred by complaint to the U.S. attorney as critical." "Agency Criminal Referrals," p. 1056. Undoubtedly, this varies by agency. One assistant confirmed this. "The FBI is interested in convictions. But the Postal Inspectors are interested in arrests. Their statistics are based on the number of arrests." I also encountered evidence that dismissal rates are used as a measure of agency performance. A U.S. attorney's attempts to dispose of a huge backlog left by his predecessor met resistance from agencies concerned that the large number of dismissals would subject them to criticism from their Washington headquarters.

8. Kaplan, "The Prosecutorial Discretion," p. 180.

9. This discussion on the uses of conviction rates is based on Rabin, "Agency Criminal Referrals," p. 1045. Because this public constituency is ill defined, U.S. attorneys are particularly sensitive to the content of newspapers. It is not unusual for papers to emphasize conviction rates. For example, the *New York Times* ran a story headed, "Conviction Rate Reported Higher" that began, "A report that 95 per cent of the Federal indictments here result in conviction was issued yesterday by United States Attorney Whitney North Seymour." January 24, 1972. Such attempts to mold opinion are not uncommon, as the description of relations with the press at the end of this chapter suggests.

10. The interdependence of a high conviction rate at trial and an efficient guilty plea

system at the local level has been described frequently. See, especially, Jerome Skolnick, "Social Control in the Adversary System," *Journal of Conflict Resolution* 11 (1967): 52–70.

11. *U.S. House of Representatives, Subcommittee of the Committee on Appropriations: Hearings on the Department of State and Justice, the Judiciary, and Related Agency Appropriations for 1971.* U.S. House of Representatives, 92nd Congress, 1st Session (1971), pp. 411–12.

12. Rabin reaches a similar conclusion. Discussing differences over what kind of cases ought to be prosecuted, he observes, "The mutual dependence of agency and prosecutor creates pressure toward convergence of enforcement policy. While the agency is dependent on the U.S. attorney for whatever level of criminal enforcement the agency deems minimally essential, the U.S. attorney is, in turn, heavily dependent on the agency's investigative and technical expertise for whatever level of criminal enforcement it deems minimally essential. Preservation of the ongoing relationship is mutually beneficial. Thus, agency–prosecutor friction is diminished, but not eliminated, by the necessity of living with each other." "Agency Criminal Referrals," p. 1056.

13. John Kaplan identifies several factors contributing to the development of such consensus: "The assistants shared a common perception of their role; each assistant had been taught the standards for prosecution by the other, more experienced hands; assistants often discussed their decisions and asked the advice of each other; and finally, prosecutorial decisions were constantly being checked by the litigative process." "The Prosecutorial Discretion," p. 177.

14. The importance of maintaining a high enough quality of investigations to elicit authorizations is presented in stark terms by Rabin. "If an agency cannot package an attractive product it will become the victim of market forces and its criminal enforcement program will be seriously impeded." "Agency Criminal Referrals," p. 1064.

15. These findings are supported nicely by Rabin's research. See, especially, his discussion of postal inspector's prior screening of mail fraud cases, "Agency Criminal Referrals," p. 1048, and the failure to screen by Agriculture and the Alcohol, Tobacco, and Firearms Division, pp. 1052 and 1055.

16. Once again, Rabin reports similar findings. "The federal prosecutor's resources are so heavily in demand that the natural reaction is to decline out of hand cases sent over by an agency with a reputation for poor quality preparatory work." "Agency Criminal Referrals," p. 1063. There is some consensus among assistants on agency performance. No one, for instance, thought highly of Agriculture Department agents. Less consensus was found on the performance of the FBI, Secret Service, and Postal Inspection Service.

17. Kaplan, "The Prosecutorial Discretion," p. 182. It should be pointed out, however, that he states the importance of this factor is often overestimated.

18. An individual mailing obscene material from Los Angeles can be prosecuted there or at any point of destination. Even if authorization were equally likely in all such districts, an Iowa or Oklahoma jury would be more likely to convict than one in California. Cases involving untaxed liquor made in Mississippi and sold in New Orleans are prosecuted in Louisiana because Mississippi's federal judges have often given moonshiners light sentences.

19. The distinction between the "crime-control" and "due process" models of the criminal process was first made in Herbert Packer, *The Limits of the Criminal Sanction* (Stanford: Stanford University Press, 1968), pp. 149–73.

20. Rabin also found U.S. attorneys were generally well satisfied with the quality of the work of investigative agents. "Agency Criminal Referrals," p. 1064. Some U.S. attorneys' enthusiasm was almost embarrassing. Speaking of the FBI, one southern U.S. attorney said that "The relationship is 100 per cent good and congenial. This is one relationship I wouldn't swap for any in the world. I also have a strong love for the Treasury Department."

21. With the passage of gun control legislation in the late 1960s, the agency's jurisdiction expanded. It is now known as the Alcohol and Firearms Division of the Internal Revenue Service.

22. For a U.S. attorney's description of the FBI's rigidity, reluctance to initiate new

investigations, and regulations which restrict their effectiveness, see Whitney North Seymour, *United States Attorney* (New York: William Morrow, 1975), pp. 99-101.

23. It should be noted that strategies to win agency cooperation are necessary because of U.S. attorneys' near total dependence on them for investigations. In recent years, a strategy to reduce this dependence has emerged—hiring investigators and researchers to serve on the U.S. attorney's staff directly. According to an article by David Burnam in the *New York Times*, there were some 250 such personnel in 1971. The deputy director of the Executive Office for U.S. Attorneys was quite candid in his explanation to Burnham of the desired impact of this strategy. "The investigators will give us a chance to initiate. You need something concrete to get an investigation going by the F.B.I. or I.R.S. In addition to gathering facts in the initial stages of some investigations, these new staff members can help in the process of maturing an agency's investigative report into an actual prosecution." "U.S. Prosecutors Hiring Own Investigators to Ferret Out Crime," *New York Times*, September 30, 1971.

24. United States Department of Justice, *Annual Report of the Attorney General of the United States: 1975* (Washington, D.C.: United States Government Printing Office, 1976), p. 27.

25. Ibid.

26. See especially Abraham Blumberg, "The Practice of Law As a Confidence Game," *Law and Society Review* 1 (1967): 15-39; David Sudnow, "Normal Crimes: Sociological Features of the Penal Code in a Public Defender Office," *Social Problems* 12 (1965): 255-76; Albert Alschuler, "The Prosecutor's Role in Plea Bargaining," *University of Chicago Law Review* 36 (1968): 50-112; David Neubauer, *Criminal Justice In Middle America* (Morristown, New Jersey: General Learning Press, 1974), ch. 9; James Eisenstein, *Politics and the Legal Process* (New York: Harper & Row, 1973), ch. 6; H. Lawrence Ross, *Settled Out of Court* (Chicago: Aldine, 1970); and James Eisenstein and Herbert Jacob, *Felony Justice: An Organizational Approach to Criminal Courts* (Boston: Little, Brown, 1977), ch. 4 and ch. 6.

27. Douglas Rosenthal, *Attorney and Client: Who's in Charge?* (New York: Russell Sage Foundation, 1974), pp. 96-99.

28. Of the forty-nine U.S. attorneys at the 1965 Annual Conference of U.S. Attorneys who returned a questionnaire which asked about career ambitions, twenty-eight (57 percent) indicated they wanted to become federal judges. The mail questionnaire sent to U.S. attorneys serving between 1961 and 1973 (described in Appendix B) asked respondents to rank in order of preference the subsequent career they hoped to pursue at the time they received their appointment. More ranked a federal judgeship first than any other career, including becoming a partner in a law firm. Thirty-one percent of the first place rankings fell into the "federal judgeship" category.

29. The major exceptions have already been mentioned—Rabin, "Agency Criminal Referrals," and Kaplan, "The Prosecutorial Discretion."

30. *Annual Report of the Attorney General, 1975,* p. 27. Of 46,467 criminal cases terminated, 5,180 involved trials.

31. See, for example, Neubauer, *Criminal Justice in Middle America*, pp. 93-96, 238; Jonathan Casper, *American Criminal Justice* (Englewood Cliffs, New Jersey: Prentice-Hall, 1972), pp. 78, 135-44.

32. For a description of such sentence bargaining, see Eisenstein and Jacob, *Felony Justice*, ch. 5.

33. For descriptions of count bargaining in Detroit and Baltimore, see Eisenstein and Jacob, *Felony Justice*, ch. 4 and ch. 6.

34. For a discussion of why defendents in Connecticut state courts fear trials, see Casper, *American Criminal Justice*, pp. 66-77.

35. "Agency Criminal Referrals," pp. 1068-70.

36. For a fairly comprehensive list of these factors, see Alschuler, "The Prosecutor's Role," pp. 53-61.

37. For one U.S. attorney's published account of his continuous stormy press relations, see Seymour, *United States Attorney*, ch. 11.

CHAPTER 9

1. For an interesting example, see John H. Langbein, "Controlling Prosecutorial Discretion in Germany," *University of Chicago Law Review* 41 (1974): 439–67. Langbein discusses the American prosecutor's "monopoly" on the decision to decline prosecution, but says little about the forces that restrain prosecutorial discretion. For a similar perspective on the limited discretion of German prosecutors, see Joachim Herrmann, "The German Prosecutor," in Kenneth Culp Davis, ed., *Discretionary Justice in Europe and America* (Urbana, Illinois: University of Illinois Press, 1976), ch. 2; and Professor Davis's comments on Professor Herrmann's chapter in the same volume, pp. 60–74.

2. Of the thirteen districts studied which could be classified, seven were normal, two judge-dominated, two department-dominated, and two fell into the "semiautonomous" pattern.

3. Richard Richardson and Kenneth Vines, *The Politics of the Federal Courts* (Boston: Little, Brown, 1970), p. 36.

4. Harold Chase, *Federal Judges: The Appointing Process* (Minneapolis: University of Minnesota Press, 1972), p. 156.

5. Evidently, no one collects such statistics for publication. According to an article in *The New Republic,* Attorney General Kleindienst testified that only one U.S. attorney had been the subject of an administrative inquiry in the Nixon administration up to 1972. Henry Peterson, with many years of experience, could recall only one assistant who was asked to resign and one who was actually prosecuted. "Kleindienst Postscript," *The New Republic,* June 17, 1972, pp. 7–9.

6. See, for example, "Kleindienst Postscript," *New Republic* (June 17, 1972): 7–9. The article asserts that the U.S. attorney in the Southern District of California blocked service of a grand jury subpoena on a close personal friend and political supporter who was reported to have been instrumental in his appointment as U.S. attorney.

NOTES TO APPENDIX A

1. Robert A. Dahl, "Power," *The International Encyclopedia of the Social Sciences* (New York: Macmillan, 1968), 12: 410.

2. Two of the districts had a population of less than one million; six had between one and one and a half million; three had between one and one-half and two and one-half million, and three had more than two and a half million. Similar variation in the proportion of non-whites in the population was obtained. Four districts had 3 percent or less, three had more than 20 percent. Eight of the districts were carried by Richard Nixon, six by John Kennedy; per capita income and percent rural farm population showed similar variation.

3. See, for example, Abraham Blumberg, *Criminal Justice* (Chicago: Quadrangle, 1967); Jonathan Rubinstein, *City Police* (New York: Farrar, Straus and Giroux, 1973); Jerome Skolnick, *Justice Without Trial* (New York: Wiley, 1966); James Q. Wilson, *Varieties of Police Behavior* (Cambridge, Mass.: Harvard University Press, 1968); Joel Grossman, *Lawyers and Judges* (New York: Wiley, 1965); John T. Elliff, *Crime, Dissent, and the Attorney General* (Beverly Hills, Calif.: Russell Sage, 1971); David W. Neubauer, *Criminal Justice in Middle America* (Morristown, New Jersey: General Learning Press, 1974); and Jonathan D. Casper, *American Criminal Justice* (Englewood Cliffs, New Jersey: Prentice–Hall, 1972).

NOTES TO APPENDIX B

1. The characteristics of the men whose biographies could not be located can be compared on two measures: the size of the district in which they served, and its location. A comparison of those located with the total roster on these two measures follows:

|  | Men whose biographies were located (%) | Total roster (%) |
|---|---|---|
| REGION: | | |
| New England | 6.7 | 7.3 |
| Mid-Atlantic | 11.6 | 10.7 |
| Mid-West | 25.0 | 25.7 |
| Old South | 25.0 | 22.2 |
| Border | 12.2 | 14.9 |
| West | 19.5 | 19.2 |
|  | 100.0 | 100.0 |
| DISTRICT SIZE: | | |
| Four assistants or less | 43.0 | 43.6 |
| Five to eight assistants | 37.3 | 38.8 |
| More than eight assistants | 19.6 | 17.6 |

2. A more detailed description of this analysis appeared in my doctoral thesis, *Counsel For The United States: An Empirical Analysis of the Office of United States Attorney* (Yale University, 1968), ch. VII.

# Index